AMERICAN CULTURE AND SOCIETY SINCE THE 1930s

AMERICAN CULTURE AND SOCIETY SINCE THE 1930s

Christopher Brookeman

Schocken Books • New York

First American edition published by Schocken Books 1984
10 9 8 7 6 5 4 3 2 1   84 85 86 87
Copyright © 1984 by Christopher Brookeman
Published by agreement with Macmillan Publishers Ltd, London and Basingstoke

Library of Congress Cataloging in Publication Data
Brookeman, Christopher.
    American culture and society since the 1930s.
    Bibliography: p.
    Includes index.
    1. United States—Civilization—20th century.
2. United States—Social conditions—1933–1945.
3. United States—Social conditions—1945–.
4. Mass media—United States—History—20th century.
I. Title.
E169.1.B79825   1984   973.91   84–10488

Printed in Great Britain

ISBN 0–8052–3939–1

To Hazel

Contents

List of Plates

1. Still from *The Man Who Shot Liberty Valance*, 1962, directed by John Ford. © Paramount Pictures
2. *Immigrants Arriving at Ellis Island*, 1937–38, detail of mural by Ben Shahn. For former Community Centre of Jersey Homesteads, Roosevelt, New Jersey. © Estate of Ben Shahn, 1981
3. *Jackson Pollock at Work*, 1951. © Hans Namuth
4. *Going Westward*, oil, *c.* 1934–38, by Jackson Pollock. By courtesy of the National Museum of American Art (formerly National Collection of Fine Arts), Smithsonian Institution. Gift of Thomas Hart Benton
5. *Isaiah* by Michelangelo. Detail from the Sistine Chapel
6. *Rosie The Riveter* by Norman Rockwell. *Saturday Evening Post* cover, 29 May 1943. Printed by permission of the Estate of Norman Rockwell. Copyright © 1943 Estate of Norman Rockwell
7. Front of the Solomon Guggenheim Museum, New York. © Ben Asen, 1984
8. *Floyd Burroughs, Southern Share Cropper* by Walker Evans, 1936. By courtesy of the Library of Congress
9. *A Jewish Giant at Home with his Parents in the Bronx, New York, 1970* by Diane Arbus

Every effort has been made to trace all the copyright holders, but if any have been inadvertently overlooked the publishers will be pleased to make the necessary arrangement at the first opportunity.

Preface

ANY survey of American culture since the 1930s is faced with the major problem of doing justice to an enormous range of activity in the American arts. The contribution this book seeks to make is to place selected developments in literary criticism, cultural theory and artistic practice within an historical context in order to provide a framework of analysis for students embarking on a study of contemporary American culture. The various uses to which the term culture is put in the book need some elaboration. Raymond Williams in *Keywords* (Fontana, 1976) has enumerated the various definitions and uses of the term. What this book aims to do is provide definitions within the context of the particular critic under review. Therefore for an art critic such as Clement Greenberg the culture of modernism functions as a shorthand way of evoking an experimental abstract tradition in painting that includes Cézanne, Picasso, Jackson Pollock and the other New York school of painters of the late 1940s and 1950s. For an anthropologist such as Margaret Mead the culture concept casts a much wider net of meaning than Clement Greenberg's arts-based tradition of abstract experimentation. One of the purposes of the book is to show how variously the term has been used by the critics whose ideas of culture are under review. Two important critiques of American culture, the feminist and the Afro-American, will be dealt with in other books of this series and therefore do not appear in this book.

I am indebted to the Polytechnic of Central London for a period of study leave to complete this book and to the many students and colleagues in both England and the United States with whom many of the ideas in the book were discussed and clarified. Thanks are also due to Chris Fowler and Marian Gleason who typed the manuscript.

C.B.

Editors' Preface

MENTION the United States and few people respond with feelings of neutrality. Discussions about the role of the United States in the contemporary world typically evoke a sense of admiration or a shudder of dislike. Pundits and politicians alike make sweeping references to attributes of modern society deemed 'characteristically American'. Yet qualifications are in order, especially regarding the distinctiveness of American society and the uniqueness of American culture. True, American society has been shaped by the size of the country, the migratory habits of the people and the federal system of government. Certainly, American culture cannot be understood apart from its multi-cultural character, its irreverence for tradition and its worship of technological imagery. It is equally true, however, that life in the United States has been profoundly shaped by the dynamics of American capitalism and by the penetration of capitalist market imperatives into all aspects of daily life.

The series is designed to take advantage of the growth of specialised research about post-war America in order to foster understanding of the period as a whole as well as to offer a critical assessment of the leading developments of the post-war years. Coming to terms with the United States since 1945 requires a willingness to accept complexity and ambiguity, for the history encompasses conflict as well as consensus, hope as well as despair, progress as well as stagnation. Each book in the series offers an interpretation designed to spark discussion rather than a definitive account intended to close debate. The series as a whole is meant to offer students, teachers and the general public fresh perspectives and new insights about the contemporary United States.

CHRISTOPHER BROOKEMAN
WILLIAM ISSEL

Abbreviations

The following abbreviations are used for books frequently cited in the text.

DE   Theodor Adorno and Max Horkheimer, *Dialectic of Enlightenment* (1944/1979)

SJ   Daniel Bell, *Sociological Journeys: Essays 1960–1980* (1980)

CCC   *The Cultural Contradictions of Capitalism* (1976/1979)

SE   T. S. Eliot, *Selected Essays* (1976)

ASG   *After Strange Gods: A Primer of Modern Heresy* (1934)

NTDC   *Notes Towards the Definition of Culture* (1948/1979)

CD   Sigmund Freud, *Civilization and its Discontents* (1930/1979)

AC   Clement Greenberg, *Art and Culture* (1961)

LPCS   Leo Lowenthal, *Literature, Popular Culture and Society* (1968)

AAG   Dwight Macdonald, *Against the American Grain* (1963)

OM   *On Movies* (1981)

UM   Marshall Mcluhan, *Understanding Media: The Extensions of Man* (1964/69)

PP   Norman Mailer, *The Presidential Papers* (1976)

AN   *The Armies of the Night: History as a Novel, The Novel as History* (1968)

EC   Herbert Marcuse, *Eros and Civilization* (1955/1974)

EL   *An Essay on Liberation* (1969)

GWT   John Crowe Ransom, *God Without Thunder: An Unorthodox Defence of Orthodoxy* (1931)

WB   *The World's Body* (1938)

PC   I. A. Richards, *Practical Criticism: A Study of Literary Judgement* (1929)

LC   David Riesman, *The Lonely Crowd: A Study of the Changing American Character* (1950/1970)

OP   Susan Sontag, *On Photography* (1980)
LD   Lionel Trilling, *The Last Decade: Essays and Reviews, 1965–75*
      (1979)
OS   *The Opposing Self: Nine Essays in Criticism*
      (1955/1980)
IE   Robert Warshow, *The Immediate Experience: Movies, Comics,*
      Theatre and other Aspects of Popular Culture (1962, 1971)
NJ   Tom Wolfe, *The New Journalism* (1975)

1. The Legacy of the Thirties

THERE are many entrances to the intellectual and cultural history of a period. One of the strongest perspectives on the cultural debates and issues of the period from Roosevelt's New Deal society of the 1930s through to the present highlights the various adjustments and changes between competing cultural ideals and political beliefs that writers and critics made in this period. This version has a dramatic storyline that disproves Scott Fitzgerald's belief that 'there are no second acts in American lives'.[1] The first act of the 1930s describes a move by a wide range of writers towards various forms of political commitment. The political spectrum of these ideological stands included liberal reformism, exemplified for many by Roosevelt's New Deal and its relief agencies, through to socialism, communism and the myriad forms of fellow-travelling. Although the movement was, in the main, towards liberal and socialist ideologies, there was a distinctive counter-movement towards conservatism. T. S. Eliot had set the model for this counter-movement with his 1928 declaration: '[My] general point of view may be described as classicist in literature, royalist in politics, and anglo-catholic in religion'.[2] However, a more representative ideological journey is that described by the playwright Lillian Hellman, in her book of memoirs, *Pentimento*. She characterises herself as: 'A child of the Depression, a kind of Puritan Socialist, I guess – although to give it a name is to give it a sharper outline than it had – and I was full of the strong feelings the early Roosevelt period brought to many people'.[3]

This first act of Lillian Hellman's personal political drama focused not only on the bankruptcy of an American political and economic system that had produced over thirteen million unemployed, but also on the dangers of totalitarian ideologies, particularly the rise of fascism in Germany, Spain and Italy. By pursuing anti-fascist

1

activities and taking a critical view of American society, Lillian Hellman was no different from many of her contemporaries who, like Ernest Hemingway and Erskine Caldwell, co-operated with many political organisations, including the Communist Party, in order to create a worldwide popular front against fascism in the period from 1935 to 1939. Of 418 American writers who gave their views on the Spanish Civil War in a pamphlet of 1938, *Writers take Sides*, 410 strongly favoured the loyalist Republicans against the rebel fascists under Franco.[4] Lillian Hellman visited Spain in 1937 and actively supported the Republican cause, particularly through the activities of a production company called Contemporary Historians Inc., who produced a pro-republican film, *The Spanish Earth*. It was directed by Joris Ivens, and scripted and narrated by Ernest Hemingway, with music by Marc Blitzstein and Vergil Thomson. The film was screened at charity performances throughout America to raise money for the Republican cause in Spain. Americans also served in the Lincoln Brigade, one of the International brigades that was raised to fight against Franco and the fascists in Spain. However, none of this activity moved the USA, Britain or France to change their positions of neutrality. Franco's ultimate victory in the Spanish Civil War, achieved with the support of the Nazis, was the first of many setbacks to the anti-fascist popular front. The Nazi-Soviet pact of 1939, by which Hitler and Stalin agreed not to attack one another, and the repressions of the Stalinist purges, set the stage for that disenchantment with communism and explicit ideological commitment that became a hallmark of the 1940s and 1950s.

For many American writers, there followed a second act in their political lives when, under the pressure of the McCarthyite purges, many publicly confessed their so-called errors and sought to protect their careers by denouncing colleagues and friends, either for being paid-up members of the Communist Party, or for giving tacit support to the communist cause by donating money to or allowing their talents to be used by the host of front organisations and left groups in which there had been communist infiltration. The ringing declarations of ideological commitment that were so characteristic of the 1930s gave way, in many cases, to evasive silence or abject conformism. Such American classics as *Let Us Now Praise Famous Men*, a documentary and photographic record of Southern tenant farming, text by James Agee and photographs by Walker Evans, written in the 1930s but not published until 1941, had been prefaced by the appeal:

'Workers of the world, unite and fight. You have nothing to lose but your chains, and a world to win.'[5] Although such sentiments were to become suspect during the Cold War, the tortuous path of politics and history took a further preliminary abrupt twist before settling into the anti-communism of the Cold War. When Hitler invaded Russia without warning in 1941, the suspicions engendered in America by the 1939 Nazi-Soviet pact were pragmatically set aside. With America's entry into the war in 1941, the stage was set for the wartime alliance between Russia and the USA as they fought a common fascist enemy together. Russian casualties in this cause were enormous and the American press were full of praise for the heroic Russians who were described in *Life* magazine (29 March 1943) as: 'One hell of a people who look like Americans, dress like Americans, and think like Americans'.[6] It was not until the Cold War of the late 1940s and 1950s that Americans were exhorted by rhetoric and anti-Red scares to change once again their view of Russia, its ideology and world role.

The problems of sustaining ideological positions and loyalties within the contradictions of world history led many American writers and intellectuals to seek what Arthur M. Schlesinger called the 'vital center', a core of agreed basic democratic values that could act as a focus of critical enquiry, not subject to the sudden ravages of history, revolution and ideological schisms. The full title of the 1949 book in which Schlesinger defined his programme is instructive in its metaphorical resonance: *The Vital Center: Our Purposes and Perils on the Tightrope of American Liberalism*. Although the book is full of a recognition that the soft underbelly of liberal democratic theory and practice had been comprehensively exposed by the ease with which totalitarianism had destroyed democratic forces in the 1930s, Schlesinger strongly emphasised the egalitarian individualism and toughness of the liberal tradition. Liberalism could be redeemed, revised and reformulated for use in a post-war era that 'is threatening to turn us all into frightened conformists; and conformity can only lead to stagnation. We need courageous men to help us recapture a sense of the indispensability of dissent, and we need dissent if we are to make up our minds equably and intelligently.'[7] This agenda was a powerful spur to a number of like-minded writers, intellectuals and cultural critics who were often sponsored either by federal or private foundations and think-tanks such as the Centre for the Study of Democratic Institutions, or the Congress for Cultural Freedom. The scale of this support for the new liberalism was international. In September 1955, the Congress for Cultural Freedom sponsored an international conference in Milan to debate 'the Future of Freedom'. The proceedings were then reported in the Congress's London-based monthly review, *Encounter*. Both the Congress and *Encounter* later proved to have been financed by the CIA as part of its attempts to persuade the elite intellectuals of the world of the virtues of democracy as opposed to the repressions of totalitarian political systems.

This debate on the nature of liberal democracy and the search for a 'vital center' had numerous echoes in literary culture. As long ago as 1915, the critic Van Wyck Brooks in his literary history *America's Coming of Age* had sought to establish 'an open skeptical, sympathetic centrality' as a core characteristic of American culture. In a society characterised by rapid expansion and a destabilising rate of social change, literature could provide 'a certain focal center – a national "point of rest" '. This challenge was specifically taken up by a number of literary critics in the 1940s and 1950s who produced a series of thesis books in which selected American writers, mainly from the nineteenth century, were seen as the promoters and guardians of a heritage of democratic and humanistic values. The contemporary relevance and worth of this nineteenth-century heritage to the twentieth century was a key unsettled issue. In a much quoted phrase of the time, there was the search for a 'usable past' that could anchor the anxieties of the present.

A seminal example of this kind of thesis book was F. O. Matthiessen's *American Renaissance*, first published in 1941. Matthiessen's 'usable past' is based on five writers: Emerson, Thoreau, Whitman, Hawthorne and Melville. This group had in 'one extraordinarily concentrated moment of expression . . . the half-decade of 1850–55'[8] produced a set of books that might constitute a 'vital center'. The five writers are united by 'one common denominator . . . their devotion to the possibilities of democracy'.[9] In many respects, Matthiessen's work on American literature parallels that of the English critic F. R. Leavis. In *The Great Tradition* Leavis singled out a group of mainly nineteenth-century novelists as the major model of literary excellence. The common quality that Leavis saw in George Eliot, Henry James and D. H. Lawrence was that of a 'marked moral intensity'.[10] One of the problems with this kind of criticism, organised around some master theme or thesis, is that it arbitrarily excludes important writers who do not happen to share the chosen group's ideological or aesthetic affiliations. Matthiessen acknowledges this problem when discussing his exclusion of Edgar Allan Poe who was 'bitterly hostile to democracy'.[11] As well as conducting an intense scrutiny of 'the possibilities of democracy', the five writers that Matthiessen selects have another important set of shared characteristics; they all employed, to varying degrees, techniques of symbolism, allegory and mythology. The dominance of these poetic devices was in part the natural literary extension of a dualistic view of the world in which neither spiritual nor material qualities dominated. It is significant that several of the writers that Matthiessen selected had mystical or transcendental views of nature. Their work thus constituted evidence for the existence and perpetuation of a mythic anti-materialist view of the world. Matthiessen's celebration of a set of nineteenth-century writers, whose techniques and themes were complex and ambiguous, offered a clear alternative to the dialectical materialism and agitprop declarations of the 1930s. James and Hawthorne, so often dismissed as redundant counter-revolutionary bourgeois mandarins by Marxist theoreticians in the 1930s, were redeemed by these revaluations of the 1940s. This recovery of James and Hawthorne also enhanced the status of writers such as Faulkner whose complex techniques and anti-democratic themes had seemed irrelevant in the 1930s when the ideological tide had run strongly in favour of writers who had a more materialist view of nature and society such as Dreiser, Steinbeck, Hemingway and Caldwell.[12] A clear division emerges in the 1940s and 1950s between critics such as Matthiessen and Northrop Frye who inclined to see 'literature in transhistorical terms, as the embodiment either of a timeless verbal symbol or of the eternal recurrences of archetypal myth'[13] and critics such as Philip Rahv who saw literature as the product of history, ideology and society. Rahv, in an essay on the reactionary implications of the myth and symbol school of criticism, first published in 1949, mounted an extended critique of this mythopeic tendency:

> the one essential function of myth stressed by all writers is that in merging past and present it releases us from the flux of temporality, arresting change in the timeless, the permanent, the ever-recurrent conceived as 'sacred repetitions'. Hence the mythic is the polar opposite of what we mean by the historical, which stands for process, inexorable change, incessant permutation and innovation.

> Myth is reassuring in its stability, whereas history is that power-house of change which destroys custom and tradition in producing the future.[14]

An important consequence of this revelation of a highly symbolist and allegorical strain in American literature was the elevation of this strain to the status of a unique national characteristic. By expanding a set of cues and hints derived in the main from D. H. Lawrence's pioneering *Studies in Classic American Literature*, a whole generation of American critics argued that American literature and culture were best understood as products of myths whose meanings were mediated through symbols and allegories. Three books that specifically followed into the same territory as that mapped out by Matthiessen were Henry Nash Smith's *Virgin Land: the American West as Symbol and Myth* (1950), R. W. B. Lewis's *The American Adam: Innocence, Tragedy and Tradition in the Nineteenth Century* (1955), and Leo Marx's *The Machine in the Garden: Technology and the Pastoral Ideal in America* (1964). The books share a common methodology in which the social critiques of a selected number of nineteenth-century writers are used as the basis for 'speculation about the entire culture'.[15] Where the books differ is over the contemporary significance and worth of the nineteenth-century value systems they investigate. Henry Nash Smith carefully documents the powerful fascination that the myth of agrarianism and the figure of the western hero have held for the American imagination, only to find the myths socially and intellectu-ally inadequate: 'the philosophy and the myth affirmed an admirable set of values, but they ceased very early to be useful in interpreting American society as a whole because they offered no intellectual apparatus for taking account of the industrial revolution'.[16] R. W. B. Lewis is less concerned to match his nineteenth-century pastoral Adam to the requirements of the twentieth century. Indeed his portrait of the ideal American seems designed to fly in the face of all known theories of the interaction between the individual and society. Lewis's Adam is 'an individual emancipated from history, happily bereft of ancestry, untouched and undefiled by the usual inheritances of family and race; an individual standing alone, self-reliant and self-propelling, ready to confront whatever awaited him with the aid of his own unique and inherent resources'.[17] Leo Marx is far more ambiguous about the relevance of the pre-industrial value systems embodied in such figures as Lewis's American Adam. He poses the following question about the value of the anti-industrial, anti-technological tradition he analyses in *The Machine in the Garden*: 'What possible bearing can the urge to idealise a simple, rural environment have upon the lives men lead in an intricately organised, urban, nuclear-armed society?'[18] In their anxieties about the value in the twentieth century of what appear to be redundant nineteenth-century ideologies, Smith and Marx seem to miss a basic point about ideology that Lewis's anachronistic idealised American Adam expresses. Ideology by its very nature is often archaic, inconsistent and nostalgic. The example of Nazi ideology with its confused amalgam of mysticism, transcendent nature and industrial efficiency is a powerful reminder of the volatility of such constructs. Ideologies do not necessarily have to conform to a particular mode of production such as agrarian or industrial.

The nineteenth century has continued to attract myth and symbol critics seeking the roots of the twentieth century in a set of founding characteristics and themes. The critic whose model of America's classic nineteenth-century past has most dramatically questioned the validity of the democratic humanist model proposed by Matthiessen and others is Leslie Fiedler with his 1960 publication, *Love and Death in the American Novel*. Fiedler sees the world of Melville, Twain and Hawthorne and their twentieth-century descendant William Faulkner as a pathological nightmare which is 'bewilderingly and embarrassingly a gothic fiction, nonrealistic and negative, sadist and melodramatic – a literature of darkness and the grotesque in a land of light and affirmation'.[19]

This brief sketch of some of the issues and controversies that emerged as literary and cultural critics came to terms with the changed conditions of post-war America indicates how pervasive and early was the concern with the ideology of culture. The chapters that follow will examine the various schools of literary and cultural analysis that sought to determine the path that American culture would take in the post-war period.

2. Daniel Bell and the Cultural Contradictions of Capitalism

ONE of the most distinctive intellectual groups that emerged as a force during the Cold War has been variously described as anti-communist liberal, and more recently as neo-conservative. Daniel Bell, a leading figure in this group, has defined this generation in terms of a particular ideological journey that began in the 1930s when many of the writers and intellectuals in the group were 'intense, horatory, naive, simplistic and passionate but, after the Moscow trials and the Soviet-Nazi pact, disenchanted and reflective'.[1] Many of the leading anti-communist liberals of the post-war period were former socialists who had rebelled against the authoritarian Stalinism of left politics. Daniel Bell sees this group as a seminal force in American life in the post-war period: 'from them and their experiences we have inherited the key terms which dominate discourse today: irony, paradox, ambiguity and complexity'.[2] Bell suggests that this post-war intellectual culture of 'ambiguity and complexity' marks an improvement on the crude sectarian extremism of the 1930s. In fact he suggests in the famous title of his book *The End of Ideology* that fixed ideological positions are both redundant and inhibit accurate analysis. Some former socialists and communists such as Max Eastman and John Dos Passos moved to the extreme right, but a more characteristic position was that of the anti-communist liberal adopted by such cultural critics as Dwight Macdonald and Lionel Trilling.

One of the main cultural issues raised and debated by this group was the fate of the individual in a mass democratic society. The nature of this debate can be clearly derived from a series of questions that the editors of *Partisan Review* posed to Lionel Trilling and other leading intellectuals in 1952. Among the questions were the following: 'Must

8

the American intellectual and writer adapt himself to mass culture? If he must, what forms can his adaptation take? Or, do you believe that a democratic society necessarily leads to a leveling of culture, to a mass culture which will overrun intellectual and aesthetic values traditional to Western civilization?' The final question of four related directly to the idea of a usable past discussed in the first chapter: 'If a re-affirmation and rediscovery of America is under way, can the tradition of critical nonconformism (going back to Thoreau and Melville and embracing some of the major expressions of American intellectual history) be maintained as strongly as ever?'[3]

Whether you formulated the issue in terms of the contemporary artist facing the dominance of what were seen as the caricatures, stereotypes and standardisation of mass culture, or in terms of the literary critic attempting to affirm the 'critical nonconformism' of Thoreau and Melville, your argument depended on a political definition of an individual and his or her rights. The founding formula for the way the relationship between an individual and society has been conceived in this version of classic liberal political theory 'begins with the individual and his rights and judging society as an arrangement to ensure these abstract rights, argues normally for only the necessary minimum of government'.[4]

This basic model and definition provided anti-communist liberals such as Lionel Trilling with an ideological perspective that powerfully influenced their literary cum-cultural analysis. The master theme that organises Trilling's 1950 collection of essays is described as follows: 'The essays deal with episodes of the literature of the last century and a half, and they all, in one way or another, take account of the idea that preoccupies this literature and is central to it, and makes its principle and unity – the idea of the self'.[5] Not only was the self a basic unit to be protected and affirmed, it could perform transcendent functions when allied to the arts. This refinement appears in Trilling's 1965 collection of essays *Beyond Culture* where he talks of the honoured belief that 'a primary function of art and thought is to liberate the individual from the tyranny of his culture in the environmental sense and to permit him to stand beyond it in an autonomy of perception and judgement'.[6] Here Trilling gives a supreme value to the process by which an individual can transcend the tyrannies and bonds of the complicated and dense system of social values, taboos and restraints that crowd in on the individual. In Trilling's literary analysis, the concept of individual transcendence was a basic source of energy and a governing methodology. However, the passionate individualism celebrated by anti-communist liberals had limitations, clearly specified in the work of Daniel Bell.

'I came to political awareness in the Depression and joined the Young People's Socialist League in 1932, at the precocious age of thirteen.'[7] From such beginnings, Bell developed a carefully delimited, and in his eyes non-ideological liberalism that was a compromise between classic liberalism and conservatism. This compromise was announced in *The End of Ideology* with its subtitle, 'On the Exhaustion of Political Ideas in the Fifties'. Bell described the inevitable coming of an age of consensus:

> Few 'classic' liberals insist that the state should play no part in the economy, and few serious conservatives, at least in England and on the Continent, believe that the Welfare State is 'the road to serfdom'. In the western world, therefore, there is today a rough consensus among intellectuals on political issues: the acceptance of a Welfare State; the desirability of decentralized power; a system of mixed economy and of political pluralism.[8]

This open system is for Bell not only a more accurate model of the nature of post-war society but it allows a diversity of views and behaviour. This diversity is not available to what he describes as the 'closed system' of Marxism in which all experience and analysis is monolithically controlled and 'integrated through the mode of production or a dominant value system'.[9] Bell argues that 'society is better understood as being composed of diverse realms, each obedient to a different "axial principle" ' (*SJ*, p. xiv). He argues that human psychology and the nature of modern society will be better understood by his descriptive model of the differing value systems that an individual can operate than by models that reduce diversity to a single socio-economic deterministic base. Bell isolates three main areas of activity in modern society, each of which is regulated by a different axial principle. In the sphere of modern economic activity the axial principle is 'functional rationality or efficiency – the idea that in the techno-economic realm the criterion for using a process or a product is whether it can be made cheaper, better, more efficiently' (*SJ*, p. xiv). In the sphere of politics, 'the axial principle is equality – equality before the law, equality of opportunity, equality of rights' (*SJ*, p. xiv). In the sphere of culture, 'the axial principle is the enhancement or the fulfilment of the self' (*SJ*, p. xiv).

Although Bell is in broad agreement with this liberal mixed system, various contradictions develop within such a system to the point of crisis, particularly in the area of individual rights. The historical sources of these contradictions are examined in detail in *The Cultural Contradictions of Capitalism* (first published in 1976). Bell's main thesis is that the energies and principles of bourgeois capitalism that released society from the controls of feudalism have now become redundant, self-conscious and inimical to progress, particularly in the arts. His account of this process highlights the historical impact of one idea: 'The fundamental assumption of modernity, the thread that has run through Western civilization since the sixteenth century, is that the social unit of society is not the group, the guild, the tribe, or the city, but the person'.[10] The economic version of this phenomenon is the bourgeois entrepreneur, pursuing laissez-faire behaviour, subject only to individual conscience as established by the protestant ethic. The cultural version of this process of liberation was the individual artist, freed from patrons and institutions, and like his businessman counterpart free to operate in a market economy.

In Bell's view this shared radicalism of artist and businessman collapsed in the nineteenth century when: 'Radical in economics, the bourgeoisie became conservative in morals and cultural taste' (*CCC*, p. 17), a taste which began to degenerate into 'the heroic and banal' (*CCC*, p. 17). An adversary relationship then developed between the artist and society. For example, the controls of censorship and morality were intensified to limit the freedom of artists. One response by artistic culture to this diminution of artistic licence is exemplified by Baudelaire, who set out to subvert bourgeois values with such declarations as: 'To be a useful man has always appeared to me as something quite hideous' (*CCC*, p. 17). Increasingly, the artistic practice that took this view attempted to disrupt and challenge the rationality, the causally related narrative sequences and the optimism of the bourgeoisie by creating a subculture of dada experiment, abstraction and the whole range of 'isms' from impressionism to surrealism and cubism that challenged the basic aesthetic of bourgeois art and culture. This traditional aesthetic centred on the idea that the arts should be based on some kind of figurative realism; a face should look like a real face, not a cubist distortion, and should be part of a solid three-dimensional world. The development, within the bourgeois world, of an adversary anti-realist experimental aesthetic was enhanced by the increasing ability of artists to justify their practice not to the general public but to a mixed grouping of fellow artists, critics and supporters who constituted an avant-garde culture and audience.

Bell sees the development of an avant-garde as a cultural demand for individualism similar to that asserted in the economic field by the laissez-faire capitalist. Its achievements have been considerable: 'The period from 1890 to 1930 was the great period of modernism, in its brilliant explorations of style and its dazzling experiments of form' (*CCC*, p. 115). However, Bell's view of the creative record of modernism since the 1930s is very different: 'Today modernism is exhausted. There is no tension. The creative impulses have gone slack. It has become an empty vessel' (*CCC*, p. 19). This decadent modernism is symptomatic of changes in the value system and practices of bourgeois capitalism that have created ideas of individualism with no restricting mechanisms such as operated in the early development of capitalism when 'the unrestrained economic impulse was held in check by Puritan restraint and the Protestant ethic' (*CCC*, p. 21). The root cause of this decadence in both cultural and economic life is an overvaluation of the rights of the individual. The original heroic energies of the individual have degenerated into a narcissistic idolatry of the self and a value system in which 'the impact on the self, not the moral consequence to society' has become 'the source of ethical and aesthetic judgements' (*CCC*, p. 19). This ideology of individualism like the other ideologies analysed in *The End of Ideology* has, in Bell's favourite metaphor, become 'exhausted', redundant and counter-productive.

Armed with this critique Bell attacks a whole range of avant-garde tendencies in contemporary American culture. The Beat Generation are a 'hopped-up, jazzed-up, souped-up, self-proclaimed group of outcasts'[11] and the counter-culture of the 1960s nothing more than 'the fantasies and sexual demands of childhood acted out during adolescence on a mass scale unprecedented in cultural history' (*CCC*, p. 144). This phenomenon of the liberation movements of the 1960s and the counter-culture of drugs, happenings and rock and roll is, in Bell's view, the inevitable consequence of an economic system in which 'the cultural, if not moral, justification of capitalism has become hedonism, the idea of pleasure as a way of life' (*CCC*, p. 21, 22). Bell connects this decadence with specific economic practices:

The greatest single engine in the destruction of the Protestant ethic was the invention of the installment plan, or instant credit. Previously, one had to save in order to buy. But with credit cards, one could indulge in instant gratification. The system was transformed by mass production and mass consumption, by the creation of new wants and new means of gratifying those wants. (*CCC*, p. 21)

Bell's proposals for rehabilitating this nightmare world of unrestrained individualism constitute a set of entrances into a discussion of what a number of critics have described as his 'neo-conservatism'. In his essay 'Liberalism in a Postindustrial Society', Bell clearly argues not for a wholesale reduction of individual rights, but for a recovery of some of the 'virtues of liberalism' that are less individualistic. One important historical element of liberalism is its 'identification with secular humanism' (*SJ*, p. 229), the traditional moral and ethical continuities of western civilisation since Aristotle and the Renaissance – what Matthew Arnold described as 'the best that has been thought or said'. This 'humane or heroic, rather than warlike, culture' provides a 'way of guarding society against religious fanaticism, ideological extremism, or mindless activism, political or cultural' (*SJ*, p. 229). This is Bell's version of a 'usable past', variously defined by such literary-cum-cultural critics as Lionel Trilling and F. O. Matthiessen. In Bell's formulation, this historic culture of liberalism was as much a system of restraints as of permissions. The new forms of individualism have transformed an historically acceptable idea of individual liberty into the idea of liberation that Bell defines as 'a psychological impulse – to be free of all restraints, to achieve extasis, freedom from the body itself' (*SJ*, p. 231). Bell clearly feels that the ideas of liberation promoted by the counter-culture in the 1960s are a decadent form of liberalism. The counter-culture threatens a cardinal feature of classic liberalism, namely that 'achievement is to be judged on the basis of merit, talent and work' (*SJ*, p. 230). Classic liberalism also maintained that ascriptive criteria 'such as birth, or race, or color, or religion, or social class are irrelevant to judging the individual' (*SJ*, p. 230). Bell's defence of the meritocratic values of 'classic liberalism' inevitably places him ideologically alongside neo-conservatives such as Irving Kristol and Daniel P. Moynahan, who have used a meritocratic ideology to reject the demands and special pleadings of under-privileged or minority groups who claim preferential entitlements or quotas on the basis of historical injustice and inequity. Classic liberalism cannot accommodate itself to rights movements that demand redress on the basis of gender, colour or other ascriptive criteria.

When one turns from the political implications of Bell's call to liberal first principles to his proposals for checking the cult of liberation in the cultural sphere, his main concern is firstly to disengage culture from economics and politics and then to recover the historic connections between culture and religion. Bell carefully establishes a more metaphysical definition of culture than either 'an anthropologist's definition of culture as the artifacts and patterned ways of life of a group' or Matthew Arnold's definition of culture as 'the achievement of perfection in the individual' (*CCC*, p. 12). For Bell culture is expressed in 'those efforts in painting, poetry, and fiction, or within the religious forms of litany, liturgy and ritual, which seek to explore and express the meanings of human existence in some imaginative form' (*CCC*, p. 12). Culture can transcend time and place because it derives its themes 'from the existential situations which confront all human beings, through all times, in the nature of consciousness' (*CCC*, p. 12). This kind of transcendental metaphysical culture has historically 'been fused with religion' (*CCC*, p. 12). The major themes in this culture as religion 'are cultural universals, to be found in all societies where men have become conscious of the finiteness of existence' (*SJ*, p. 333). Bell's list of key recurrent and universal themes recalls Aristotle's classic elevation of tragedy over comedy, pain over pleasure in its high moral and spiritual tone, 'how one meets death, the meaning of tragedy, the nature of obligation, the character of love' (*SJ*, p. 333).

His belief that culture is not inextricably linked to a particular mode of economic production or the ideology of a particular political system can be seen in the way he differentiates between the operations of technology and those of culture:

> A machine or a process that is more efficient or more productive replaces one that is less efficient. This is one meaning of progress. But in culture, there is always a ricorso, a return to the concerns and questions that are the existential agonies of human beings. (*CCC*, p. 13)

Nothing is more characteristic of the psychological and aesthetic divide between Daniel Bell's generation and a succeeding generation of critics such as Susan Sontag than the contrast between Bell's high-toned spiritual Messianism and Susan Sontag's belief developed in her essay 'Against Interpretation' that: 'In place of a hermeneutics, we need an erotics of art'.[12] Daniel Bell singled out Sontag as a promotor of cultural hedonism in his essay 'The Sensibility of the Sixties' in which he dismisses the counter-culture as 'the pathetic celebration of the self – a self that had been emptied of content and which masqueraded as being vital through the playacting of Revolution' (*CCC*, p. 144).

Bell's ideas of both religion and culture stress their role as part of 'a dialectic of release and restraint', with individual creativity and exploration at one pole and a traditional system of curbs, limits and controlling standards at another. In his view the pendulum has swung too far towards the idea of release and liberation and 'the fear of the demonic, of human nature unchecked' that was a cardinal feature of 'the great historical religions' has been displaced by the 'idea that experience in and of itself was the supreme value, that everything was to be explored, anything was to be permitted' (*CCC*, p. 19). Bell's definition of religion specifically excludes 'the multiplicity of exotic consciousness-raising movements – the Zen, yoga, tantra, I Ching, and Swami movements' (*SJ*, p. 348). For critics like Sontag, Bell's fusion of restraining religions and culture creates a value system that denies a whole range of human experience. Bell's formulation denies both Dionysus and Eros, favours the tragic over the comic and erotic, the mind over body, pain over pleasure, and moral content over formal innovation.

It would be dangerous and uncritical to give the impression that Bell seeks to reverse the historical process by which the idea of the individual has become the basis of how western society has organised its socio-political system, but he does wish to disengage culture, religion and the arts from the idea of individual liberation and return them to a more communal spiritual role. There is an atavistic element to his thinking, strongly expressed in his essay 'The Return of the Sacred?' where he looks to 'new religions' that will 'return to the past, to seek for tradition and to search for those threads which can give a person a set of ties that place him in the continuity of the dead and the living and those still to be born. Unlike romanticism, it will not be a turn to nature, and unlike modernity it will not be the involuted self; it will be the resurrection of Memory'. These sentiments parallel the revival of what Bell calls 'moralizing religion' (*SJ*, p. 349) among the

Fundamentalist 'silent majority', a revival which Bell sees as being in part a reaction to the excesses of the counter-culture. Bell has consistently favoured the role of voluntary associations as important mediating structures between the individual and the state. In his essay, 'America as a Mass Society', included in *The End of Ideology*, Bell rejects the notion that American society has become a 'Lonely crowd' of atomised, alienated individuals. He claims that: 'In no other country in the world, probably, is there such a high degree of voluntary communal activity, expressed sometimes in absurd rituals, yet often providing real satisfaction for real needs'.[13] This strain of populism is a characteristic of Bell's theorising that links him to the considerable revival of conservatism in the United States in the 1970s and 1980s.[14]

In many ways, this celebration of voluntary associations and transcendental bonding is at odds with the investigative rationalism that is another key strain in Bell's theorising. This more empirical aspect of his analysis was particularly influential during the Kennedy era in the early 1960s. In a speech given at Yale in June 1962, Bell's 'end of ideology' thesis took on the status of Presidential doctrine. Kennedy analysed the current condition of America as follows:

> What is at stake in our economic decisions today is not some grand warfare of rival ideologies which will sweep the country with passion but the practical management of a modern economy. What we need are not labels and clichés but more basic discussion of the sophisticated and technical questions involved in keeping a great economic machinery moving ahead . . . political labels and ideological approaches are irrelevant to the solutions . . . technical answers – not political answers – must be provided.[15]

This contradictory mixture of rationalism and atavism is not illogical in Bell's own system of argument. When he was a postgraduate student, Bell was once asked by a professor: 'What do you specialize in?' Bell replied: 'I specialize in generalizations'. Bell has also increasingly specialised in contradictions. He firmly believes that the realms of economics, politics and culture can be separated and has defined his own position as follows: 'I am a socialist in economics, a liberal in politics, and a conservative in culture' (*CCC*, p. xi).

3. The Foundations of Anglo-American Literary Theory

IF Daniel Bell's and Lionel Trilling's work is characterised by an attempt to revise and rehabilitate the liberal imagination, there were other self-conscious groups who in roughly the same historical period, the 1930s to the present, fundamentally rejected liberalism. A major figure in this conservative group was T. S. Eliot, whose poems, plays and literary criticism reverberate throughout twentieth-century discussions of the relationships between art and ideology. His work and that of a group of Southern critics and writers that included John Crowe Ransom, Allen Tate, Robert Penn Warren and Cleanth Brooks will serve to exemplify a tradition that was often seen as the opposing tendency to both Marxism and Liberalism. This conservative group, like their socialist and liberal contemporaries, underwent a series of theoretical adaptations and transformations as they reacted to the political and economic changes of the period from the 1930s to the present, a process succinctly described by Malcolm Bradbury: 'They display, almost, a modern way of dealing with a history that will not stay still, a world in which the most felt opinions, the most committed life-styles, the most perfect marriages, can be as suddenly rescinded as contracted'.[1] The rate and scale of ideological change has seemed more abrupt and dramatic among writers and critics such as Dwight Macdonald and Irving Kristol who have journeyed from communism, through Trotskyism and anti-communist liberalism to their present ideological positions. Irving Kristol, the godfather of neo-conservatism, is now a registered Republican and with Daniel Bell has edited, since its foundation in 1965, the magazine *Public Interest*, one of neo-conservatism's semi-official publications. The movements within the conservative tradition have been less seismic, but it would be a mistake to underestimate the divisions and varieties of conservatism in this historical period.

17

Among the most consistent of the critics of liberalism has been T. S. Eliot. His early literary criticism clearly took issue with the idea, popularised by Romanticism and liberalism, that the individual artist should turn against the dead hand of tradition and seek inspiration in his own emotions and sensibility. In Eliot's essay 'Tradition and the Individual Talent' (1919), poetry 'is not a turning loose of emotion; it is not the expression of personality, but an escape from personality'.[2] Parallel to this rejection of romantic individualism in the arts was an attack on protestant individualism as promoted by such liberal thinkers as John Middleton Murry. Eliot disparagingly quotes Murry's formulation: 'The English writer, the English divine, the English Statesman, inherit no rules from their forbears; they inherit only this: a sense that in the last resort they must depend upon the inner voice' (*SE*, p. 27). Eliot continues his characterisation of the individualist inner voice as one 'which breathes the eternal message of vanity, fear and lust' (*SE*, p. 27) and contrasts it with the practices and beliefs of writers like himself 'who shamefully depend upon tradition and the accumulated wisdom of time' (*SE*, p. 29). He sets against this overvaluation of individualism his own conservative model in which the artist works within a tradition in which 'the historical sense compels a man to write not merely with his own generation in his bones, but with a feeling that the whole of the literature of Europe from Homer and within it the whole of the literature of his own country has a simultaneous existence and composes a simultaneous order' (*SE*, p. 14). For Eliot there can be no revolutionary break with the past, rather any new work has to be sufficiently in tune with the cultural values of the past that it can be incorporated into the 'existing monuments' which 'form an ideal order among themselves' (*SE*, p. 15). This process of absorption and modification is crucial in controlling the vagaries of individual personality, a process that involves 'a continual surrender of himself as he is at the moment to something which is more valuable. The progress of an artist is a continual self-sacrifice, a continual extinction of personality' (*SE*, p. 17). It is relevant here to point to a radically different formulation of the role of past history and tradition in the 'Eighteenth Brumaire' of Karl Marx:

> The tradition of all the dead generations weighs like a nightmare on the brain of the living. And just when they seem to be engaged in revolutionizing themselves and things, in creating something that

has never yet existed, precisely in such periods of revolutionary crisis, they anxiously conjure up the spirits of the past to their service and borrow from them names, battle cries and costumes in order to present the new scene of world history in this time-honored disguise and this borrowed language.[3]

Eliot's literary criticism is directly influenced by his sense of social and historical change. The rise of protestant individualism and capitalism disrupted what Eliot saw as the organic, unified social and cultural order of Christian feudalism. Once European society had taken this decision to set the individual free from the traditions and controls of feudalism, certain psychic and cultural consequences followed: 'In the seventeenth century a dissociation of sensibility set in, from which we have never recovered' (*SE*, p. 288). Before this dissociation poets like Dante could naturally and organically use ideas of unity and coherence in their work. The last English poets who wrote in this organic tradition that acknowledged no dualistic split between thought and feeling, mind and body, were Donne and Marvell. Donne's poetry 'is constantly amalgamating disparate experience . . . always forming new wholes' (*SE*, p. 287). After Donne, the process of dissociation set in: 'The poets revolted against the ratiocinative, the descriptive; they thought and felt by fits, unbalanced' (*SE*, p. 288). A poetry of synthesis is replaced by one of fragmentation and alienation. As a result of Eliot's arguments, Dante and Donne became monuments of artistic excellence, the 'ideal order' that modern poets should follow. It is no coincidence that Eliot's dividing line between unification and dissociation coincides with the demise of feudalism and Roman Catholicism, and the rise of capitalism and protestantism. Eliot's ideas are basic to a whole generation of critics who celebrated the arts, and poetry in particular, as elaborate linguistic structures that were not expressions of a single unsubstantial self but were rather complex treatments of inherited traditions.

A crucial component to this conservative tradition is the role of myth. The general tendency in critics of Eliot's persuasion was towards the unconscious, the non-material world of spirit and mythopeic consciousness. For Eliot a mythic structure makes 'the modern world possible for art' by bringing order. Myth 'is simply a way of controlling, of ordering, of giving a shape and a significance to the immense panorama of futility and anarchy which is contemporary history'.[4] Writers and critics in this tradition look out on a world of chaotic individualism and mass democracy and conclude that the role of art should be to redeem the world from chaos and endless diversity by ideal mythic meditations on organisation, balance, and controlling structural form, which constitute the means of reunifying dissociated sensibility. Ezra Pound and T. S. Eliot represent the international expatriate dimension of this conservative ideology. The native American dimension is most dramatically represented by a group of twelve Southerners that included John Crowe Ransom, Allen Tate, Donald Davidson and Robert Penn Warren, who published a collection of essays *I'll take my Stand: the South and the Agrarian Tradition* (1930). The main problem and grand theme that the twelve contributors addressed was announced by Ransom in an earlier essay of 1928: 'How can the Southern communities, the chief instance of the stationary European principle of culture in America, be reinforced in their ancient integrity as centers of resistance to an all – but – devouring industrialism?'[5]

Eliot's links to this group can be seen most clearly in his lectures given at the University of Virginia in 1933, published as *After Strange Gods*. The subtitle was *A Primer of Modern Heresy* and the lectures analyse the work of a number of heretical authors that include W. B. Yeats and D. H. Lawrence. Eliot declares that 'the chief clue to the understanding of most contemporary Anglo-Saxon literature is to be found in the decay of Protestantism'.[6] Yeats is castigated for substituting 'a highly sophisticated lower mythology' for a 'world of real good and evil, of holiness or sin' (*ASG*, p. 46). D. H. Lawrence's story *The Shadow in the Rose Garden* exhibits 'the absence of any moral or social sense' (*ASG*, p. 37). Only Joyce has created works 'penetrated with Christian feeling' (*ASG*, p. 48). This parlous state of cultural affairs is the consequence of a modern social system 'worm-eaten with liberalism' (*ASG*, p. 13) from which 'the idea of original sin' and the 'idea of intense moral struggle' (*ASG*, p. 42) have disappeared. In this climate, Eliot particularly welcomes the anti-industrial programme of the authors of *I'll Take my Stand* although he accepts that: 'It will be said that the whole current of economic determinism is against them' (*ASG*, p. 17). Eliot goes on to specify the roles of culture, tradition, religion and region in preserving the homogeneity of the South from the outside impact of an unnatural degree of industrialisation:

Stability is obviously necessary. You are hardly likely to develop tradition except where the bulk of the population is relatively so well off where it is that it has no incentive or pressure to move about. The population should be homogeneous; where two or more cultures exist in the same place they are likely either to be fiercely self-conscious or both to become adulterate. What is still more important is unity of religious background; and reasons of race and religion combine to make any large number of free-thinking Jews undesirable. There must be a proper balance between urban and rural, industrial and agricultural development. And a spirit of excessive tolerance is to be deprecated. (*ASG*, pp. 19–20)

Most of the elements that make up Eliot's model community are standard themes in such Southern writers as William Faulkner.

Eliot's exclusion of 'free-thinking Jews' touches on a question that has been debated throughout American history. Should all Americans be assimilated to the values and culture of such dominant founding groups as the puritans and their WASP descendants or should American culture be plural and diverse? Although Eliot and the Southern Agrarians did represent, in their own eyes, an admirable set of traditional aristocratic values, and did maintain considerable influence over American intellectual life, Daniel Bell has no doubts as to which group finally achieved the position of cultural hegemony. In his genealogical tree of the New York Jewish intellectuals (*c.* 1935–65) Bell charts the rise of Jewish intellectuals to leading arbitrating roles in American culture. Bell argues that through the achievements of literary critics such as Lionel Trilling, and art critics such as Clement Greenberg, Jewish intellectuals 'have inherited the cultural establishment in ways that they, and certainly their fathers, could never have dreamed of'.[7] Although many of the New York Jewish intellectuals have recanted on their ideological commitments of the 1930s, communism was for many of them an important influence. It is therefore significant that one of the rejected titles for the group of essays that were eventually published as *I'll Take my Stand* was *A Tract Against Communism*. Eliot's view of the fate of his type of American intellectual in an American culture that was rapidly adapting to industrialisation and free-thinking liberal ideas is also significant:

The American intellectual of today has almost no chance of

continuous development upon his own soil and in the environment which his ancestors, however humble, helped to form. He must be an expatriate: either to languish in a provincial university, or abroad, or, the most complete expatriation of all, in New York.[8]

If Eliot's despairing analysis is set against the development of New York as a major international cultural centre in the 1950s and 1960s, particularly in the field of painting, there is no doubt as to which group has flourished since the 1930s.

One of the problems with a neat division between an avant-garde free-thinking culture of experiment promoted by artists and intellectuals of the left, and an opposing culture of reactionary values and artistic forms promoted by conservative artists and intellectuals, is that both T. S. Eliot and Ezra Pound employed the experimental techniques of modernism in their poetry. T. S. Eliot's work exhibits a range of formal devices that are basic to twentieth-century modernism; ambiguous multi-dimensional levels of consciousness and points of view; a fragmentary idea of cultural continuity that mixes Zen Buddhism, vegetation myths, Christianity and discontinuous periods of English and European history, expressed in an elliptical, symbolic and surrealistic poetic language. It is also true, however, that Eliot's later poetry and plays after *The Wasteland* increasingly reduced the level of experimentation and became dependent on classical and historical mythology to provide controlling ethical and aesthetic structures as in *Murder in the Cathedral* and *The Family Reunion*. Poems such as *The Four Quartets* reveal the extent to which an overall ordering form that could absorb and control consciousness was paramount in his later work. Also it would be erroneous to see Eliot's status as that of an expatriate figure in decline. He found a powerful cultural base in English society, often arbitrating the nature of literary debate from his position as a major partner in the publishing house of Faber and Faber.

Despite their access to opinion-forming journals and publishers, both T. S. Eliot and the Southern Agrarians modified their entrenched conservatism in the face of the major economic and political transformations that occurred in both American and British society. The acceptance of a New Deal ideology of Federal intervention in the USA, and the coming of the Welfare State in post-war Britain, reinforced the trend towards liberal state capitalism and towards that industrialisation of mind and body that Eliot and the

Southern Agrarians saw as a fatal disruption of organic agrarian consciousness. Eliot's essay 'Notes toward the Definition of Culture' (1948) redefines a far less adversary position towards industrial democracy, and the work of John Crowe Ransom in the 1940s, when he was refining the techniques of the New Criticism, marks a distinct adaptation of the programme enunciated in *I'll Take my Stand*.

4. From Southern Agrarianism to Criticism Inc.

IN 1953, the poet and critic Randall Jarrell announced that he was living in an 'age of criticism'. In 1956, T. S. Eliot gave a reserved ticket only public lecture entitled *The Frontier of Criticism* in a sports arena at the University of Minnesota before an audience of 13,723. Under the bye line 'What makes a newspaper great?', the *Minneapolis Star and Tribune* gave the following account of the event:

> T. S. Eliot probably is the only poet in history to face an audience of 13,723 in a cavernous sports arena.
> The event: the third in the series of Gideon Seymour Memorial Lectures, presented by the University of Minnesota and sponsored by the *Minneapolis Star and Tribune*. The subject: a brilliant discourse on 'The Frontier of Criticism', which earned for the 67-year-old Nobel Prize winner an ovation remindful of those that rattle the same Williams Arena rafters during a Big Ten basketball game.[1]

This establishment of critical analysis and interpretation as a major activity in American intellectual life has been described by John Crowe Ransom as the advent of 'Criticism, Inc., or Criticism, Ltd.' This development was in part due to the needs of the massive extension of higher education in the USA after the Second World War. In the general professionalisation, systematisation and refinement of teaching skills and strategies that took place to meet the needs of an expanding curriculum and student market, the pursuit of knowledge took on a new missionary and semi-scientific character. In the study of literature there was a trend towards making the business of literary analysis and interpretation a more precise discipline.

Various critical tendencies emerged to meet these demands for an expanded academic study of literature and the arts. One approach that found particular favour was to see, in various authors and traditions, valuable moral and cultural critiques. The basis for this approach had been famously laid in the nineteenth century by Matthew Arnold who felt that a selected tradition of texts and ideas, drawn from the ancient Greek and Latin classics, could provide the content of a national educational curriculum of 'the best which has been thought and said'.[2] The need for such a programme was acute in a society that was rapidly coming under the dominance of a mechanical 'philistine' industrial culture that showed no respect for spiritual or aesthetic values. Arnold's belief that classical humanist culture could preserve and convey an important 'criticism of life'[3] went through several adaptations in the twentieth century. F. R. Leavis significantly adapted Arnold's position with his belief that the non-conformist intellectual tradition represented by such figures as William Blake, George Eliot and D. H. Lawrence was as valuable as and more organically indigenous than the classical tradition of Aeschylus and Virgil proposed by Arnold. Instead of humanistic 'sweetness and light',[4] Leavis celebrated 'moral intensity'.[5] The specifically American versions of these developments can be seen in the work of F. O. Matthiessen and Lionel Trilling.

Considerable impetus was given to this development of literature as a 'criticism of life' by the growth of a commercial mass culture of cinema, radio and press that was invariably seen as a threat to civilised values. The rise of literature to a pre-eminent arbitrating role in discussions about the quality of western civilisation was also in part due to the retreat from such evaluations by sociology. The social sciences became empirically-minded, more concerned with the gathering of data than with the making of value judgements about the quality of modern civilisation. There were notable exceptions to this tendency, particularly in the work of Freud, but the general retreat from explicit social or moral commentary on the part of social science left, in both America and Britain, 'an objective vacuum at the centre of the culture'[6] which literature and the humanities increasingly came to occupy.

Another important dimension to the rise of literary criticism to positions of arbitration was the work associated with the English critic, I. A. Richards. Although Richards often contrasted the subtle discriminations to be found in poetry with the crude 'stock responses'[7] of a mass culture, he was less explicit about the particular historical tradition, classical or non-conformist, that could provide alternative values and experiences to those on offer in a mass industrial society. His approach and methods were so important to many of the positions that developed in Anglo-American criticism that they merit particular attention.

I. A. Richards joined the faculty of the Harvard School of Education in 1939 after playing a major role in establishing the academic study of English literature as an autonomous discipline at the University of Cambridge in the 1920s. At the centre of his belief in literary studies is the idea that 'language is the instrument of all our distinctively human development, of everything in which we go beyond the animal'.[8] To Richards a logical extension of this idea is that literature and in particular poetry represent forms of complex linguistic organisation and development that can play a crucial role in preserving and enhancing civilised values. The various technical devices developed within poetry, rhyme, imagery, symbolism and so on, constitute the developmental instruments and tools of culture. Many of these positions are described in *Practical Criticism* (1929).

One of the first issues that Richards tackles is the division of labour between the various forms of knowledge that modern civilisation has developed. The dominant mode of cognition in modern society is that provided by science which can explain a whole range of phenomena in terms of 'verifiable facts and precise hypotheses' (*PC*, p. 5). However, there are whole areas of human concern such as 'ethics, metaphysics, morals, religion' (*PC*, p. 6) which are not susceptible to scientific investigation. These areas are fraught with subjective and unverifiable questions: 'To this world belongs everything about which civilised man cares most' (*PC*, p. 6). Richards describes these value-laden questions of debate and morality as 'tricksy components' (*PC*, p. 6) which are nevertheless as crucial to the quality and maintenance of civilisation as those empirical questions whose nature and status can be settled scientifically. At the point where science cannot provide analysis and guidance, Richards suggests that poetry can play an important role. Poetry, unlike science, is organised around a series of hypothetical statements and states that cannot be tested or proved scientifically. Poetry is full of what Richards calls 'pseudo-statements', imaginative speculations rather than scientifically verifiable descriptions. Poetry, therefore, in a modern society dominated by scientific modes of cognition, has a crucial role in dealing with an inherent crisis that Richards describes as follows: 'We do not and, at present, cannot order our emotions and attitudes by true statements alone. Nor is there any probability that we ever shall continue to do so. This is one of the great new dangers to which civilization is exposed.'[9] A further argument in favour of poetry is that many of the unscientific ethical and religious beliefs so crucial to civilisation are embodied in mythologies. Poetry has always had a special relationship to mythic consciousness. Richards maintains that 'the poetic function is the source and the tradition of poetry is the guardian of the supra-scientific myths'.[10]

As well as giving poetry an important role as a medium in which non-verifiable ideas can be explored, Richards argues that the process of analysing and responding to a poem rehearses and reinforces that crucial evolutionary stage by which, through language, we become civilised. Certain qualities of language predominate in Richards' account of the ways that poetry duplicates and enhances the shift from animal to human, from nature to culture. First and foremost poetry is a language in which subtlety and complexity are present in abundance. Poetry is 'our chief means by which subtle ideas and responses may be communicated' (PC, p. 249). It is this ability to embody and stimulate virtuoso displays of linguistic activity that earns poetry this high status:

> Making up our minds about a poem is the most delicate of all possible undertakings. We have to gather millions of fleeting semi-independent impulses into a momentary structure of fabulous complexity, whose core or germ only is given us in the words. (PC, p. 317)

In Richards' system, it is not sufficient just to stimulate linguistic activity through poetry; he has definite views as to the state of awareness that such activity should promote. A poem should provide a series of hieratically organised mental experiences. This ability of poetry to take the reader through various levels of consciousness fortuitously coincides with the way Richards conceives of the mind as a system of interests which 'must come into play and remain in play with as little conflict among themselves as possible'. Poetry is an ideal stimulus for this first level of consciousness which should be characterised by a rich diversity in which each impulse has 'the greatest possible degree of freedom'.[11] From this stage of consciousness the mind, and poetry, its surrogate, should undergo a transformation that Richards describes as follows: 'If the mind is a system of interests, and if an experience is their movement, the worth of any experience is a matter of the degree to which the mind, through this movement, proceeds towards a wider equilibrium'.[12] The admired idealised state that poetry can induce is that of 'equilibrium', a kind of balancing act in which a rich range of often contradictory impulses and ideas are held together and reconciled. The inference that a number of critics have drawn from this 'balance and conciliation model that posits an infinity of particulars held together in perfect equilibrium as the ideal'[13] is that it offers a paradigm of conservative social control and ideology. In Richards' model poetry is not a medium in which experience and analysis are allowed to remain at the level of disruptive conflict. The insights produced by the first stage of consciousness in which contradictory impulses are set in motion, are refined and moved towards an ideal of balance, harmony, of 'equilibrium'.

Richards and T. S. Eliot became the key influences on a whole generation of Anglo-American critics. To Eliot's defence of tradition, Richards added the central idea that poetry could be defended in an age of science if its special linguistic status could be established. Richards had no doubt that the complex linguistic devices, ideas and subtle emotional states that could be explored in poetry were essential to modern society:

> Nine-tenths, at the least, of the ideas and the annexed emotional responses that are passed on – by the cinema, the press, friends and relatives, teachers, the clergy . . . – to an average child of this century are – judged by the standards of poetry – crude and vague rather than subtle or appropriate. (*PC*, p. 248)

The sense in which T. S. Eliot and I. A. Richards set the terms of reference for twentieth-century Anglo-American criticism can be clearly seen in the work of John Crowe Ransom and Cleanth Brooks, two American critics who played major roles in what became a dominant school of literary analysis, the 'New Criticism' movement.

The various stages of Ransom's career pivot around a process in which there is a changing interaction between the search for a set of stable social and political ideas and a parallel search for an aesthetic system that could be internally validated without recourse to a particular idea of society. The first phase of his career was as a prime mover behind the Fugitives, a group of Southerners who founded a magazine, the *Fugitive*, in 1922. They based themselves in Nashville, a city which considered itself the Athens of the South, complete with its own full-size replica of the Parthenon. Although the title of the Fugitives suggested a group at odds with the world, alienated from the dominant creeds of progress, it took a specific event in history to clarify and hasten the creation of an ideological programme around which the Fugitives could gather. The event was the Scopes Monkey Trial of 1925 when John T. Scopes was convicted at Dayton, Tennessee, for teaching Darwinian theory in the public schools, contrary to State Statute. In *God Without Thunder*, Ransom refers to 'the affair of Dayton, Tennessee' as 'a bit of recent religious history'.[14] The ridicule that descended on the South as a backward superstitious region served to stimulate the Fugitives into making a stand on behalf of a Southern Society which they felt not only embodied admirable social values and benign forms of economic organisation that were being wantonly destroyed by Northern industrial capitalism, but was also a society that valued art and the aesthetic life. It was these characteristics of agrarian society that became the basis of their defence of the South against 'an all-but-devouring industrialism',[15] a defence launched by the twelve unsigned essays of *I'll Take My Stand*.

For Ransom, the programme enunciated by the twelve Southerners enabled him to combine his aesthetic concerns with his social beliefs: 'I subordinate always Art to the aesthetic life; its function is to initiate us into the aesthetic life, it is not for us the final end. In the *Old South* the life aesthetic was actually realized. . . .'[16] Ransom's 'Old South' is his selected historical version of the pre-Civil War plantation economy of the eighteenth century, a world that valued leisure and the life of the mind as a balance to the world of work. Ransom envisions 'the Old South' in terms of the

> social arts of dress, conversation, manner, the table, the hunt, politics, oratory, the pulpit. These were arts of living and not arts of escape; they were also community arts, in which every class of society could participate after its kind. The south took life easy, which is itself a tolerably comprehensive art.[17]

Although there is a strongly anti-industrial element in the programme described by the contributors to *I'll Take My Stand* in 1930, it was not totally Luddite, as a retrospective gloss on *I'll Take My Stand* by one of the authors, Donald Davidson, makes clear:

> We did not, of course, mean that the term industrialism should include any and every form of industry and every conceivable use of machines; we meant giant industrialism, as a force dominating every human activity: as the book says, 'the decision of society to invest its economic resources in the applied sciences'.[18]

The applied sciences of industrialism are for both I. A. Richards and Ransom the forms of cognitive knowledge against which the forms of knowledge provided by art and in particular by poetry, are to be measured, defined and justified. Richards concedes the dominance of scientific knowledge while reserving a special status for poetry as responsible for bearing 'the burden of constituting an order for our minds'.[19] Ransom takes up a far more aggressive stance towards the applied sciences and his instancing of the agrarian South as a social order to be defended against the ravages of industrialism and the applied sciences is only part of his general indictment of the course of western civilisation. The major statement of these views comes in *God Without Thunder*, which connects the rise of protestantism with the disappearance of religious orthodoxy and the triumph of secular science and industrialism. The title of the book declares its major theme which traces the cultural consequences of the demise of 'the stern and inscrutable God of Israel, the God of the Old Testament' and the advent of an 'amiable and understanding God' (*GWT*, p. 5) of the New Testament. The humanism of a Christ-centred New Testament 'adapts itself to the requirements of our aggressive modern science' (*GWT*, p. 5). This dilution of religious orthodoxy promotes an attenuation of strict orthodoxy 'into Unitarianism; into many local Congregational units; into Christian Science; and into philanthropic societies with a minimum of doctrine about God, like the Young Men's Christian Association, welfare establishments, fraternal organizations, and Rotary' (*GWT*, pp. 4–5). Ransom, like T. S. Eliot, sees religion losing its mystery and tapering off into a purely secular code of ethical conduct with neither a central orthodoxy of faith nor a mythology and set of rituals. Ransom, like Richards, attaches great value to myth: 'Religious doctrines are embodied in myths, and myths attempt to express truths which are not accessible to science. They are necessarily super-scientific, or super-natural, but they are not necessarily anti-scientific and unnatural' (*GWT*, pp. 11–12). Ransom concedes that there are ideas in Christian mythology that seem incompatible with scientific knowledge as 'when science substituted the Copernican for the Ptolemaic universe' (*GWT*, p. 12). Both parties to the dispute over whether the Ptolemaic or the Copernican system was the correct model of the universe fell into error according to Ransom's account. The defenders of the faith are faulted in that when disputing the validity of the Copernican system 'the myths in their hands did not prove sufficiently elastic, they were not modified gracefully in points that were not quite critical'. The scientists compounded the faults of their opponents by attacking the 'purely natural features' of the Ptolemaic mythology. Presumably Ransom means by this that the scientists did not intellectually recognise that the myths of religion are not to be interpreted literally. Rather they contain moral truths and meanings that can only be revealed by the techniques of allegorical and metaphorical interpretation. If the defenders of the Ptolemaic mythology had chosen to argue their case on the level of allegory, they 'might conceivably have modified the myths and represented God as presiding over a Copernican universe'. The debate might not have reached a conclusion that forces 'upon us now the necessity of choosing between a religion which seems to repudiate science from the start, and a science which seems never to rise into a religion' (*GWT*, p. 12).

Ransom's argument implies that there is a possible accommodation between science and religious orthodoxy if each were to accept that their constituent essences should be subject to different techniques of interpretation and criteria for verification. This dualistic separation of powers anticipates the ways in which Ransom, in the 1940s and 1950s, adapted and revised his view of science as his own programme for the future of literary criticism became more scientific in spirit. However, at the stage of his career represented by *God Without Thunder*, his rejection of science as a mode of cognition is reinforced by the connections he sees between science and protestantism. Like so many versions of the theme of the decline of the West, Ransom contrasts a prelapsarian world of unity with a later one of fragmentation. The religious orthodoxy of the Old Testament 'held together till the close of the period we call medieval'.

But upon that date rose Protestantism, and rose also modern science. The two have been quite contemporaneous, and it is hardly possible to find in this fact nothing but a coincidence. For

Protestantism has always figured to itself as a determination to rationalize the antiquated religious doctrines. And as for modern science, that, of course, is the developing rationalization of the universe under a minimum of definitive principles known as 'scientific'. (*GWT*, p. 28)

Ransom continually compares religion as a mode of experience and cognition with that of science.

> Religion is an order of experience under which we indulge the compound attitude of fear, respect, enjoyment, and love for the eternal nature in the midst of which we are forced to live. We were born of earth – why should we spurn it? But in science we cultivate quite a different attitude. Science is an order of experience in which we mutilate and prey upon nature. . . . (*GWT*, p. 139)

This mutilation of nature by science is manifest in the procedures and philosophy of scientific investigation:

> When our thinking is scientific or conceptual, we fail to observe the particular objects as particulars, or as objects which are different and contain a great many features not at all covered by the given concept. We attend only to what is constant or like among them, or to what has repetition – value. (*GWT*, pp. 60–1)

In contrast to these scientific modes of rationalisation are the procedures of poetry, religion and myth in which: 'The universe in every local detail is evidently of inexhaustible fullness or particularity' (*GWT*, p. 69). The recovery and description of this rich universe is the work of poets who 'are constantly creating little local myths, in their rebellion against the destructive terms of a routine presentation. "The waves outdid themselves in glee". They did not actually. It is simply a way of saying to the reader, "look very hard – did you ever see waves laughing – try then for yourself" ' (*GWT*, p. 68). Memory becomes a crucial faculty in this process:

> The myth-maker is a desperate man, for he has a memory. He remembers the remarkable individual in the richness of his private existence. He sees very little relation between that individual and

the dry generalization into which science would fit him. (*GWT*, p. 67)

In Ransom's programme, 'a myth must be institutionalised or become a social possession' (*GWT*, p. 93). Mythology needs to be intimately associated with religion: 'You must concentrate on one myth and say to it, "I believe" ' (*GWT*, p. 98). As an example of mythology without religion Ransom gives Wordsworth's pantheism which has only the status of 'a vague yearning . . . looking at nature without the benefit of a creed' (*GWT*, p. 90). Ransom demands a religion and a God 'fully equipped with his thunderbolts' (*GWT*, p. 89). His model is Jaweh, the Old Testament God of the ancient Jews who 'cannot be identified with a principle of human service. He is awful, unpredictable, unappeasable, and his works issue frequently in human suffering' (*GWT*, p. 54). This true orthodox religiosity is also manifest in its forms of worship: 'Their ritualistic practices, their Sabbath observances, and their burnt offerings were a sort of mnemonic discipline. By its help, they reminded themselves ceaselessly of their metaphysical destiny as men' (*GWT*, p. 38).

Many of the qualities that Ransom wishes to rescue and rehabilitate are preserved in agrarian communities where 'the infinite individualism of nature' is recognised, and a social temper exists which 'is humble, religious and conservative' (*GWT*, p. 128). Ransom argues that in an ideal agrarian economy, 'all labour should be effective without being arduous; and with that general proviso the best labour is the one which provides the best field for the exercise of sensibility – it is clearly some form of pastoral or agrarian labour' (*GWT*, p. 201). Ransom's homily on the pleasures of rural life concludes with the thought that: 'There may easily be more true culture in circumscribing one field with a plough than in the Grand Tour itself as it is sometimes conducted in these days'. Culture, in other words, is not a material commodity to be bought and consumed but is 'the by-product of a humane kind of life' (*GWT*, pp. 206–7).

As an example of his account of social evolution, in which the pastoral is the highest form of civilisation, Ransom cites Milton's *Paradise Lost*. In their pre-lapsarian state, Adam and Eve, in the main, work together in the garden. Ransom then comments that 'it was only when they had separated in the process of specialization that the blandishments of Satan stood a chance to succeed'. From that fatal division of labour ensued the forbidden act of eating the apple of knowledge which for Ransom represents 'the adoption of a secular attitude; in having unlimited faith in the powers of human science; in regarding nature not romantically but possessively, and as an enemy' (*GWT*, p. 131).

Ransom's pessimistic critique of western society does include a programme that will enable the individual to resist the industrialisation of mind and body that has been consequent on the relentless secularisation and specialisation of the applied sciences. Recovery depends on creating a society 'which governs itself with an orthodox religious code' (*GWT*, p. 153) and which displays a less aggressive attitude towards nature. Modern industrial urban man needs to 'hold himself back from an unthinking belligerence against nature' (*GWT*, p. 153). The role of the arts in recovering this more metaphysical view of nature is crucial in Ransom's programme. The arts should promote: 'The romantic attitude to nature . . . in which we regard the endless mysterious fullness of this object' (*GWT*, p. 129). This romantic attitude can for example be found in 'Pastoral poetry, which reached a beautiful perfection with the ancient Jews' and which represents 'the protest of a people that is being industrialized and thinks it is making a mistake' (*GWT*, p. 128).

Another more personal example of a 'romantic attitude to nature' is the way ideas of romantic love and courtship transform lust into love: 'The technique of love is not the technique of a science but the technique of an art. The lover is the man who opposes and stops the drive of his lust in order to enrich and solidify the experience. He has sensibility (*GWT*, p. 197). The same process of materialist demystification that lust represents can be seen in the way anthropology, in its pursuit of a scientific understanding of man and his cultures, relegates Christianity from the status of a theological spiritual system to that of a detritus of primitive cults that mixes 'a vegetation-myth' (*GWT*, p. 95) with solar and phallic myths.

The shift in Ransom's thought away from a controlling commitment to Southern Agrarianism to an acceptance of scientific modes of analysis can be traced in *The World's Body*, a collection of his literary criticism. In one of the essays from the book, 'Poets Without Laurels', Ransom begins to identify not with a set of social ideas but with 'the possibility that an aesthetic effect may exist by itself, independent of morality or any other useful set of ideas'.[20] Ransom demonstrates this ability of art to create virtuoso displays of technical and aesthetic complexity through an analysis of two poems, 'Sea Surface Full of

Clouds' by Wallace Stevens and 'Death of Little Boys' by Allen Tate. Stevens in particular creates in words a purely pictorial world of shifting planes and 'surface effects' (*WB*, p. 58). Ransom argues that this kind of 'pure' poetry that displays no concern with 'moral, political, religious or sociological values' (*WB*, p. 59) is a legitimate development in that it is a complex display of linguistic virtuosity. The poem by Allen Tate, though occasioned by a human tragedy, shares many of the qualities to be found in the poem by Stevens. Despite what Ransom calls 'the contagious fury of the poem', he admires the way that Tate 'conscious that he is close to moralising' draws back from commentary by employing 'an effect of obscurity' (*WB*, p. 60). Ransom likens the shift away from a concern with moral content to 'strict aesthetic effects' (*WB*, p. 59) to the ways the Impressionist painters turned their backs on the great social and sacred themes of European art and instead concentrated on virtuoso effects of technique and heightened visual perception: 'Cézanne, painting so many times and so lovingly his foolish little bowl of fruits' (*WB*, p. 62). Ransom is clearly beginning to identify with and to celebrate the role and achievements of an experimental avant-garde which is part of what he calls the 'modern program . . . to perfect the parts of experience separately or in their purity, and is a series of isolated perfections' (*WB*, p. 63).

The delight that Ransom takes in special technical effects seems at first sight at odds with his rejection of the specialising, industrialising, applied sciences. The ways in which he comes to terms with the specialising techniques of industrial society while preserving the artistic values that in *God Without Thunder* depended on an organic, religiously orthodox agrarian society can be gleaned from his essay 'Forms and Citizens', included in *The World's Body*. The essay establishes a contrast between agrarian 'societies of the old order' (*WB*, p. 31) which maintained a balance between work and play, and modern industrial societies governed by utility and efficiency in which work either excludes leisure or leaves workers too exhausted to enjoy their leisure. In modern industrial society leisure and culture are increasingly geared to the built-in instant consumer gratifications of mass commercial culture. By contrast the arts and culture of agrarian societies depend on deferred, suspended gratification: 'an art is usually, and probably of necessity, a kind of obliquity; that its fixed form proposes to guarantee the round-about of the artistic process, and the "aesthetic distance" ' (*WB*, p. 32). Ransom calls this ability to suspend immediate gratification 'aesthetic distancing', enabling the individual to 'transform instinctive experience into aesthetic experience' (*WB*, p. 42). The arts in this formulation become important guarantees of this deferred gratification through their ability to create complex aesthetic structures that can only be appreciated at leisure. Art presents a vision of elaborate plenitude 'so radical that the scientist as a scientist can scarcely understand it, and puzzles to see it rendered, richly and wastefully, in the poem, or the painting' (*WB*, p. 45). The specific example that Ransom gives of a literary text that embodies both the principle of abundance and the techniques of 'aesthetic distancing' is Milton's pastoral poem, 'Lycidas'. The pastoral genre guarantees that the spirit of the poem will be one of agrarian abundance 'rendered, richly and wastefully'. What Ransom increasingly begins to assert as he accommodates his ideology to that of a specialising industrial society is that the complex structures of modernist art can provide a vision of 'fulness' (*WB*, p. x) that is not dependent on an agrarian economy or on pastoral genres. Impressionist or cubist paintings are particularly representative of this 'fulness' in that they offer the spectator multiple planes, illusions and perspectives on reality. The experimental, highly technical disciplines of avant-garde modernist art not only offered Ransom a vision of 'fulness' independent of agrarianism but also gave the arts many of the characteristics of modern science.

Ransom's abandonment of the ideology of Agrarianism can be clearly seen in a letter he wrote to Allen Tate in 1941:

> I am forced to regard poetic theory as science, though a new science, because about a new or 'different' kind of discourse. That's why I don't want any taboos, restrictions, philosophical censorship, against analytic work. If that is positivism, I guess I'm a member of the tribe. But, as far as the absurd emphasis on scientific discourse as the only discourse goes, I'm far from being one.[21]

The final essay in *The World's Body*, 'Criticism, Inc.' outlines the new post-agrarian critical regime: 'Criticism must become more scientific, or precise and systematic, and this means it must be developed by the collective and sustained effort of learned persons – which means that its proper seat is in the Universities' (*WB*, p. 329). In his search for an apt description of the new regime, Ransom is aware of offending humanist sensibilities: 'Perhaps I use a distasteful figure but I have the idea that what we need is Criticism, Inc. or Criticism, Ltd.' (*WB*, p. 329). The 'professionals' who will carry out the new critical programme do not include the creative artist whose 'understanding is intuitive' (*WB*, p. 327), or the philosopher who specialises in general theories rather than 'an acute study of particulars'. The responsibility for carrying out the new programme is on the university teacher of literature, but not on the literary historian who spends 'a lifetime in compiling the data of literature and yet rarely or never commits himself to a literary judgement' (*WB*, p. 328). Judgement will be based on the new criticism's ability 'to define and enjoy the aesthetic or characteristic values of literature' (*WB*, p. 332). This is the core of Ransom's approach; the idea that poetry is a special kind of discourse with its own techniques, devices and frameworks of reference. Again his argument exhibits a modernist emphasis on the nature of the medium rather than on content. This elevation of aesthetics over all other qualities is in part Ransom's reaction against ideology. The ideological commitments and clashes of the 1930s have, in Ransom's view, excluded almost any discussion of form in the arts, and led to a monolithic concern with content. He claims that: 'Debate would never occur between a Humanist and a Leftist on aesthetic grounds, for they are equally intent on ethical values' (*WB*, p. 334). Instead of concerning itself with discussing social and political content, literary criticism should concern itself with technical studies. In terms of the analysis of poetry, these studies would be of 'its metric, its inversions, solecisms, lapses from the prose norm of language, and from close prose logic; its tropes; its fictions, or inventions, by which it secures "aesthetic distance" and removes itself from history' (*WB*, p. 347). Ransom urges poetry towards its own autonomous realm of meaning, not subject to the contingencies of history and ideology. Poetry, in this formulation, is liberated from materialist consciousness, free to create its own fictional world and displays of technical virtuosity.

As well as pointing the direction in which literary criticism should go, Ransom isolates several current heresies that divert attention away from 'what the poem says as poem'. The first of these heretical approaches is described by Ransom as the school of 'personal registrations', a critical method in which the emotional 'effect of the artwork upon the critic as reader' is more important than describing 'the nature of the object' (*WB*, p. 342). This diversionary approach involves the use of 'an extensive vocabulary which ascribes to the object properties really discovered in the subject as moving, exciting, entertaining, pitiful' (*WB*, p. 343). In this school of personal registrations the psychological and emotional responses of the reader take wrongful precedence over an objective analysis of the formal nature of the art-work which stimulates these subjective responses. Ransom lists other heretical approaches that detract from the aesthetic criticism he wishes to promote such as 'synopsis and paraphrase, Historical Studies, Linguistic Studies and Moral Studies' (*WB*, pp. 344–5).

The technical scientific bias that has become paramount in Ransom's work by the late 1930s does not mean that he has abandoned his basic equation of art versus science. He does, however, temper the sharpness of his original opposition to science. The relationship between art and sciences is now more that of a dialectic than a life and death struggle. The original struggle which science was clearly winning is replaced by a formulation in which the arts are 'an equal and opposite activity'. However, in order to survive in a scientific age 'poetry has to be a technical art, of extreme difficulty' (*WB*, p. xi). The complexities of Modernism can provide the technical means of survival but, as a movement, it should still be motivated by Ransom's unchanging commitment to the idea that the arts can reconstruct 'a world which is made of whole and indefeasible objects', a vision of 'fulness' (*WB*, p. x) that is inaccessible to scientific forms of enquiry.

Although there was general agreement among the new critics that the role of the arts in a scientific society should be to provide models of 'fulness' to compensate for the reductive thinness of an empirical scientific culture, there were a number of disagreements as to the technical means by which 'fulness' could be achieved. Once Ransom had abandoned Agrarianism and begun to advocate that 'criticism must become more scientific', he also began to question the idea that poetic truth was necessarily in conflict with scientific truth. As has been described, the main advocate of a clear distinction being drawn between the world of poetic 'pseudo-statements' and the world of scientific and 'verifiable hypotheses' was I. A. Richards. In Richards' formulation, poetry explores and sustains a whole complex of linguistic and moral possibilities. Science, however, is governed by reductive principles that demand logical denouements to arguments or enquiries, a linear process which excludes some avenues and options. Ransom's unease with this view that the poetic imagination has some special mystical status not subject to the same laws of explanation that govern scientific enquiry is raised in his essay on I. A. Richards that he included in *The New Criticism*. Instead of advocating like Richards that a poem should create states of 'equilibrium' and reconciliation, Ransom calls for a more rigorous approach and argues that:

> opposites can never be said to be resolved or reconciled merely because they have got into the same poem, or into the same complex of affective experience to create there a kind of tension; that if there is a resolution at all it must be a logical resolution; that where there is no resolution, we have a poem without a structural unity. . . .[22]

In his post-Agrarian phase, Ransom demands that 'the logic of a human purposiveness is necessary for poetic as for any other discourse'.[23]

Despite Ransom's personal reservations, the drive to assert the unique non-scientific status of the poetic imagination continued unabated within the 'new criticism' movement. A good example of this drive in which the superior status of poetry is continually emphasised is *The Well Wrought Urn* by Ransom's fellow-Southerner, Cleanth Brooks. The ten poems from different historical periods that Brooks selects for close critical analysis in this book do not represent a particular 'criticism of life' in the Arnold–Leavis tradition. They are linked by the degree to which they employ three connected literary devices: paradox, irony and ambiguity. Out of these three formal devices, the poets create a rich world of linguistic 'fulness'. This dense world of the poetic imagination is contrasted with the one-dimensional world of science 'whose truth requires a language purged of paradox'.[24] The flood of connotations and denotations released by this poetry of paradox, ambiguity and irony need not as Ransom argues eventuate in a 'logical conclusion'.[25] Brooks, in a spirit much closer to I. A. Richards, sees poetry as 'a dramatic process, not a logical; it represents an equilibrium of forces, not a formula'.[26] In Brooks the tendency of the new criticism to relegate disruptive conflict to a lower order of consciousness in favour of a model of the social role of art in which the vagaries of consciousness are synthesised and integrated, reaches a grand climax:

the essential structure of a poem (as distinguished from the rational or logical structure of the 'statement' which we abstract from it) resembles that of architecture or painting: it is a pattern of resolved stresses. Or, to move closer still to poetry by considering the temporal arts, the structure of a poem resembles that of a ballet or musical composition. It is a pattern of resolutions and balances and harmonizations, developed through a temporal scheme.[27]

Depending on whether you see the arts as a harmonising synthesising force or as a disruptive force in which conflict and struggle are as important as any final experience of reconciliation, Cleanth Brooks' version of aesthetic harmony has the status either of a transcendent paradise or of a monolithic fetish of control.

Throughout the 1940s and 1950s the new criticism gathered momentum. In 1939 John Crowe Ransom moved away from the South to Ohio where he founded the influential *Kenyon Review* which he edited for twenty years. Other journals that promoted the new criticism were the *Hudson Review* (from 1948), the *Sewanee Review*, which Allen Tate edited from 1944 to 1946, and the *Southern Review*, founded by Cleanth Brooks and Robert Penn Warren in 1935.[28] Brooks and Penn Warren were the real popularisers of the theories and training methods of the new criticism. In a series of teaching anthologies, beginning with *Understanding Poetry: An Anthology for College Students* (1938), they provided basic training texts for generations of college students that survived well into the 1960s. These anthologies seemed to meet the methodological requirements of the expanding higher education sector that an affluent post-war America had sanctioned. Students were trained first and foremost to appreciate the technical complexities of poetry and the subtle discriminations that a poetic discourse full of paradox, irony and ambiguity can effect. Malcolm Bradbury has summarised the continuing legacy of the new criticism as follows:

For New Criticism it was the text itself that was postulated as an empirical experience independent of the persons experiencing – an ideal text to which all critics, provided they purge themselves of quirks of personality, misfortunes of upbringing, environmental, social and political preferences, might share in as a common fund.[29]

5. The Debate on Mass Culture

It is perhaps premature to envisage a collapse of values, a transvaluation by which popular taste replaces trained discrimination. Yet commercialism has done stranger things: we have not yet fathomed the more sinister potentialities of the cinema and the loud-speaker . . .[1]

IF the new criticism established a specific role in American culture for literary analysis, it also provided one of the co-ordinates for a view of the quality and nature of the mass culture of press, radio, cinema and television. Paul Lazarsfeld, a pioneer of the debate on mass culture and its effects, has commented on the fact that the role of mass culture and its relationship to other cultural forces such as those of high culture was a major preoccupation of intellectual life from 1935: 'In this country we attained a peak of discussions about mass culture between 1935 and 1955'.[2] The purpose of this chapter and several of those that follow it is to describe the development of this debate in the work of a number of literary, cultural and sociological investigators of the impact of mass culture on American society. One emphasis will be on the proponents of the conservative critique of mass culture which stressed the low level of aesthetic complexity and intellectual content in mass culture. The work of this group, from T. S. Eliot to Dwight Macdonald, proceeded by a comparative method in which the products of mass culture were evaluated in a balance against those of high or avant-garde culture. The balance invariably tilted in favour of the latter. This conservative critique intersects at a number of points with the Marxist critique of the Frankfurt School of Theodor Adorno, Max Horkheimer and Herbert Marcuse who, in the 1930s, took up residence in the USA as a result of the rise of Nazism. This group produced a damning critique of the agencies and effects of what they described in a famous essay as 'The Culture Industry: Enlightenment as Mass Deception'.

Both these traditions see mass culture as transmitting distorted consciousness through the use of repetitive stereotypes and mechanical narrative formulae. The effects of mass culture are to induce passive alienation and anomie into the mass audience, and to exclude the majority of people from active participation by manipulating an artificial consensus of beliefs. Implicit in both the conservative and Marxist critiques is the assessment that the joint processes of industrialisation and mass democracy, of which mass culture is a product, reinforce a rationalisation and dehumanisation of all forms of social and personal being into systems that destroy the autonomy of the majority while allowing a degree of individuality to privileged groups. For the Frankfurt School theoreticians this process of rationalisation begins at an earlier stage of world history than the onset of industrialisation and mass democracy in the nineteenth century which is the favoured moment of cultural decline for T. S. Eliot and Dwight Macdonald.

T. S. Eliot's *Notes Towards the Definition of Culture* locates the cultural fall of the USA as 'a consequence of the Civil War; after which arose a plutocratic elite; after which the expansion and material development of the country was accelerated; after which was swollen that stream of mixed immigration, bringing (or rather multiplying) the danger of development into a caste system which has not yet been quite dispelled'.[3] Dwight Macdonald's version of the grand moment of decline is similar: 'The turning point in our culture was the civil war, whose aftermath destroyed the New England tradition almost as completely as the October Revolution broke the continuity of Russian culture'. Macdonald's account includes a note of liberal despair at what might have been:

> New England culture dwindled to provincial gentility and there was no other to take its place; it was smothered by the growth of mass industry, by westward expansion, and above all by the massive immigration from non-English-speaking countries. The great metaphor of the period was the melting pot; the tragedy was that it melted so thoroughly. A pluralistic culture might have developed enriched by the contributions of Poles, Italians, Serbs, Greeks, Jews, Finns, Croats, Germans, Swedes, Hungarians and all the other peoples that came here from 1870 to 1910.[4]

For Eliot and Macdonald it is the destruction of a minority aristocratic high culture by the coming of mass industrial society that is the occasion for an irreversible disintegration and decline of culture. For Theodor Adorno and Max Horkheimer this process dates from a much earlier historical period. In an intricate reading of the *Odyssey* they show how the features of a mass culture in modern industrialised societies are anticipated in the poem. The classic encounter between Odysseus and the sirens prefigures the ways pleasure will be organised and distributed in a mass society. Odysseus outwits the temptations of the singing sirens not by taking another route that will pass beyond their vocal range but by stopping the ears of his rowers with beeswax and then binding himself to the mast. By these manoeuvres Odysseus has controlled access to pleasure himself while his proletarian oarsmen row on mindlessly like the consumers of mass culture.[5] This early model of the process of mechanical rationalisation suggests that Adorno and Horkheimer view industrialisation as only the latest phase of a process that began much earlier. Also the process of rationalisation that industrial democracy intensifies is not wholly detrimental and contains a contradictory promise:

> The fallen nature of modern man cannot be separated from social progress. On the one hand, the growth of economic productivity furnishes the conditions for a world of greater justice; on the other hand it allows the technical apparatus and the social groups which administer it a disproportionate superiority to the rest of the population.[6]

The pessimism of T. S. Eliot and Dwight Macdonald is clearly different from the notion of the contradictory promise of industrial capitalism developed by the Frankfurt School theorists.

This opening sketch of reactions to mass culture would not be complete without mention of a diverse group of sociologists and anthropologists who began to study mass society using a range of investigative techniques derived from three main sources: opinion polling and marketing research, anthropological field work, and psychoanalytic testing strategies derived from Freud. Much of this work was federally financed and inspired and coincides with the expansion of government involvement in all aspects of American life that was a marked characteristic of the period from the New Deal onwards. This awareness of mass society was intensified by the experience of mobilisation and government-directed life during the Second World War. The range and quality of these mass observation studies varied in scale and scope from studies of particular socio-economic groups and communities, to studies of distinct subcultures, and on to general assessments of the condition of the American psyche on a national scale. These kinds of concerns also became central to the work of a number of writers and artists. Norman Mailer's novel *The Naked and the Dead* (1948) is a particularly representative study of the totalitarian potential of a mass society in arms. The trend towards these kinds of studies led, in the view of one of the major practitioners of this form of analysis, C. Wright Mills, to a situation where: 'The sociological imagination is becoming, I believe, the major common denominator of our cultural life and its signal feature'.[7]

The following selected list of studies does not include the work of novelists and new journalists that will be covered elsewhere but does bear witness to the scale of the activity among social scientists, anthropologists and psychologists:

The Gold Coast and the Slum (a study of social life and mobility in a district of Central Chicago), Harvey Warren Zorbaugh (1929)

Middletown (a study in Contemporary American Culture), Robert S. Lynd and Helen M. Lynd (1929)

Middletown in Transition (a study in Cultural Conflicts), Robert S. Lynd and Helen M. Lynd (1937). (Middletown was a pseudonym for the town Muncie in Indiana.)

Caste and Class in a Southern Town, John Dollard (1937)

Management and the Worker (a pioneering work of industrial sociology based on an analysis of the Hawthorne Works of the Western Electric Company, Cicero, Chicago), F. J. Roethlisberger and William J. Dickson (1939)

And Keep Your Powder Dry (an analysis of how to define and deal with fascism in a democratic society), Margaret Mead (1942)

Street Corner Society (a study of gangs and rackets in a district of Chicago), William Foote Whyte (1943)

An American Dilemma (a study of the Negro problem) organised by the Swedish writer, Gunner Myrdal (1944)

The American People (an analysis of American character by a British anthropologist), Geoffrey Gorer (1948)

The two Kinsey Reports: *Sexual Behaviour in the Human Male* (1948);
Sexual Behaviour in the Human Female (1949)

Studies in Social Psychology in World War II, Vol. I, *The American Soldier:
Adjustment during Army Life*, S. A. Stouffer, E. A. Suchman, L. C.
De Vinney, S. A. Star and R. M. Williams, Jr. (1949). (There
were four volumes in all.)

The Authoritarian Personality (a study of prejudice focusing on
anti-Semitism), T. W. Adorno, Else Frenkel-Brunswick, Daniel
J. Levinson and R. Levitt Sanford (1950)

The Lonely Crowd (a study of the changing American character),
David Riesman (1950)

White Collar (a study of the professional middle class), C. Wright
Mills (1951)

Hustlers, Beats and Others (a study of pool room society), Ned Polsky
(1967)

The list is not exhaustive and the books embrace a multiplicity of
research methods and theoretical speculations but this small selection
of investigative work sponsored by such diverse groups as the
Carnegie Foundation, the American army, the Rockefeller Foundation and the American Jewish Committee shows the extent to which
social and cultural behaviour in a mass society had become a central
concern of American intellectuals and their sponsors. The American
people had become used to being questioned and analysed, particularly in the years of the New Deal when armies of documentary
investigators and photographers sought to provide Washington with
an accurate portrait of Americans in a state of economic depression.
Erskine Caldwell found that these kinds of investigations had reached
saturation point when an attendant at a petrol station, in reply to
some political questions, handed Caldwell a neatly printed card
which read:

I am 36 years old. I smoke about a pack of cigarettes a day,
sometimes more and sometimes less, but it evens up. I take an
occasional drink of beer. I am a Baptist, an Elk, and a Rotarian. I
live with my own wife, send my children to school, and visit my
in-laws once a year on Christmas Day. I wear No. 9½ shoes, No. 15½
collar and No. 7¼ hat. I shoot a 12-gauge shotgun and have a
27-inch crotch. I like rice, sweet potatoes, and pork sausage. I vote

for F. D. R., pull for Joe Louis, and boo Diz Dean. I wouldn't have anything against Hitler if he stayed in his own backyard.[8]

Despite these signs of popular indifference, the debate on mass culture seemed to focus many of the anxieties of post-war society. The purpose of the analysis of Dwight Macdonald and the chapters that follow is to particularise various contributions to the mass culture debate either in the work of a single person, or as became an increasingly more typical research model, a group of investigators with access to teams of interviewers and research data, compiled from questionnaires.

Daniel Bell in *The End of Ideology* gives a portrait of Dwight Macdonald as a 'journalist-cum-intellectual, not a social scientist or a philosopher. The intellectual takes as a starting point his self and relates the world to his own sensibilities; the scientist accepts an existing field of knowledge and seeks to map out the unexplored terrain.'[9] This portrait gives the impression of a romantic maverick intelligence with a distaste for any concept of a party line or collective activity. This image may be an accurate guide to Macdonald's style during the period from 1944 onwards when he founded his own monthly, later quarterly, periodical *Politics* which ran until 1949, but it is not a very good guide to his involvement in cultural politics which began with the founding of *Miscellany* magazine in 1929.

Macdonald's commitment to individualism was a position he finally reached after immersion in the ideological battles waged amongst left intellectuals in the 1930s. Macdonald was a frequent contributor to *Partisan Review*, a magazine that became closely associated with a more critical view of Russian communism than that adopted by the American Communist Party. In order to expose the evils of Stalinism, Macdonald and other socialist cultural critics such as the art critic, Clement Greenberg, gave their support to the leader of the opposition to Stalin, the exiled Trotsky. *Partisan Review* published Trotsky's positions including a letter from Trotsky entitled *Art and Politics*, translated by Macdonald and published in December 1937. Macdonald's support of Trotskyite positions was based on his growing disenchantment with such developments in Russia as the purges and show trials of dissidents, and the silence of the American Communist Party on these events. The Nazi-Soviet non-aggression pact of 1939 completed the betrayal of the course of the Russian

Revolution in the eyes of radicals such as Macdonald who began to use the word totalitarian to describe the nature of the Stalinist state bureaucracy and its repressive ideology.

These political arguments had been accompanied by a series of related debates on the role of the artist in the revolutionary process. Both in Stalin's Russia and in artistic circles in America that followed the Communist Party line, there was a distrust of artistic experiment and the achievements of the avant-garde. The favoured official aesthetic was that of Socialist Realism which led to a populist art depicting the heroic labours of industrial and agricultural workers. Avant-garde abstract art was seen as negative and pessimistic and was therefore potentially counter-revolutionary. The popular-front consciousness which dominated the arts in America during the 1930s when radicals of all persuasions buried their differences and united in a common struggle against fascism, created an affirmative mood in which the experimental disruptions of modernism seemed out of place. In Macdonald's view this repression of the avant-garde was the cultural equivalent of the Stalinist purges and show trials. Again the pages of *Partisan Review* provide examples of this debate. In 1941, Van Wyck Brooks gave a paper on 'Primary Literature and Coterie Literature' which condemned the work of T. S. Eliot, Ezra Pound, James Joyce, Gertrude Stein and the theories of the new criticism on the grounds that they had lost touch with mainstream democratic values and had degenerated into an unhealthy pessimism. Macdonald's reply to Van Wyck Brooks, *Van Wyck Brooks and Kulturbolschewismus*, was included in the November–December issue of *Partisan Review*, 1941.

In his reply Macdonald defends Eliot, Joyce, Proust, Henry James and Valéry on the grounds that the avant-garde 'is still the most advanced cultural tendency that exists, and in a reactionary period it has come to represent again relatively the same threat to official society as it did in the early decades of the century'. He describes the various attacks on the avant-garde as 'an ominous sign of the drift towards totalitarianism'. *Partisan Review* is seen as 'fighting a rearguard action against this growing official aesthetic, first as it manifested itself in the Stalinist writer's front, then, after the Nazi Pact disillusioned the main body of American writers with Stalinism (unfortunately, purely on the political level, without raising the broader cultural issues at all), as it has cropped up in the swing behind the government in the war crisis'.[10]

'The swing behind the government' has not only created an unthinking support for Stalinism, it has also devalued the liberties of the individual, and the achievements of democratic liberalism. As an example of this betrayal of liberalism, Macdonald cites Roosevelt's Vice-President, Henry Wallace. Wallace's pro-Russian sympathies and support for Roosevelt's programme of Federal intervention in all areas of America life signify the decay of liberalism: 'A "liberal" used to be one who favoured the spread of liberty. Today it has become one who favours the extension of governmental authority for reasons of efficiency, especially in wartime'.[11] The original promise of liberalism was as a counter to the power of a centralised state. In the political and economic crises of the 1930s, the liberal has become ' "the social engineer" who gets things done and thinks in terms of the efficient conduct of modern mass society. Fiorella La Guardia and Henry Wallace are examples'.[12] Classic liberalism has been replaced by populism and the rhetoric of the popular front. Macdonald is highly critical of this reduction of the idea of individual rights: 'The notion of the common man can be summed up: become like everybody else, become nothing. This is a long way from the western concept of the citizen'.[13]

Macdonald emerges from the ideological battles of the 1930s and 1940s as an anti-Stalinist liberal. He resigned from *Partisan Review* in 1943 mainly because his pacifism was contrary to the main editorial line, but this did not lead to a retreat from political and cultural debate. His position during the Cold War can be gleaned from his contribution to a public debate at the Holyoake College in the winter of 1952 on the conflict between East and West, between Soviet communism, and American liberalism. In answer to Norman Mailer's attack on the West, Macdonald argues his case as to 'why I choose the West' as follows:

> I choose the West because I see the present conflict not as another struggle between basically similar imperialisms as was World War I but as a fight to the death between radically different cultures. In the West, since the Renaissance and the Reformation, we have created a civilization which puts a high value on the individual, which has to some extent replaced dogmatic authority with scientific knowledge, which since the 18th Century has progressed from slavery and serfdom to some degree of political liberty, and which has produced a culture which, whilst not as advanced as that

of the ancient Greeks, still has some appealing features. I think Soviet Communism breaks sharply with this evolution, that it is a throw back not to the relatively humane middle ages, but to the great slave societies of Egypt and the Orient.[14]

In the light of the rise of fascism in Europe in the 1930s, Macdonald's claim that western liberalism and its culture of enlightenment are guarantees of individual rights, is an extremely suspect equation. Macdonald was to abandon this idea that there were different cultural traditions of freedom in the East and West in favour of a view that economic transformations could obliterate and assimilate cultural diversity into monolithic structures: 'The tendency of modern industrial society whether in the U.S.A. or the U.S.S.R. is to transform the individual into the mass man' (*AAG*, p. 8). Increasingly Macdonald turned his interests towards the effects of mass culture and became a leading figure in the debate.

The various permutations of meaning that the term 'mass' generated in the course of the mass culture debate have been usefully summarised by Daniel Bell and can provide a context in which to examine Macdonald's analysis. Bell isolates five different, and sometimes contradictory, usages:

(1) Mass as undifferentiated number as commonly used in the expression 'mass media' implying that standardised material is transmitted to all groups of the population uniformly.

(2) Mass as signifying low, vulgar quality, a usage mainly derived from Ortega y Gasset's *The Revolt of the Masses* (1931) in which mass is used not to denote a group such as the workers but the low level of modern industrial civilisation which resulted from the decline of the aristocracy of discerning gentleman patrons who once constituted a controlling educated elite.

(3) Mass as the mechanised society, a usage which idealises nature and the pastoral and contrasts an organic face to face rural *gemeinshaft* with an atomised anonymous industrial *gesellschaft*.

(4) Mass as denoting the bureaucratised state in which all activities have been regulated and centralised into a seamless web of control.

(5) Mass as mob, a usage popularised by Hannah Arendt's *The Origins of Totalitarianism* (1951) which sees the mass as the majority of those large numbers of neutral politically indif-

ferent people who never join a party or hardly ever go to the polls.[15]

Daniel Bell's reservations about the mass culture thesis are that as a model it does not 'reflect or relate to the complex richly striated social relations of the real world'.[16] However, the fact remains that a consciousness of mass cultural forces has become a central concern and part of the folklore of western culture.

Macdonald's most theoretical contribution to the mass culture debate appears in its final form as an essay on 'Mass Cult and Mid Cult' in *Against the American Grain*. The essay in its earliest version was published in Macdonald's magazine *Politics* in February 1944 under the title of 'A Theory of Popular Culture'. It was this 1944 version that Eliot described as 'the best alternative'[17] to the one he advanced in *Notes Towards the Definition of Culture*. At the centre of Macdonald's argument is a basic distinction between high culture which was originally a minority aristocratic culture dependent on a patron, and mass culture which is often parasitic on the forms and content of high culture, but is marketed to be consumed by a mass audience, not to be individually appreciated by a minority. Before mass culture emerged, high culture existed separately from folk culture in 'fairly water-tight compartments' which 'corresponded to the sharp line once drawn between the common people and the aristocracy' (*AAG*, p. 34). This relationship was transformed by the coming of mass cult which altered the production and distribution of culture: 'Mass cult first made its appearance in eighteenth century England where also, significantly, the industrial revolution was just beginning. The important change was the replacement of the individual patron by the market' (*AAG*, p. 15). This process, the industrialisation of culture, occurred in the USA after the Civil War. Once mass cult has appeared, a whole set of destructive interactions between the various cultural categories of high, folk and mass takes place. The blurring of the lines between the folk culture of the common people and the high culture of the aristocracy 'however desirable politically, has had unfortunate results culturally. Folk art had its own authentic quality, but mass cult is at best a vulgarized reflection of High Culture and at worst a cultural nightmare, a Kulturkatzenjammer' (*AAG*, p. 34). The unwholesome ménage à trois of high, folk, and mass then spawns an even more sinister hybrid, called 'Mid cult', which in the period since the 1930s has posed a greater threat to high culture than that posed by mass cult. Macdonald describes the threat as follows:

> The danger to High Culture is not so much from mass cult as from a peculiar hybrid bred from the latter's unnatural intercourse with the former. A whole middle culture has come into existence and it threatens to absorb both its parents. This intermediate form – let us call it Mid cult – has the essential qualities of mass cult – the formula, the built-in reaction, the lack of any standard except popularity – but it decently covers them with a cultural figleaf. (*AAG*, p. 37)

This last quotation introduces the main way in which Macdonald distinguishes between high, mass and mid cult, in terms of their effects on their audiences. The standardised products of mass and mid cult are programmed to produce 'the Built-In Reaction'. Macdonald borrows this formulation from Clement Greenberg's article in *Partisan Review* (1939), 'Avant-Garde and Kitsch'. Macdonald applies Greenberg's analysis of kitsch and its effects as follows:

> The special aesthetic quality of kitsch – a term which includes both Masscult and Midcult – is that it 'predigests art for the spectator and spares him effort, provides him with a short cut to the pleasures of art that detours what is necessarily difficult in the genuine art' because it includes the spectator's reactions in the work itself instead of forcing him to make his own responses. (*AAG*, pp. 28–9)

Among the examples of the insidious workings of mid-cult kitsch, Macdonald gives some lines spoken by the stage-manager in Thornton Wilder's play, *Our Town*. Sucking on his pipe, the stage-manager confides to the audience:

> Now there are some things we all know, but we don't tak'm out and look at'm very often. We all know that something is eternal. And it ain't houses and it ain't names. . . . There's something way down deep that's eternal about every human being.

The folksy populist tone of the speech provokes Macdonald to comment: 'The last sentence is an eleven-word summary in form and content of Mid cult. I agree with everything Mr Wilder says but I will fight to the death against his right to say it in this way' (*AAG*, p. 40).

This ability of mid cult and mass cult to create mass circulation commodities that appeal to the lowest common denominator is well understood by the owners and editors of *Life* magazine which:

> mixes, scrambles everything together, producing what might be called homogenized culture, after another American achievement, the homogenization process that distributes the globules of cream evenly throughout the milk instead of allowing them to float separately on top . . . the process destroys all values, since value judgements require discrimination, an ugly word in liberal-democratic America.

Life, Macdonald notes, is purchased by rich, middle class and poor alike, creating an illusion of social consensus which is mirrored in the way 'the same issue will present a serious exposition of atomic energy, followed by a disquisition on Rita Hayworth's love life'. Macdonald ironically concludes: 'Mass cult is very, very democratic; it refuses to discriminate against or between anything or anybody' (*AAG*, p. 12).

The only counters to the corrosive effects of mass and mid cult are the residual achievements of the 'old avant-garde of 1870–1930, from Rimbaud to Picasso' (*AAG*, p. 56). This tradition of avant-gardism provides the only models of artistic excellence in modern industrial society. In its heyday, this avant-garde had managed to separate 'itself from the market and was in systematic opposition to it'. Despite becoming famous and successful the avant-garde figures that Macdonald names 'like Stravinsky, Picasso, Joyce, Eliot, and Frank Lloyd Wright' created works of art not for a mass audience but for a 'small audience that sympathized with their experiments because it was sophisticated enough to understand them' (*AAG*, p. 20). This avant-garde art and its effects can be distinguished from the in-built effects of mass cult because avant-garde art is 'an expression of feelings, ideas, tastes, visions that are idiosyncratic and the audience similarly responds to them as individuals. Those who consume mass cult might as well be eating ice-cream sodas' (*AAG*, p. 5).

Macdonald's proposals for the future of culture in modern industrial society contain two main strategies. One is to accept mass cult and high culture but reject mid cult: 'So let the masses have their mass cult, let the few who care about good writing, painting, music, architecture, philosophy, etc. have their High Culture, and don't fuzz up the distinction with Mid cult' (*AAG*, p. 73). The second strategy consists of attempting 'to raise the level of our culture generally' (*AAG*, p. 70) (presumably according to the models provided by the avant-garde). However, Macdonald's essay ends with a revision of these proposals which will be 'a compromise between the conservative and liberal proposals'. This third strategy is based 'on the recent discovery – since 1945 – that there is not One Big Audience but rather a number of smaller, more specialised audiences that may still be commercially profitable . . . the mass audience is divisible, we have discovered – and the more it is divided, the better' (*AAG*, p. 73).

This reluctant acceptance of a diversity of specialised audiences existing side by side without conflict is reminiscent of the world of reconciliation of contradictions, achieved in the aesthetic equilibriums of I. A. Richards and Cleanth Brooks. Macdonald has reached a position where he accepts the commercially profitable cultural divisions and levels created by the American market economy. This commitment to pluralism clearly signals the demise of Macdonald's Marxist sympathies. It is the difference between working for *Partisan Review* in the 1930s and Macdonald's career as a staff writer for the *New Yorker* and *Esquire* magazines, mainly on cinema, after his own journal *Politics* closed in 1949. Like so many one-time Marxist intellectuals in the post-war period, Macdonald created a career for himself as a journalist-cum-cultural critic shuttling between part-time teaching in universities and staff-writer positions on weekly magazines and journals of opinion. This world of journals was the milieu within which many of the cultural debates of the post-war period were conducted. The columns of the *New Yorker, Partisan Review, the New York Review of Books, Esquire, Harper's, Village Voice* and *Rolling Stone*, among others, play a significant role in mediating taste and cultural opinion to their largely college-educated, middle-class readerships. None of these journals called for the revolutionary transformations demanded by radical journals in the 1930s, but they did provide platforms for disenchanted Marxists like Macdonald. On occasions, particularly during the period of urban riots and anti-Vietnam marches of the 1960s, there was a renewal of ideological commitment by some of these journals of opinion. In 1967, at the time of the Detroit and Newark riots, the *New York Review of Books* 'printed a diagram showing a Molotov cocktail on its cover and its lead article called for revolution and dismissed Martin Luther King as an amiable, do-gooding relic from the past'.[18]

Macdonald's contributions to this process of mediating cultural opinion, with regard to film, were gathered in his volume of essays and reviews *Dwight Macdonald on Movies*. The book repeats many of the formulations of mass cult and mid cult particularly the attack on the mass-cult productions of the Hollywood studio system. The book also reveals the extent to which Macdonald's historical assessment of world cinema, forged in the ideological battles of the 1930s and 1940s, became a standard post-war liberal orthodoxy until challenged by auteur critics such as Andrew Sarris.

In line with the theories of mass cult and mid cult, the main source of artistic excellence in world cinema is provided by an avant-garde group of individual geniuses. A basic source of this view is Macdonald's essay 'The Soviet Cinema 1930–40; A History', which he contributed to *Partisan Review* in 1938 and 1939. The theme of the essay is the crushing of the cinematic genius of the Eisenstein generation of 1925–29 by Stalinism:

> The 1917 Revolution, sweeping aside the old order, opened a wide field to avant-garde art. In the first decade after 1917, the Soviet Union was the scene of a veritable renaissance of such tendencies: Mayakovsky and the LEF group in literature, Malievitch and Kandinsky in painting, the formalist and the constructivist schools of architecture, Eisenstein, Pudovkin and Dovschenko in the cinema, Tairov and Meyerhold in the theatre. . . . Finding no stable base in Russian society, the avant-garde in one field after another was ousted by the reactionaries, just as the old Bolsheviks, whose advanced political theories similarly clashed with a backward society, were gradually reduced to impotence by the Stalin bureaucracy.[19]

This reading of the history of Russian cinema directly influences the way he constructs his history of world cinema and the role of Hollywood. Macdonald's periodisation coincides with technological developments. In his view cinema has passed through three major periods: Classic Silent (1908–29), Early, or Medieval, Sound (1930–55), and Later, or Renaissance, Sound (1956 to date). All aesthetic achievement in cinema flows from the first period 'which subdivides into American (Griffith, Stroheim, and the makers of silent comedies); Weimar German (Murnau, Lang, Pabst, and Caligari); NEP Russian (Eisenstein, Pudovkin, Dovzhenko, et al)' (*OM*, pp. xvii–xviii). The second period, 1930–55, which coincides with the coming of sound and the studio system of Hollywood is in Macdonald's view a cultural wasteland of mass kitsch when the artistic genius of individual autocrats like Griffith was replaced by the anonymous industrialisation of 'craftsmen, specialists, technicians who turn out, perhaps with stifled boredom or indignation, whatever the industry requires of them' (*OM*, p. 76).

The particular aesthetic qualities that Macdonald focuses upon to mirror the decline of artistry in cinema are the 1930s conventions of sound and characterisation that are still dominant in post-Second World War Hollywood production. A good example of the continuing travesty of the original promise of American cinema and the extent to which directors like Elia Kazan have not escaped the melodramatic conventions of the 1930s is Macdonald's review of Elia Kazan's 1961 film *Splendor in the Grass*:

> It seems impossible that *Splendor in the Grass* could be contemporaneous with *L'Aventura*. Technically, it could have been made in 1930 . . . (Kazan) knows about the close-up, he uses waterfalls as a background for sexy scenes (all that torrential noise), and he blurs the focus to indicate violence, but that is about the extent of his cinematic savvy. He is, furthermore, as vulgar a director as has come along since Cecil B. De Mille; in his movies – and his direction of such plays as *J.B.* and *Sweet Bird of Youth* – the emotional pitch is always fortissimo, the hard sell is always in, and passions are torn to tatters to split the ears of the groundlings. (*OM*, p. 141)

The film's music is typical of Hollywood overkill, 'shameless crescendos to back up the "big" moments' (*OM*, p. 137) and is a sure sign for Macdonald of the programmed built-in reactions of mass cult that anticipate and comprehensively regiment the audience's emotional responses.

Macdonald's other quarrel with the aesthetic conventions of the Hollywood studio system is with the nature of characterisation inherent in the action-dominated genres of Hollywood:

> One mark of a bad movie or play is that the characters exist only as

functions of the plot, which means they have lots of Big Moments, but no small ones. Real people, however, exist all the time – that is known as the time-space continuum and is rigidly enforced everywhere except in Hollywood. (*OM*, p. 142)

These Hollywood conventions of sound and characterisation have the effect of eliding the process of individual response to a work of art: a blind man could follow a film by Kazan. In Macdonald's view the conventions of Hollywood impose a very limited repertoire of effects on the director, who is forced to make everything very clear, nudging the audience to the proper response.

Although Macdonald concedes that his second historical period of cinema, 1930–55, does include 'some good American films by Hawks, Ford, and others, but only two masters – Lubitsch and Welles', the cinema industry only recovers the promise of the silent period with the advent of a new non-American high art cinema represented by ' "old masters" like Bergman, Fellini, Antonioni, Truffaut, Resnais, Bunuel, and Kurosawa'. This group of directors have created a new 'esthetic of the sound film' (*OM*, p. xviii). In contrast to the heavy-handed use of sound and action-dominated plots in Hollywood, this new international school 'subordinates plot to character; it uses images and sound to suggest a mood rather than tell a story; and it has restored montage and the camera to the dominance they had before they were dethroned by stage dialogue in 1930' (*OM*, p. 375). This new cinema also recreates the process of unprogrammed individual response to art that distinguishes an avant-garde work from a kitsch one:

> Antonioni's sound tracks, on the contrary, are miracles of understatement, mostly using natural sounds, including the human voice and often reversing the Hollywood pattern and stepping the sound down, or even eliminating it completely, during the 'big scenes'. He doesn't nudge, he states. The odd thing is that some of us in the movie audience, an increasing number of late years, rather enjoy doing some work, perhaps because we are used to books and music and paintings that require some effort from the consumer. (*OM*, p. 36)

Complexity is clearly a quality that Macdonald values both in art and in the nature of the response it evokes but, in his later reviews, he retreats from his commitment to the experimental aesthetic of 'the old avant-garde of 1870–1930 from Rimbaud to Picasso' (*AAG*, p. 56) to a more traditional realist high culture aesthetic. In a 1964 review of Fellini's film *8½*, Macdonald likens the film not to Picasso but to traditional representational painters, not to Stravinsky but to classical composers: 'like Baroque art, of which it is a belated golden ray, *8½* is complicated but not obscure. It is more Handel than Beethoven – objective and classical in spirit as against the romantic subjectivism we are accustomed to. It's all there, right on the surface, like a Veronese or a Tiepolo' (*OM*, p. 30). Fellini's aesthetic is not seen in the experimental disruptive tradition of the avant-garde, it is closer to the synaesthetic fulness of classical art that Ransom finds in Milton's *Lycidas*. *8½* becomes a dense encyclopaedic structure of high-culture cross-references:

Finally, in *8½*, Fellini steals from everybody, just like Shakespeare. 'Theft' on this scale becomes synthesis. *8½* is an epitome of the history of cinema . . . the general structure – a montage of tenses, a mosaic of time blocks – recalls Intolerance, Kane, and Marienbad, but in Fellini's hands it becomes light, fluid, evanescent. And delightfully obvious. (*OM*, p. 31)

After such high *plaisir du texte* no wonder Macdonald's vision of aesthetic hell is an echo chamber full of Elia Kazan's soundtracks.

Macdonald's argument is that, given the industrialised studio system that achieved control over American cinema in the 1930s, it necessarily followed that any film packaged as a commodity by such a culture industry would cater to the lowest common denominator of appreciation in its mass-consumer audience. This is a view shared by the Frankfurt School theoreticians Adorno and Horkheimer. As a view it prevailed as the dominant intellectual perspective on mass culture and its products until a whole range of developments such as Pop Art and the revaluation of Hollywood directors undertaken by the French critics and film-makers of the *Cahiers du Cinéma* group and Andrew Sarris of the *Village Voice* dissolved the critical categories that had been established by a generation of Marxists, liberals and conservatives. The aesthetic Chinese wall that had separated the products of high from mass art began to crumble. Macdonald, however, has remained unrepentant in his view of Hollywood:

The only great films to come out of Hollywood were made before industrial elephantiasis had reduced the director to one of a number of technicians, all operating at about the same level of authority. Our two greatest directors, Griffith and Stroheim, were artists, not specialists; they did everything themselves, dominated everything personally. (*OM*, p. 446)

Despite Macdonald's views, one of the continuing debates on the artistic status of Hollywood has centred on the degree to which an individual director can impose his own personal vision and style on the commercially determined genres and aesthetic conventions of the Hollywood studio system. Auteur critics such as Andrew Sarris of the *Village Voice* have named a whole tradition of directors from John Ford to Nicholas Ray who have managed to create artistically distinguished films within the commercial structures of the Hollywood studio and star systems. The terms of the auteur rehabilitation of Hollywood will be examined in a later chapter but there were other affirmations of Hollywood's aesthetic and sociological status that developed in the 1940s and 1950s. The work of Robert Warshow is significant in this context.

6. Robert Warshow and the Legacy of the 1930s

IN his genealogical chart of the intelligentsia in American society, 1935–65, Daniel Bell places Robert Warshow in the second generation, coming of age in the late 1930s and early 1940s. The coming of age of this generation coincided with a general disenchantment with the idea that adherence to a pre-determined party line on questions of political and cultural policy was a necessary prerequisite of left-wing radicalism. Dwight Macdonald's defence of high culture and the avant-garde was one outcome of this period of disenchantment, and could either be seen as an important defence of the principle of artistic freedom or a counter-revolutionary collapse of radicalism. Robert Warshow began to publish at a particular phase of these ideological debates. *Partisan Review*, founded in 1934, where Warshow published a number of his essays on aspects of mass culture, had been a semi-official organ of the American Communist Party. By the time Warshow began to contribute to its columns in 1946 *Partisan Review* had become a focus for attacks on Stalinist authoritarianism. This emphasis on a defence of individualism that came to be characterised as anti-communist liberalism was a feature of the other main publication to which Warshow contributed, *Commentary*. This monthly magazine had originally been called *Contemporary Jewish Record*, founded in 1938 'to promote Jewish cultural interests and creative achievement in America', but widened its scope with a change of name to *Commentary* in 1945. Contributors to the magazine in its pursuit of a non-sectarian plural image included James Baldwin. Warshow's contributions to the various ideological revisions and assessments that emerged in the post-war period were abruptly terminated by his early death in 1955, at the age of 37, but his basic positions were outlined in an essay he contributed to the December 1947 issue of *Commentary*, significantly called 'The Legacy of the 30s'.

The essay is mainly concerned with the pervasive impact of the communist movement on the cultural climate and production of the 1930s. In Warshow's view the impact was corrosive and destructive:

> in the 1930s radicalism entered upon an age of organised mass disingenuousness, when every act and every idea had behind it some 'larger consideration' which destroyed its honesty and its meaning.[1]

The machiavellian tactics of Stalinism, the subordination of means to ends, are seen by Warshow as decisive corruptions of 'the character of American liberalism and radicalism' (*IE*, p. 33). Elia Kazan in recalling his early political life gives a portrait of how party lines were enforced:

> Our behaviour in the Group Theatre was conspiratorial and, I thought, disgusting: our cell would discuss what we were going to do, then we would go to Group Theatre meetings or Actors' Equity meetings and pretend we were there with open minds.[2]

This subordination of individual to group response was not only characteristic of the Communist Party, but showed itself in the ways genuine political debate was pre-empted by Roosevelt's manipulation of public opinion. This trend became acute and pernicious during the period of the popular front when political differences were suppressed in favour of what Dwight Macdonald called the 'swing behind the government'. Communists, New Deal Democrats and fellow travellers buried their differences in support of a broadly-based anti-fascist reforming ideology.

The cultural consequences of 'the Communist-liberal-New Deal movement of the 1930s' (*IE*, p. 35) which Warshow argued were still pervasive in post-war intellectual life are clearly visible in the compromises of the new cultural category that this popular front created: 'the mass culture of the educated classes – the culture of the "middlebrow", as it has sometimes been called' (*IE*, p. 34). This middlebrow culture which is Warshow's version of Dwight Macdonald's mid cult uses the techniques of mass culture 'to distort and eventually to destroy the emotional and moral content of experience, putting in its place a system of conventionalised "responses" ' (*IE*, p. 38). This 'mass culture of the educated classes' is a particularly difficult form to analyse in that it has many characteristics of serious or high culture:

> It was not possible to ignore *The Grapes of Wrath* as it was possible to ignore Edna Ferber or Amos and Andy. *The Grapes of Wrath* had all the surface characteristics of serious literature and it made all the 'advanced' assumptions. (*IE*, p. 35)

For Warshow, John Steinbeck's 1939 portrait of American working-class life, and John Ford's 1940 film adaptation of the novel, represent a 'disastrous vulgarization of intellectual life' (*IE*, p. 33) full of the populist rhetoric and false messages of 'middle-class "popular front" culture' (*IE*, p. 36). The mélange of Nietzschean ideas of a collective oversoul, biological determinism and humiliated but heroic workers that Steinbeck constructs in *The Grapes of Wrath* is as inauthentic as the affirmative 'New Deal' sequence that comes at the end of John Ford's film. Steinbeck's novel ends with Rose of Sharon, having lost her baby, turning to offer her breast full of milk to a starving hobo in a box-car. The film ends with Ma Joad looking forward through a car windscreen bathed in sunlight. With her head tilted defiantly upwards she declares: 'We'll go on forever, Pa. We're the people'. Warshow argues that these middlebrow cultural hybrids with their built-in 'fixed system of moral and political attitudes' (*IE*, p. 38) are the cultural counterparts of Stalinism, 'a kind of willing mortification of the self' (*IE*, p. 37). The possibility of art providing 'an enrichment of experience' is denied by a Stalinist mass culture whose 'chief function . . . is to relieve one of the necessity of experiencing one's life directly' (*IE*, p. 38).

The coalition of interests that created and supported a populist 'mass culture of the educated classes' has survived into the post-war period and constitutes in Warshow's view the main audience for the themes and dramatic methods of Arthur Miller. Warshow argues that plays such as *Death of a Salesman* and *The Crucible* which attempt to deal with the ruthless success ethic of capitalism and McCarthyism respectively, in fact falsify and reduce 'the frightening complexities of history and experience' (*IE*, p. 194) to simple-minded parables and allegories. The main aim of the plays is to provide a liberal 'fossilized audience' (*IE*, p. 195) with 'a generalized tone of affirmation' (*IE*, p. 194). Warshow sees this sentimental search for solidarity, stimulated by Miller, as no different from the blind support given to the party lines demanded by the Communist Party. The liberals who find satisfaction in Miller's parables are not really confronting capitalism or McCarthyism, their real motives are described by Warshow as follows:

> In however inchoate a fashion, those who sat thrilled in the dark theater watching 'The Crucible' were celebrating a tradition and a community. No longer could they find any meaning in the cry of 'Strike!' or 'Revolt!' as they had done in their younger and more 'primitive' age: let it be only 'Bravo!' – a cry of celebration with no particular content. The important thing was that for a short time they could experience together the sense of their own being, their close community of right-mindedness in the orthodoxy of 'dissent'.
> (*IE*, p. 202)

Although Warshow's critique of the way liberalism has allied itself with mass culture to produce a culture of emotional alibis shares many of the elements of Dwight Macdonald's critique of mass culture, he does offer a range of strategies that while including Macdonald's commitment to high culture and avant-garde art, also, unlike Macdonald, extends a creative role to selected mass cultural forms. The main issue that affects all Warshow's strategies is of how 'we regain the use of our experience in the world of mass culture' (*IE*, p. 48). One of the ways out of this impasse that Warshow approvingly notes is the use in modern poetry of irony which:

> by a kind of negative connotation, can also convey some of the quality of fresh and meaningful experience – or, more accurately, it can indicate what fresh and meaningful experience might be like if there existed a context and a vocabulary for it.

However, Warshow doubts that 'a whole literature can be built on irony'. A writer who has managed 'to evolve some method of understanding and communicating experience directly' (*IE*, p. 40) in the modern world of mass culture without an overt use of irony is the dramatist Clifford Odets. In such plays as *Awake and Sing* Odets limits himself to the dramatic presentation of a specific ethnic and socio-economic group, 'the New York Jews of the lower middle class' (*IE*, p. 57). He does not sentimentalise or vulgarise them like other Jewish writers who 'must dignify the Jews, or plead for them or take revenge upon them' (*IE*, p. 55). Not only has Odets rooted himself in a particular milieu, he has invented a 'special type of dramatic poetry' (*IE*, p. 58) that involves the audience not in a group solidarity or a generalised tone of affirmation but in a dialectical critical process that Odets describes as follows:

> In the end you really get something like a direct apprehension of sociological truth, the whole picture built up out of the words spoken on the stage, the tones of speech and thought, all is added to the knowledge already possessed by the audience. (*IE*, p. 60)

As an example of this density of interaction, Odets quotes this passage of dialogue from *Awake and Sing*:

> RALPH: I don't know . . . Every other day to sit around with the blues and mud in your mouth.
> MYRON: That's how it is – life is like that – a cake-walk.
> RALPH: What's it get you?
> HENNIE: A four-car funeral.
> RALPH: What's it for?
> JACOB: What's it for? If this life leads to a revolution it's a good life. Otherwise it's for nothing.
> BESSIE: Never mind, Pop! Pass me the salt.
> RALPH: It's crazy – all my life I want a pair of black and white shoes and can't get them. It's crazy! (*IE*, pp. 65–6)

Odets does not force his bleak picture of Jewish family life into a universal statement. It is just one stage of Jewish history from which some have escaped but in which others remain living 'on top of one another, in that loveless intimacy which is the obverse of the Jewish virtue of family solidarity, and their discontentment is expressed in continual and undisguised personal hostility' (*IE*, p. 66).

Clifford Odets' plays dealing with Jewish life were not part of a commercial popular theatre and therefore were not subject to the economics and procedures of the mass-culture industry. The extent to which Warshow attributed a more creative role to certain forms of mass culture than Dwight Macdonald can be seen in his assessment of two forms, the western and the gangster films that were produced from the Hollywood heartland of mass production. Warshow's analysis of the gangster film in his essay 'The Gangster as Tragic

Hero' can serve as an introduction to the ways he redeemed parts of Hollywood production from the cultural wasteland to which critics such as Dwight Macdonald had consigned the Hollywood studio system and all its works. Warshow's first strategy is to see the Hollywood mode of production as no different from the ways earlier art forms had been developed, thus collapsing in this respect the artificial barrier between high and mass art. Warshow argues that: 'the gangster film is simply one example of the movies' constant tendency to create fixed dramatic patterns that can be repeated indefinitely with a reasonable expectation of profit' (*IE*, p. 129). This characteristic of repeatability is no different from the process by which such high-culture forms as 'Elizabethan revenge tragedy and Restoration comedy' developed 'specific and detailed conventions'. Warshow then describes the conventions that operate within the gangster thriller; the setting is usually urban, the activities of the gangster are some 'form of rational activity' (*IE*, p. 131), based on the model of business enterprise, and follow an invariable narrative pattern: 'the typical gangster film presents a steady upward progress followed by a very precipitate fall' (*IE*, p. 132). The way a director can use these conventions is shown by Warshow's reading of the opening scene of Howard Hawks' 1932 film *Scarface*:

> In the opening scene of 'Scarface', we are shown a successful man; we know he is successful because he has just given a party of opulent proportions and because he is called Big Louie. Through some monstrous lack of caution, he permits himself to be alone for a few moments. We understand from this immediately that he is about to be killed. No convention of the gangster film is more strongly established than this: it is dangerous to be alone. (*IE*, pp. 132–3)

Having established to his own satisfaction the artistic status of the Hollywood gangster thriller, Warshow's other claim on behalf of the form is that: 'From its beginnings, it has been a consistent and astonishingly complete presentation of the modern sense of tragedy' (*IE*, p. 129). Warshow argues that the idea of tragedy is politically embarrassing to 'modern egalitarian societies' who are committed 'to a cheerful view of life' (*IE*, p. 127). This official affirmative optimism is transmitted through the organs of mass culture where, 'at a time when the normal condition of the citizen is a state of anxiety, euphoria spreads over our culture like the broad smile of an idiot'. It is in the gap between an official optimism and 'an actual sense of desperation and inevitable failure which optimism itself helps to create', that a tragic sense of modern life can appear. Warshow claims that this 'current of opposition' can appear within the forms of mass culture such as 'the continually reasserted strain of hopelessness that often seems to be the real meaning of the soap opera' (*IE*, p. 128). This 'current of opposition' to the positive consensus norms of democratic society shows itself most strikingly in the gangster film's ability to make contact with a dark urban underworld of status anxiety, fear of failure, dangerous success, constant treachery and relentless nervous activity. This 'dangerous and sad city of the imagination' (*IE*, p. 131) is a reverse image of the affirmative optimism that mass culture so often projects and reveals the degree to which the euphoric messages of mass culture can be subverted from within.

These disruptive possibilities of the gangster film and the sense in which as a form it conveys a modern sense of tragedy are focused in its contradictory treatment of the cult of individualism that often lies at the core of the form. When the dying Little Caesar supplies his own epitaph with the words: 'Mother of God, is this the end of Rico?' he talks about himself in the third person 'because what has been brought low is not the undifferentiated man, but the individual with a name, the gangster, the success'. The tragic irony that these dying words convey is central to the gangster form which demands that individuals strive for solo pre-eminence, a status that ironically 'automatically arouses hatred' (*IE*, p. 133) and leads to inevitable death. In Warshow's view the gangster film is a dramatic metaphor for a basic drive in American society: 'one must emerge from the crowd or else one is nothing' (*IE*, p. 132). Yet the almost inevitable consequences of this drive are, in the conventions of the gangster film and classical Greek tragedy, fatal.

The kind of revaluation that Warshow made of the gangster film has been followed by the revaluation of a whole range of Hollywood genres that, it is argued, subvert the official optimism of mass culture. The same nightmarish qualities that Warshow found in the gangster film have also been found in the genre of *film noir*[3] where the conventions of ordinary life become threatening; even the simple action of taking a shower in a motel becomes in Alfred Hitchcock's *Psycho* a dangerous venture.

Warshow's contributions to the mass-culture debate gathered in

The Immediate Experience testify to the transformations he was attempting to effect within the debate, to move beyond the rigid categories of high and mass that were both crippling the debate and preventing the close analysis of mass-culture genres that he was beginning to write himself. His work is powerfully influenced by his distaste for the agit-prop aesthetics and popular front messages of the 1930s and his almost pathological loathing for the cultural legacy of the popular front as it manifested itself in the vague ahistorical dissent of such plays as Arthur Miller's *The Crucible*. The import and influence of these ideological quarrels and perspectives will remain part of the process of analysis that 'will not stand still', and willy-nilly involves students of this period in an art and politics debate.

7. T. S. Eliot and Mass Society

In his study of *The Conservative Intellectual Movement in America Since 1945*, George H. Nash describes Eliot as 'virtually a patron saint of the new conservatism'.[1] The problem with this kind of assessment is that one of the main arguments in the new conservatism that was defined in the Cold War called for a restoration of power to the individual, an emphasis alien to Eliot. Roosevelt's New Deal had dramatically increased the role of the Federal government in regulating the economy and providing welfare and educational services to the people. A whole range of business and traditional liberal interests could be enlisted against the New Deal, in support of programmes that sought to roll back the powers of the state over individual initiatives. In contrast with this tendency that the New Deal had generated, Eliot's work in this period sought to reduce the extent to which the promotion of individual initiative and energy took precedence over more collective principles in a transformed modern society that he saw as increasingly dependent on the idea of personal achievement and merit for its guiding ideology. This disruptive atomising trend led Eliot to define his own version of conservatism in *Notes Towards the Definition of Culture* which while acknowledging the importance of the meritocratic achievement principle still reserves a higher status for principles of integration that can assimilate and transcend an individualistic meritocratic ideology. A major concern of Eliot's work in this period was an examination of the role and sources of culture in modern democratic society that led him to an involvement in the mass-culture debate. Eliot increasingly saw culture as the source of communal values that could check the rampant individualism of modern western societies.

Eliot's contributions to the mass-culture debate appeared as early as his 1923 essay on the music-hall comedienne Marie Lloyd and continued into *Notes Towards the Definition of Culture*. In the essay on Marie Lloyd Eliot praises her ability through her art to be an 'expressive figure of the lower classes' (*SE*, p. 458). Her art consists in the intimate collaborations of thought, feeling and gesture that she establishes with 'the working man who went to the music-hall' (*SE*, p. 458). The onset of mass entertainment industries will, in Eliot's view, destroy this kind of interaction: 'With the decay of the music-hall, with the encroachment of the cheap and rapid-breeding cinema, the lower classes will tend to drop into the same state of protoplasm as the bourgeoisie' (*SE*, p. 458). Instead of collaboration at the music-hall, the working man's leisure time will be spent at:

> the cinema, where his mind is lulled by continuous senseless music and continuous action too rapid for the brain to act upon, and will receive, without giving, in that same listless apathy with which the middle and upper classes regard any entertainment of the nature of art. (*SE*, pp. 458–9)

Eliot's argument depends on a contrast between a vital working-class culture and a middle-class culture of passive entertainment. The aristocracy is powerless to intervene in this mechanical industrialisation of culture in which it will be 'possible for every child to hear its bedtime stories from a loudspeaker' (*SE*, p. 459). The inevitable tendency of industrial democracy is to make the aristocracy: 'subordinate to the middle class which is gradually absorbing and destroying them' (*SE*, p. 458).

Eliot's clearest expression of this idea that the industrialisation and mechanisation of culture will create a one-dimensional cultural and social order comes in *The Idea of a Christian Society*: 'Britain will presumably continue to be governed by the same mercantile and financial class which, with a continual change of personnel, has been increasingly important since the fifteenth century'.[2] This coalition of economic and class interests will terminate in a dominantly petit-bourgeois commercial culture which Eliot defines as follows: 'I mean by a "lower middle class society" one in which the standard man legislated for and catered for, the man whose passions must be manipulated, whose prejudices must be humoured, whose tastes must be gratified, will be the lower middle class man'.[3] Eliot's despairing vision of a monolithic petit-bourgeois world that will ultimately extinguish and absorb a decaying aristocracy and working class is a strikingly similar analysis to that made of twentieth-century French culture by the French Marxist Roland Barthes:

> The whole of France is steeped in this anonymous ideology: our press, our films, our theatre, our pulp literature, our rituals, our Justice, our diplomacy, our conversations, our remarks about the weather, a murder trial, a touching wedding, the cooking we dream of, the garments we wear, everything in everyday life is dependent on the representation which the bourgeoisie has and makes us have of the relations between men and the world.[4]

Eliot's position in the 1920s and 1930s is largely that of a high-culture Canute attempting in vain to combat

> the steady influence which operates silently in any mass society organised for profit, for the depression of standards of art and culture. The increasing organization of advertisement and propaganda – or the influencing of masses of men by any means except through their intelligence – is all against them.[5]

Apart from this standard jeremiad against a mass-entertainment culture economically promoted by the middle classes and consumed by the working classes, Eliot's only set of proposals to combat this tendency consist in the kind of support he gave to the Southern Agrarians in *After Strange Gods: A Primer of Modern Heresy*. Despite Eliot's defence of Southern Agrarianism, his work at this stage of his career is controlled by a pessimistic theory of cultural decline and of an inevitable and fatal embourgeoisement of economic and cultural production. These controlling structures of analysis show no sign of change until the publication of *Notes Towards the Definition of Culture* in 1948.

In the preface to the first edition of *Notes Towards a Definition of Culture* Eliot notes that Dwight Macdonald's 'theory strikes me as the best alternative to my own that I have seen'.[6] The main difference between their positions is that Eliot's definition of culture is less dependent on the achievements of high culture than Macdonald's. Eliot summarises Macdonald's position as maintaining:

> either that culture can only be the concern of a small minority, and that therefore there is no place for it in the society of the future; or

that in the society of the future the culture which has been the possession of the few must be put at the disposal of everybody. (*NTDC*, p. 33)

Macdonald's view that only 'the old avant-garde of 1870–1930, from Rimbaud to Picasso' can provide models of excellence for the whole society (a view he later revised), places one section of society in a dangerously individualistic and adversary role with regard to the majority. Eliot's alternative to this position is to extend the status of culture to a whole range of activities and phenomena which makes it impossible to isolate individual groups as being more important guardians or carriers of culture than any other groups. Although Eliot is more concerned to establish general categories than to provide illustrative examples of his main thesis, he does offer the following admittedly random cross-section of:

> The characteristic activities and interests of a people, that consti-tute its culture: Derby Day, Henley Regatta, Cowes, the twelfth of August, a Cup final, the dog races, the pin table, the dart board, Wensleydale cheese, boiled cabbage cut into sections, beetroot in vinegar, nineteenth-century Gothic churches and the music of Elgar. (*NTDC*, p. 31)

Eliot argues that these activities can emerge from their specific and separate class bases to create a dense web of interconnectedness throughout the whole society. This continuum of activities constitutes a cultural grist that can bind separate groups into overlapping but not identical sets of pursuits and behaviour patterns. Eliot's definition of culture as 'the whole way of life of a people' (*NTDC*, p. 31) enables him to enlist culture as a crucial humanising agency of socialisation that can mediate and transcend individual and class division. Raymond Williams's observation on Eliot's list that its 'categories are sport, food and a little art – a characteristic observation of English leisure'[7] is a useful commentary on the synthesising inadequacy of Eliot's false continuum of activities. There are wide class and economic gulfs between those who follow greyhound racing and those who can afford the expensive yachts to participate in Cowes week. Culture as a universalising tendency rarely transcends the mutual class exclusiveness of most leisure pursuits in western capitalist society. However, Eliot is seeking to establish the importance of socially cohesive and recurrent patterns of behaviour, not to integrate them into a cosmetic universalism. He believes in 'a healthily stratified society' (*NTDC*, p. 84) in which there are ritual occasions of 'an overlapping and sharing of interests, by participation and mutual appreciation' (*NTDC*, p. 24). The rituals of 'Derby Day' and 'a Cup final' which symbolically unite a whole range of different classes and socio-economic groups exemplify this process of overlapping in ways that the 'healthily stratified' pursuits of Henley Regatta and Cowes do not.

Eliot's conception of culture as an agency of integration is derived from his reading in social anthropology, and in particular the work of the American anthropologist Ruth Benedict. Her *Patterns of Culture* (1934) popularised the idea that societies should be studied not in terms of separate discrete institutions, classes and traits but in terms of the structures and patterns that bind them together. Benedict argued that cultures should be viewed holistically for none of their specific features could be adequately grasped without reference to the pattern of which they formed a part. This kind of approach gives a more positive account of the 'anonymous ideology' that integrates the various elements of a society than that given by Roland Barthes in the passage already quoted. To Barthes this social grist produces a disfiguring caricature of social relationships and is created and controlled by the bourgeoisie. Despite Eliot's awareness that western society is increasingly under the domination of this bourgeois class, he commits himself to an anthropological form of analysis because in his view it can transcend the limitations both of a bourgeois liberalism that focuses on the individual as the basic unit of society, and of a Marxism that employs a class analysis. This belief in the transcendence of culture and his debt to Ruth Benedict can be seen in the following quotation: 'We shall look for culture, not in any individual or in any group of individuals, but more and more widely; and we are driven in the end to find it in the pattern of society as a whole' (*NTDC*, p. 23). The role of culture as an integrating force in society is in part based on the way culture is more than the sum of its separate modes of production and can include both the liberal idea of 'the self-cultivation of the individual' (*NTDC*, p. 21), and a working-class set of leisure activities such as the music-hall of Marie Lloyd, 'Derby Day and the dog track' (*NTDC*, p. 32). The ability of the culture concept to provide the common descriptive denominator for these disparate activities leads Eliot to see 'the culture of a people as an incarnation of its religion' (*NTDC*, p. 33). As an example of the extent to which anthropology has revealed the role of culture as a powerful form of social integration Eliot describes how:

> Among the more primitive communities the several activities of culture are inextricably interwoven. The Dyak who spends the better part of a season in shaping, carving and painting his barque of the peculiar design required for the annual ritual of head-hunting, is exercising several cultural activities at once – of art and religion, as well as of amphibious warfare. (*NTDC*, p. 24)

Unlike many romantic conservatives Eliot realises that this is a world that has been lost and that modern democratic society functions according to different principles. This awareness of the inevitability and indeed the desirability of change and conflict does not in Eliot's mind cancel out the necessity for culture to have as important a role in modern society as it had in the Dyak head-hunting community.

When one turns from Eliot's review of the various definitions of culture to his analysis of the process of modernisation in western society, he concentrates on one main phenomenon: the way modern industrial and democratic 'society develops towards functional complexity and differentiation' (*NTDC*, p. 25). The various activities of the Dyak head-hunter that were once integrated become in modern society separated and specialised. Art, religion and amphibious warfare become the responsibility of separate expert professionals. The artist in his studio, the priest in his church, the captain in his nuclear submarine replace the single figure of the Dyak who could combine all these activities in his own person. The 'radical transformation of society' that ensues as a result of 'the doctrine of elites' is, in Eliot's view, a transition from an organic to an 'atomic view of society' (*NTDC*, p. 37). An ideology that demands 'that all positions in society should be occupied by those who are best fitted to exercise the functions of the positions' (*NTDC*, p. 37) is, in Eliot's view, dangerously disruptive and centrifugal. If individuals in their honourable pursuit of meritocratic achievement spin themselves off from a common organic centre in all directions, social organisation and stability are continually threatened. It is at this point where meritocratic professionalism comes into conflict with traditional values that culture can intervene to prevent the disintegration of society into a whole series of alienated subcultures. Eliot wishes to preserve some of the modes of integration that existed in primitive communities such as the Dyak while accepting the progressive possibilities of a meritocratic society of 'functional complexity and differentiation' (*NTDC*, p. 25) and the 'duty incumbent upon us, to bring about a classless society' (*NTDC*, p. 36). The ways he suggests that the interconnectedness of pre-meritocratic societies can be preserved emerge in the qualifications he has regarding the theories of Karl Mannheim in *Man and Society*. While accepting Mannheim's account of how 'the achievement principle increasingly tends to become the criterion of social success' (*NTDC*, p. 39) in modern democratic societies, he disputes Mannheim's assertion that 'a sociological investigation of culture in liberal society must begin with the life of those who create culture, i.e. the intelligentsia and their position within society as a whole' (*NTDC*, p. 37). He then proceeds to offer the following model of how the culture concept can mitigate the effects of 'the achievement principle':

> The function of what Dr Mannheim would call the culture-creating groups, according to my account, would be rather to bring about a further development of the culture in organic complexity: culture at a more conscious level, but still the same culture. This higher level of culture must be thought of both as valuable in itself, and as enriching of the lower levels: thus the movement of culture would proceed in a kind of cycle, each class nourishing the others. (*NTDC*, p. 37)

Eliot supported this somewhat mystical vision of the transcendent qualities of culture with specific proposals as to how elite groups can be organically attached to a social system in which entrenched class structures are being transformed by meritocratic tendencies. The atomising tendencies of a meritocratic achievement ideology can be deflected if elites are 'attached to some class whether higher or lower; but so long as there are classes at all it is likely to be the dominant class' (*NTDC*, p. 42). Having conceded the vitality and worth of the achievement principle, Eliot sets limits to this meritocratic tendency with a defence of the status quo. The majority of society from whose number emerge selected talented professionals serves as a feeder reservoir for a 'governing elite' which would consist 'of those whose responsibility was inherited with their affluence and position, and whose forces were constantly increased and often led, by rising individuals of exceptional talents' (*NTDC*, p. 84). Clearly Eliot's image of society is one in which power is exerted downwards by a governing elite whose energies are constantly replenished by merito-cratic professionals. Beneath the controls exerted by a governing elite Eliot allows for all kinds of movements and conflicts. In the third chapter of *NTDC*, 'Unity and Diversity: The Region', Eliot speaks of:

> the vital importance for a society of friction between its parts. Accustomed as we are to think in figures of speech taken from machinery, we assume that a society, like a machine, should be as well-oiled as possible provided with ball bearings of the best steel. We think of friction as waste of energy. (p. 58)

Armed with this notion of the creative potential of conflict which is 'quite necessary for civilization' (*NTDC*, p. 59), Eliot reviews a whole series of developments in world history in the light of this model of productive friction. In Chapter four, 'Unity and Diversity: Sect and Cult', instead of Ransom's indictment of protestantism, Eliot ack-nowledges 'that many of the most remarkable achievements of culture have been made since the sixteenth century, in conditions of disunity' (*NTDC*, p. 71). The division of the once universal Roman Catholic church into warring sects is one of the most creative threads in European history. In *After Strange Gods*, Eliot had dismissed the non-conformist culture in which D. H. Lawrence had grown up as 'vague hymn-singing pieties' (*ASG*, p. 39). In *Notes Towards the Definition of Culture* Eliot rehabilitates and redeems this tradition of non-conformism when he asks: 'whether Methodism did not, in the period of its greatest power, revive the spiritual life of the English, and prepare the way for the Evangelical Movement and even for the Oxford Movement' (p. 81). These adaptations and revisions within a central organic orthodoxy are described as a process in which 'a sub-culture' which is not 'necessarily an inferior culture' creatively separates itself 'from the main body' (*NTDC*, p. 74). As long as these subcultures remain in creative conflict with the mainstream culture, they represent genuine definitions of dissent and are part of the process by which a society develops 'organic complexity'.

Eliot's use of the term subculture has become standard practice in describing the ways in which the codes and values of particular cultural and socio-economic groups can act as self-contained struc-turing coherent visions or world views. Ned Polsky's study of the world of the pool room, included in *Hustlers, Beats and Others* (1967) and Hunter Thompson's study of *The Hell's Angels* (1966) are applications of the same thesis and methodology that Eliot uses to examine 'the cultural significance of religious divisions' (*NTDC*, p. 67). Although Eliot concedes and supports the rights of subcultural dissent, he places a number of restrictions upon the scale and nature of dissent. The major limitations are that any specialised expert group has to accept the leadership of the governing elite and that the expert skills of any meritocratic elite must promote the organic complexity of the existing social order, not its divisive atomisation. Eliot does not offer many examples of how to discriminate between organic complexity and divisive atomisation but in his discussion of the role of the family in the transmission of culture he gives the following example that contrasts a modern atomic advertising image of reductive one-dimensional thinness with his own sense of what the features of an organically complex image of family might resemble:

> Even of living members, it is a rare exception when an advertisement depicts a large family or three generations: the usual family on the hoardings consists of two parents and one or two young children. What is held up for admiration is not devotion to a family, but personal affection between the members of it: and the smaller the family, the more easily can this personal affection be sentimentalised. But when I speak of the family, I have in mind a bond which embraces a longer period of time than this: a piety towards the dead, however obscure, and a solicitude for the unborn, however remote. (*NTDC*, pp. 43–4)

This transcendent, almost mystical idea of family co-exists with other contradictory elements in Eliot's cultural criticism that belong to a scientific process of demystification. His acceptance of the doctrine of professional elites, of social science methodology as used by anthropologists and Karl Mannheim, is an empiricist materialist transition similar to those made by John Crowe Ransom in accepting scientific methods.

Eliot's emphasis on the ways the atomised individual could be socialised was shared by two important groups of social scientists who became prominent in the 1930s. Anthropologists of Margaret Mead's and Ruth Benedict's persuasion, and the sociologists of Robert Park's Chicago school of sociology all affirmed the value of inherited cultural and group values in providing the individual with ideas of personal development and a self that could cope with a hostile mass society. All this work on socialisation and the role of ideology in mass society had increasingly to take account of the frightening spectacles of mass politics in action provided by Stalin's Russia and Hitler's Germany. The totalitarian obliteration of individual rights, the suppression and censorship of artistic expression, led to a whole series of investigations as to what constituted a potentially fascist society. The ease with which various forms of dictatorship had subverted and destroyed the forms and apparatus of liberal democracy posed a whole range of questions about the course and nature of western industrial society, of which system America was considered a prime example. Eliot in *Notes Towards the Definition of Culture* had commented in passing how: 'In Italy and Germany, we have seen that a unity with politico-economic aims, imposed violently and too rapidly, had unfortunate effects upon both nations' (p. 59).

Eliot's view of fascism as the imposition of a crude totalitarian unity on a society by force was a standard response. The work of a group of refugee scholars from Nazi persecution known as the Frankfurt School made several studies of the nature and psychology of mass society in America that reached the conclusion that the false unities of totalitarianism were clearly visible in the products of America's mass-culture industries. The implications of their work were that the inequities of industrial capitalism inexorably led to a fascist mentality and potential. Using a theoretical and investigative apparatus derived from Freud and Marx the Frankfurt School produced an analysis of American society that seriously questioned whether any programme of reform or adjustment such as that proposed by T. S. Eliot could counter 'the steady influence which operates in any mass society organised for profit, for the depression of standards of art and culture'.[8]

8. The Frankfurt School: Marxism, Fascism and Mass Culture

THE validity and impact of Marxist analysis of American society has clearly been powerfully influenced by the Cold War era in which the master metaphor of a moral struggle between a Christian democratic United States and a godless Marxist Soviet Russia led to the vilification of Marxist theoreticians as traitors and un-American. The rehabilitation of Marxist analysis from these caricatures also involves an assessment of the role of the émigré scholars who fled to America from fascist persecution. One of the major historians of this phenomenon, H. Stuart Hughes, has described what he calls 'the great migration' in the following challenging terms:

> In the perspective of the 1970s, the migration to the United States of European intellectuals fleeing fascist tyranny has finally become visible as the most important cultural event – or series of events – of the second quarter of the twentieth century.[1]

Many of these European scholars had specifically encountered fascist harassment in the twin forms of anti-semitism and anti-Marxism and therefore H. Stuart Hughes' claim on behalf of a group he broadly categorises as 'European intellectuals' includes as a significant and specific section the various Marxist theoreticians who found academic refuge in America. The work of the group of émigrés known as the Frankfurt School clearly falls into this Marxist category. The group in terms of the debate on mass culture included Max Horkheimer, Theodore Adorno, Leo Lowenthal, Paul Lazarsfeld and Herbert Marcuse.

With the rise of Nazism in Germany the position of left intellectuals, and particularly of these men who worked in a privately funded research institute attached to the University of Frankfurt, became highly precarious. As Martin Jay, the historian of this group, has written:

> With the Nazi assumption of power on January 30, 1933, the future of an avowedly Marxist organization, staffed almost exclusively by men of Jewish descent – at least by Nazi standards – was obviously bleak.[2]

With the help of Columbia University's president Nicholas Murray Butler, the institute was re-established in America. Although Adorno and Horkheimer returned to Germany in 1950, Marcuse, Lowenthal and Lazarsfeld remained in America and took citizenship. Lowenthal became a professor of sociology at the University of California, Berkeley, and Lazarsfeld continued his dominant interest in applied quantitative work at the University of Columbia in the Office of Radio Research, later transformed into the Bureau of Applied Social Research. Marcuse, like H. Stuart Hughes, worked for the Federal government in departments that provided political analysis of European affairs. He later moved into academic life first at Brandeis University and then at the San Diego campus of the University of California. This fragmentation of what was originally a group enterprise should not obscure the degree to which they shared and developed, in a number of publications, various theoretical models and evaluations of the role of the mass media in American society. There were, however, a number of disagreements within the group as to the various strategies necessary to preserve intellectual freedom and the quality of their work. In a letter of 5 February 1946 Lazarsfeld comments negatively on the practice of the institute in exile of continuing to publish their analysis of American mass society in their native German and their reluctance to be integrated with the academic structure of the University of Columbia:

> The whole mess is due to the idiocy of the Institute group. I told them for years that publishing in German will finally destroy them. But they had the fixed idea that their contribution to America will be greater if they preserve in this country the last island of German culture.[3]

Despite these family quarrels a number of their collaborative and single-author publications can exemplify the kind of critique they developed of mass culture. Marcuse's work will be treated as a separate but linked case-study.

The most sustained and thoroughgoing of the Frankfurt School's critiques of mass culture appears as 'The Culture Industry: Enlightenment as Mass Deception' in a collection of essays, *Dialectic of Enlightenment*, first published in German in 1944. These joint essays by Adorno and Horkheimer examine the ways one particular form of social and economic development has dominated world society. This monolithic process is characterised as a 'scientific attitude'[4] that evaluates and exploits all phenomena according to reductive ideas of measurement, standardisation, manipulation and utility. The only lesson and model of development that this scientific form of investigation proposes is one in which 'what men want to learn from nature is how to use it in order wholly to dominate it and other men' (*DE*, p. 4). This tendency is described as a process of rational enlightenment by which 'the human mind, which overcomes superstition, is to hold sway over a disenchanted nature' (*DE*, p. 4). This enlightenment ideology finds expression in the capitalist form of economic production and employs technology to achieve 'the exploitation of others' work, and capital' (*DE*, p. 4). The mastery that this one form of scientific knowledge and economic productivity has achieved in world society does not invalidate the rational pursuit of knowledge or the idea of a creative economic use of the world's resources. Adorno and Horkheimer acknowledge that 'the growth of economic productivity furnishes the conditions for a world of greater justice' (*DE*, p. xiv). Their quarrel is with the way an ideology of technical rationality with its monolithic reductive drive towards total control over nature has created a social system which allows: 'the technical apparatus and the social groups which administer it a disproportionate superiority to the rest of the population' (*DE*, p. xiv). The mass entertainment industries in America, symbolised by the studio system of Hollywood in the 1930s and 1940s, are, for Adorno and Horkheimer, the latest audio-visual versions of this process of enlightenment writ large, a vast amplification, mechanisation and marketing of deception on a mass scale. This Marxist interpretation of the way the capitalist system has given undemocratic controlling powers over all areas of life including that of cultural production to the bourgeoisie is similar to the 'mass-cult' and 'mid-cult' theories of

Dwight Macdonald, and Eliot's theories of the embourgeoisement of society by which the whole society falls 'into the same state of protoplasm as the bourgeoisie'. The main difference between the critique of Adorno and Horkheimer and those of Macdonald and Eliot lies in the specific ideological analysis they make of the ultimate political tendency of the mass media. For Adorno and Horkheimer the use of violence in animated cartoons is a paradigm of the way the structures of monopoly capitalism:

> hammer into every brain the old lesson that continuous friction, the breaking down of all individual resistance, is the condition of life in this society. Donald Duck in the cartoons and the unfortunate in real life get their thrashing so that the audience can learn to take their own punishment. (*DE*, p. 138)

Their analysis of what Robert Warshow saw as 'the euphoria' spreading 'over our culture like the broad smile of an idiot' (*IE*, p. 128) gives the products of mass culture a more sinister gloss: they are shot through with the features of proto-fascism.

The belief that there existed in all industrialised societies a fascist potential was the main organising thesis behind another Frankfurt School work, *The Authoritarian Personality*, published in 1950. On the basis of questionnaires that measured on an F scale nine personality variables, Adorno and his team of native-born psychologists, based at Berkeley, produced a profile of fascist potentiality. The final total of those interviewed was 2099, the majority being white, native-born, gentile, middle-class Americans. The model of authoritarian character against which the research findings were measured had, in Horkheimer's words, the following characteristics:

> A mechanical surrender to conventional values; blind submission to authority together with blind hatred of all opponents and outsiders; anti-introspectiveness; rigid stereotyped thinking; a penchant for superstition; vilification, half-moralistic and half-cynical, of human nature; projectivity (the disposition to believe that wild and dangerous things go on in the world; the projection outwards of unconscious emotional impulses).[5]

The product of this complex of characteristics in the individual was, in psychoanalytic terms, 'an authoritarian syndrome'. This syndrome was seen in Freudian terms as 'a Sado-masochistic resolution of the Oedipus complex' and resulted in an unconscious 'hatred against the father . . . transformed . . . into love' for those perceived as the strong and directed against the weak and defenceless. The characteristics of this authoritarian syndrome which more obviously relate to the role of the mass media in reinforcing and perpetuating proto-fascist qualities were a tendency to think in stereotypes and to be taken in by the facile 'personalizing'[6] of public rhetoric, whether in politics or in advertising. The application of the theoretical assumptions underlying the authoritarian syndrome to the operations of the mass media is a complex process examined in the essay 'The Culture Industry: Enlightenment as Mass Deception', and will be dealt with separately.

The discovery of proto-fascist, anti-democratic resentments in American society was clearly based on the Frankfurt School's assessment that the rise of fascism was the most strikingly contemporary example of the technical rationality that had been dominant as early as the society which produced Odysseus. The control over his crew that Odysseus displayed when stopping the ears of his proletarian rowers with wax in the sirens episode is, in the Frankfurt School's critique, an early example of technical rationality. The latest incarnations of this ideology are the fascist regimes in Europe. The specific economic and political developments that have led to the rise of fascism are described by Adorno and Horkheimer as follows: 'After the short intermezzo of liberalism, in which the bourgeois kept one another in check, domination appears as archaic terror in a fascistically rationalised form' (*DE*, p. 87). Power in this model: 'passes from the dispossessed bourgeoisie to the totalitarian cartel-lords, whose science has become the inclusive concept of the methods of reproduction of the subjugated mass society' (*DE*, p. 87). This kind of Marxist interpretation of the socio-economic basis of the fascist system does not argue that fascism is the sole or necessary expression of monopoly capitalism. The main argument is that specific connections emerged between fascism and big business. The various suggested connections took a variety of forms. The most extreme asserted that fascist leadership was no more than a façade for the rule of monopoly capitalism. The second more moderate variant of this thesis argued merely that the system intentionally and systematically worked for the benefit of big business. A corollary of both these variants argued that fascism was the appropriate expression of monopoly capitalism and that those major industrial states which had not yet become fascist were in imminent danger of becoming so. Adorno and Horkheimer primarily viewed American society as a variant of industrial capitalism, rather than a unique democratic experiment or a city on a hill devoted to the pursuit of egalitarian liberty. Though they were impressed by the degree to which democratic institutions and ideology did exist in America, the increasing cartelisation of the American economy was self-evident. One historical fact does emerge from the connections between monopoly capitalism and fascism in the cases of Germany and Italy; the greater capitalists: 'Were able to ride through the fascist experience unscathed, while the members of the lower middle class who had put their trust in the rhetoric of a Mussolini or a Hitler found themselves sacrificed to the 'higher' exigencies of a nation girding for war.'[7]

The degree to which American mass society was proto-fascist according to the various psycho-social, economic and political theories developed by the Frankfurt School, is the burden of Adorno and Horkheimer's essay on the products of the Hollywood studio system 'The Culture Industry: Enlightenment as Mass Deception'. The first danger sign is clearly visible in the economics of Hollywood production. Behind the individualist façades of the two studios specifically mentioned in the essay, Warner Brothers and Metro-Goldwyn-Mayer, lies a system of cartels which results in 'the dependence of the most powerful broadcasting company on the electrical industry' and of 'the motion picture industry on the banks' (*DE*, p. 123). This high degree of control in financial matters is duplicated in the carefully monitored streamlining of films into 'a hierarchical range of mass-produced products' (*DE*, p. 123). The thrillers, musicals and social problem films produced by Hollywood are guaranteed to meet audience expectations by the use of commercial marketing techniques: 'Consumers appear as statistics on research organization charts, and are divided by income groups into red, green and blue areas; the technique is that used for any type of propaganda' (*DE*, p. 123). This kind of control over and manipulation of audiences results in repetitive narrative formulae: 'As soon as the film begins, it is quite clear how it will end, and who will be rewarded, punished, or forgotten. In light music, once the trained ear has heard the first notes of the hit song, it can guess what is coming and feel flattered when it does come' (*DE*, p. 125). A process of synthetic organisation 'integrates all the elements of the production, from the novel (shaped with an eye to the film) to the last sound effect' (*DE*, p. 124). The scale and precision of this 'triumph of invested capital' derisively fulfils 'the Wagnerian dream of the *gesamtkunstwerk* – the fusion of all arts into one work' (*DE*, p. 124). Adorno and Horkheimer are almost stunned by the degree of control that Hollywood productions can exert over every production detail:

> No medieval theologian could have determined the degree of the torment to be suffered by the damned in accordance with the *ordo* of divine love more meticulously than the producers of shoddy epics calculated the torture to be undergone by the hero or the exact point to which the leading lady's hemline shall be raised. (*DE*, p. 128)

The total monolithic orchestration and stylisation of the separate factors in Hollywood film production are achieved by a cinematic technology that specialises in built-in reactions. The background music of Hollywood melodrama, nudging the audience to the correct emotional response, is symptomatic of the means employed to achieve mesmeric control over audience response.

When Adorno and Horkheimer turn from the economic and technical controls employed by Hollywood to the ways the films can be read as 'indicators of the socio-psychological characteristics of the multitude',[8] they discover a whole series of effects and characteristics that reinforce an authoritarian syndrome. The Hollywood system in particular continues to efface whatever individual characteristics still remain in a mass society. What is offered by the star system is a carefully regulated

> Pseudo-individuality . . . from the standardized jazz improvisation to the exceptional film star whose hair curls over her eye to demonstrate her originality. What is individual is no more than the generality's power to stamp the accidental detail so firmly that it is accepted as such. The defiant reserve or elegant appearance of the individual on show is mass-produced like Yale locks, whose only difference can be measured in fractions of millimeters. The peculiarity of the self is a monopoly commodity, determined by society; it is falsely represented as natural. It is no more than the moustache, the French accent, the deep voice of the woman of the world, the Lubitsch touch. (*DE*, p. 154)

The tendency of a mass society to accept 'the deceitful substitution of the stereotype for the individual' (*DE*, p. 156) had been a visible characteristic of Nazism. The 'secret satisfaction' (*DE*, p. 156) that the star system offers is that the complex but crucial struggle to develop an authentic personality is abandoned in favour of stereotypical imitations. The deliberate obliteration of ideas of self by transcendent ideas of nature and nationalism had been a stated aim of Hitler's National Socialism:

> National Socialism takes as the starting point of its views and its decisions neither the individual nor humanity. It puts consciously into the central point of its whole thinking the *Volk*. This *Volk* is for it a blood-conditioned entity in which it sees the God-willed building-stone of human society. The individual is transitory, the *Volk* is permanent. If the Liberal *Weltanschaung* in its deification of the single individual must lead to the destruction of the *Volk*, National Socialism, on the other hand, desires to safeguard the *Volk*, if necessary even at the expense of the individual. It is essential that the individual should slowly come to realize that his own ego is unimportant when compared with the existence of the whole people . . . above all he must realize that the freedom of the mind and will of a nation are to be valued more highly than the individual's freedom of mind and will.[9]

The star system reinforces and partially completes the liquidation and displacement of the self that has occurred since the beginning of civilisation: 'For centuries society has been preparing for Victor Mature and Micky Rooney. By destroying they come to fulfil' (*DE*, p. 156). The kind of humiliation of individual human potentialities that the star system promotes is also discerned in the reductive formulae that govern Hollywood's presentation of sexuality where the dominant level is one of titillation and repression:

> By repeatedly exposing the objects of desire, breasts in a clinging sweater or the naked torso of the athletic hero (the culture industry) only stimulates the unsublimated fore-pleasure. There is no erotic situation which, while insinuating and exciting, does not fail to indicate unmistakably that things can never go that far. The Hays Office merely confirms the ritual of Tantalus that the culture industry has established anyway. Works of art are ascetic and

unashamed, the culture industry is pornographic and prudish. (*DE*, p. 140)

Appetites are aroused and then repressed: 'the real point will never be reached . . . the diner must be satisfied with the menu' (*DE*, p. 139).

The controls of the culture industry extend over all areas of cultural production. The experimental techniques of Orson Welles that attempt to disrupt the standardised genres and formulae of commercial cinema are easily assimilated into Hollywood's aesthetic repertoire. Welles' departures from the norm are regarded as calculated mutations which 'serve all the more strongly to confirm the validity of the system' (*DE*, p. 129). Adorno's analysis of jazz shows how completely he believed that all forms of cultural activity had been penetrated by a deadening technical rationality. Because of the marginal status of Afro-American culture in American society, blues and jazz have often been seen as disruptive and rebellious protests against the norms of white Anglo-Saxon protestant culture.[10] Adorno rejects this view of the revolutionary potential of Afro-American musical culture. Once black music has been absorbed into the record industry, he doubts whether the so-called creative improvisations in jazz can transcend the basic monotonous rhythms of industrialisation. Jazz is:

> music which fuses the most rudimentary melodic, harmonic, metric and formal structures with the ostensibly disruptive principles of syncopation, yet without ever really disturbing the crude unity of the basic rhythm, the identically sustained metre, the quarter note.[11]

All these mass cultural effects accumulate to produce a grotesque social vision: 'a parody of the never-never land, just as the national society is a parody of the human society' (*DE*, p. 156).

This tendency of the culture industry to mediate pseudo-individualism is the subject of another classic piece of applied Frankfurt School analysis, Leo Lowenthal's essay 'The Triumph of Mass Idols', first published in 1944 as 'Biographies in Popular Magazines'. Lowenthal used the psycho-analytic tools of the Frankfurt School for his content analysis of the ways the presentation of popular hero figures had changed in popular magazines from the beginning of the twentieth century to 1943. He describes the most dramatic change in the following way:

> If a student in some very distant future should use popular magazines of 1941 as a source of information as to what figures the American public looked to in the first stages of the greatest crisis since the birth of the Union, he would come to a grotesque result. While the industrial and professional endeavours are geared to a maximum of speed and efficiency, the idols of the masses are not, as they were in the past, the leading names in the battle of production, but the headliners of the movies, the ball park, and the night clubs. (*LPCS*, p. 116)

Lowenthal's analysis reveals that capitalist entrepreneurs have been replaced by show business and entertainment stars. Heroic figures of production have given way to idols of consumption. This change in heroic models coincides with the transformation of the economic system from one in which individual entrepreneurs and family firms exerted control to one in which corporate cartels and monopolies dominate. This new phase of monopoly capitalism is faceless and bureaucratic but senses that heroes are necessary, and therefore creates a star system of pseudo-individualism to satisfy the psychic needs of a mass consumer market: 'It is neither a world of "doers" nor a world of "doing" for which the biographical curiosity of a mass public is evoked' (*LPCS*, p. 122).

Many of the characteristics of these new idols of consumption as presented in such magazines as the *Saturday Evening Post* and *Collier's* fit the model of the authoritarian syndrome that the Frankfurt School used in their studies of prejudice. The biographies of this latter period of consumption continually play upon one of the cardinal features of anti-democratic ideology: the belief in mystical determinants of the individual's fate. Clark Gable's 'stubborn determination' is always magically related to his 'Pennsylvania Dutch ancestors' (*LPCS*, p. 119), Greer Garson succeeds in becoming a star on the basis of having wanted 'to be an actress from the time she could walk' (*LPCS*, p. 124). Success in this world is achieved by a mystical contradictory process of 'hardships and breaks' (*LPCS*, p. 126). Once individuals have achieved star status, the environment they inhabit is described and controlled by a specific discourse. Clark Gable's life is seen as a 'saga', taking place in 'Olympian regions' where all events and experiences are either 'fabulous' or a 'miracle'. This heroic scale is sometimes democratised by such qualifications as 'the crown of Roosevelt fitted him like a five and ten toupee' (*LPCS*, pp. 131–2). Eccentricity and individuality outside the prescribed norms are not allowed because the stars must be models of social adjustment for their publics. Stars can always cope with their fame and fortune; they do not become suicidal. This high degree of adjustment is achieved 'by exhibiting amiable and social qualities and by repressing all other traits' (*LPCS*, p. 129). Lowenthal's commentary on the damage such images do to human relations is unequivocal:

> What at first sight seems to be the rather harmless atmosphere of entertainment and consumption is, on closer examination, revealed as a reign of psychic terror. The already weakened consciousness of being an individual is struck another heavy blow by the pseudo-individualising forces of the superlative. (*LPCS*, p. 129)

From the preceding account it should be clear that the Frankfurt School's analysis of American mass culture in the 1930s and 1940s is locked into their reading of the ways monopoly capitalism had systematically destroyed the limited freedoms of the nineteenth-century bourgeois liberal state. In their view the state, in alliance with business interests in America or as a Stalinist party bureaucracy in Russia, directly controls the mass of individuals, without even the mediations of family or class to intervene as counters to the power of monopoly capitalism. In this phase of history: 'Everyone became an employee; and in this civilization of employees, the dignity of the father (questionable anyhow) vanishes' (*DE*, p. 153). Family, social group, ethnic heritage are replaced by models of development mediated by mass culture. The idea that this mass culture could provide valid cultural forms or authentic aesthetic pleasure was beyond the belief system of Adorno and Horkheimer. Adorno in particular suffered extreme culture shock in America, an experience he later reflected upon:

> I still remember the shock that a housemaid, an emigrant like ourselves, gave me during our first days in New York when she, the daughter of a so-called good home, explained: 'People in my town used to go to the Symphony, now they go to Radio City.' In no way did I want to be like her.[12]

Radio City, a lavish picture palace in New York which showed the latest films and live musical revues in the 1930s, was to Adorno the embodiment of the 'stylised barbarism' of Tin Pan Alley and Hollywood. For intellectual émigrés of Adorno's generation, steeped in a humanist high culture, the encounter with the mass-entertainment culture of America posed 'the question whether the concept of culture, in which one was brought up, has not itself become obsolete'.[13]

9. Herbert Marcuse: from Affirmation to Liberation

MARCUSE'S analysis of the effects of mass society proceeds from the same structure of Marxist and Freudian ideas that Adorno and Horkheimer developed, but Marcuse modifies their picture of world society under the wholesale repressive domination of technical rationality with a set of proposals that questions: 'the terrible necessity of the inner connection between civilization and barbarism'.[1] It is in Marcuse's revision and adaptation of Freud and to a lesser degree of Marx that possibilities of liberation from a civilisation of technical rationality appear. Freud's account of the process by which the individual is socialised and integrated into a repressive civilisation can be usefully abstracted from *Civilization and Its Discontents*. The imposition of civilisation upon the individual, in the main, involves circumscribing the individual with a whole series of restraints designed with the socially useful purpose of preserving the species and 'to protect men against the violence of the forces of nature and to adjust their mutual relations'.[2] This civilisation of restraints mediated by such institutions as the family, private property and law, protects the individual from his own aggressive nature and that of other men. The tragic cost of this process in which a whole range of natural human instincts are adjusted and controlled in the name and justification of an inhibiting civilisation is described by Freud in the following way: 'It is impossible to overlook the extent to which civilization is built up upon a renunciation of instinct, how much it presupposes precisely the non-satisfaction (by suppression, repression or some other means?) of powerful instincts' (*CD*, p. 34). Despite his analysis of the costs of this repressive civilisation, Freud saw no alternative to this process. He was particularly severe on the alternative models proposed by: 'The Communists [who] . . . believe that they have found the path to deliverance from our evils. According to them, man is wholly good and is well-disposed to his neighbour; but the institution of private property has corrupted his nature' (*CD*, pp. 49–50). Freud argues that property is one of the 'instruments' of human aggression, not its cause: 'Aggressiveness was not created by property. It reigned almost without limit in primitive times, when property was still very scanty, and it already shows itself in the nursery' (*CD*, p. 50). Freud does modify this severity towards utopian political programmes:

> I too think it quite certain that a real change in the relations of human beings to possessions would be of more help in this direction than any ethical commands; but the recognition of this fact among socialists has been obscured and made useless for practical purposes by a fresh idealistic misconception of human nature. (*CD*, p. 80)

Freud is basically pessimistic about the possibilities of man's liberation from a civilisation built upon repression, ironically created to curb aggression but showing no signs of achieving that kind of control. There are glimpses of the existence of individual freedom in Freud's account of the evolution of human society but they are usually located in a period before man was integrated into a repressive civilisation: 'The liberty of the individual is no gift of civilization. It was greatest before there was any civilization, though then, it is true, it had for the most part no value, since the individual was scarcely in a position to defend it' (*CD*, p. 32). Such liberties as existed were the privilege of elite minorities and were extremely precarious: 'In fact, primitive man was better off in knowing no restrictions of instinct. To counterbalance this, his prospects of enjoying this happiness for any length of time were very slender' (*CD*, p. 52).

As this brief account of Freud's theory of human evolution attempts to make clear, it is extremely difficult to find utopian models of personal and social liberation in Freud. Adorno and Horkheimer in their analysis of the culture industry faithfully reproduce Freud's pessimism and devote very little space in their work to the idea and shape of liberation: 'In every product of the culture industry, the permanent denial imposed by civilization, is once again unmistakably demonstrated and inflicted on its victims' (*DE*, p. 141). Marcuse in contrast attempted to imagine the landscape of an unrepressive civilisation and expand Freud's tentative glimpses of the character of liberation into a programme of action. Marcuse's revision of Freud appears in his *Eros and Civilization*, and was one of the many adaptations of Freud's theories that took place. The speed with which Freud's ideas and terminology became an established discourse in America had created a fertile climate for debate:

> The first popular article on psychoanalysis appeared in *Good Housekeeping* in 1915; its title was 'Diagnosis by Dreams', and it carefully avoided any allusion to sex. Such reticence was soon abandoned. Journalism, television, plays, films, musicals, and jokes, made sex, libido, oedipal complex, defense mechanism, and the unconscious the common vocabulary of urban society to such an extent that Lionel Trilling could rightly call psychoanalysis 'the slang of our culture'.[3]

The adaptation and revision of Freud's ideas had led in the work of several writers to serious distortions of his work and Marcuse in an epilogue to *Eros and Civilization*, 'Critique of Neo-Freudian Revisionism', specifically attacked Wilhelm Reich, Carl Jung and Eric Fromm for their attempts to modify Freud's pessimistic assessment of 'the basic unchangeability of human nature' (*EC*, p. 238). Reich's attempt to make 'sexual liberation per se . . . a panacea for individual and social ills' (*EC*, p. 239) and Fromm's belief that therapy can modify the severity of the pain incurred in establishing a repressive civilisation, are both rejected by Marcuse on the grounds that both positions seek to adjust the individual to a repressive status quo without disturbing the economic inequities of a mass society. Jung's idea of a collective unconscious is no more than 'an obscurantist pseudo-mythology' (*EC*, p. 239).

Marcuse's revision of Freud does not evade Freud's uncompromising belief that a non-repressive civilisation is impossible, but Marcuse does uncover a hopeful 'hidden trend in psychoanalysis' (*EC*, p. 11) that reveals a progressive dimension within Freud's theories. Marcuse argues that, if in Freud's account, man creates an inhibiting civilisation at the cost of his own instinctual freedom, that civilisation must contain, in a sublimated form, repressed memories of instinctual freedom. These memories constitute the shadows of an unrepressive civilisation. In Freudian theory man's instinctual aspirations are first blocked and then transformed into socially acceptable consciousness through the process of sublimation. The great storehouse of these repressed aspirations is the unconscious: 'the deepest and oldest layer of the mental personality' (*EC*, p. 18). Each individual enacts this process in which the: 'Promises and potentialities which are betrayed and even outlawed by the mature, civilized individual, but which had once been fulfilled in his dim past . . . are never entirely forgotten' (*EC*, p. 19). Marcuse specifically identifies the arts as a source of contradictory sublimated versions of man's former happiness, particularly as the arts rely on the faculties of memory and fantasy through which man can remember and reconstruct the shadowy impressions of liberation. The extent to which this is both a revision and a refinement of Freud's attitude towards the role of art can be deduced from Freud's less than enthusiastic recognition of the promise of art in *Civilization and Its Discontents*: 'Nevertheless the mild narcosis induced in us by art can do no more than bring about a transient withdrawal from the pressure of vital needs, and it is not strong enough to make us forget real misery' (p. 18).

This ability of the arts to embody, in however distorted and contradictory a fashion, the possibility of alternative social systems, had been an early feature of Marcuse's work. In an essay, 'The Affirmative Character of Culture' (1937), Marcuse described how 'great bourgeois art' despite its techniques of sublimation has:

> continually shattered in the hearts of men the facile resignation of everyday life. By painting in the luminous colors of this world the beauty of men and things and transmundane happiness, it has planted real longing alongside poor consolation and false consecration in the soil of bourgeois life.[4]

Marcuse accepts that this 'culture of the bourgeois epoch' includes an element of false consciousness in that it hives off 'the mental and spiritual world as an independent realm of value that is also considered superior to civilization'. This process of sublimation does not, however, in Marcuse's view, invalidate the 'decisive characteristic' of 'affirmative culture': 'The assertion of a universally obligatory, eternally better and more valuable world'.[5] Art through the faculty of memory can give intimations of an unrepressive civilisation: 'The *recherche du temps perdu* becomes the vehicle of future liberation' (*EC*, p. 19).

Despite Marcuse's recovery of a progressive 'hidden trend in psychoanalysis', he finds no hidden progressive trend in the economic system which dominates in 'this acquisitive and antagonistic society in the process of constant expansion' (*EC*, p. 45). The system of capitalism imposes additional forms of repression on to those modifications of the instincts that, in classic Freudian theory, are 'necessary for the perpetuation of the human race in civilization' (*EC*, p. 35). Over and above the social controls that man institutes to protect himself from the aggressions of nature and other men, the capitalist system demands 'surplus repression' enforced by such additional controls as 'a hierarchical division of labor' and 'the monogamic-patriarchal family' (*EC*, pp. 37–8). Under capitalism: 'Society is stratified according to the competitive economic performances of its members'. This 'performance principle' (*EC*, p. 44) forces most men to 'perform pre-established functions' (*EC*, p. 45) in alienated assembly line production. Nowhere is Marcuse's exploration of the interplay between Marx and Freud more evident than in his assessment of the instinctual damage that the capitalist idea of work does to the human body. The 'performance principle' that governs the idea of work in capitalist society: 'achieves the necessary desexualization of the body: the libido becomes concentrated in one part of the body, leaving most of the rest free for use as the instrument of labor' (*EC*, p. 48). Although Marcuse is unequivocal in his indictment of the capitalist mode of production, work and exploitation, he recognises that capitalism has fulfilled many of its promises and that: 'Its profitable utilization of the productive apparatus fulfils the needs and faculties of the individual' (*EC*, p. 45). Marcuse's analysis of the ways capitalism has gained popular support to the point where in modern mass society there is: 'an immediate identification of the individual with his society and, through it, with society as a whole'[6] appears in his *One-Dimensional Man; Studies in the Ideology of Advanced Industrial Society*.

The argument in *One-Dimensional Man* was a contribution to the 'end of ideology' debate and offered a critique of the thesis associated with Daniel Bell and other apologists for liberal capitalism who argued that ideological commitment was a redundant divisive force in modern advanced capitalist societies. This thesis had become Presidential doctrine in a number of speeches by John F. Kennedy. In June 1962 at Yale, Kennedy gave the following analysis of post-war America:

The central domestic problems of our time . . . do not relate to basic clashes of philosophy and ideology, but to ways and means . . . sophisticated solutions to complex and obstinate problems.

What is at stake in our economic decisions today is not some grand warfare of rival ideologies which will sweep the country with passion but the practical management of a modern economy.

Marcuse detects behind these apologies an increasing centralisation of control, and a dangerous cult of technical rationality that is attempting to liquidate the legitimate roles of individual and class struggles. He characterises this process as one-dimensional in that ideological and class struggles and antagonisms within society are ridiculed as irrelevant in order to produce a single integrating consensus. The kind of total integration that one-dimensional societies seek to achieve is described by Marcuse as follows:

If the worker and his boss enjoy the same television program and visit the same resort places, if the typist is as attractively made up as the daughter of her employer, if the negro owns a Cadillac, if they all read the same newspaper, then this assimilation indicates not the disappearance of classes, but the extent to which the needs and satisfactions that serve the preservation of the Establishment are shared by the underlying population.[7]

Adorno and Horkheimer had anticipated Marcuse's idea of a one-dimensional society in their essay on the Culture Industry. The huge cartels of monopoly capitalism that control the entertainments industry are part of a system that seeks to control and liquidate all other forms of economic production. Supermarkets, cinemas and mail order firms monotonously retail the standardised commodities of the monopolies to a 'civilization of employees' (*DE*, p. 153). Dissent, conflict and individual freedom are comprehensively eroded by a 'technical apparatus of production and distribution' that institutes 'new, more effective, and more pleasant forms of social control and social cohesion'.[8] The process of assimilation and integration that Marcuse delineated as a primary characteristic of advanced capitalist societies made a mockery of the claims advanced by the system's apologists that a pluralist liberal democracy open to diversity and individualism could maintain itself within such an economic struc-ture. In an essay entitled 'Repressive Tolerance' Marcuse took issue with the claims of post-war liberalism, and showed how tolerance, a cardinal component of liberal ideology, was no guarantee of equality and often functioned as a token cover for institutionalised inequality. The claims made by liberal apologists for advanced capitalism have been succinctly summarised by Robert Paul Wolff:

> America, according to this account, is a complex interlocking of ethnic, religious, racial, regional and economic groups, where members pursue their diverse interests through the medium of private associations, which in turn are co-ordinated, regulated, contained, encouraged, and guided by a federal system of representative democracy, not 'one man – one vote' but rather 'every legitimate group its share'.[9]

Marcuse rejects the democratic claims of such a system because the basis of the supposed democracy tolerant of diversity is economic inequality and therefore:

> The conditions of tolerance are 'loaded': they are determined and defined by the institutionalised inequality (which is certainly compatible with constitutional equality), i.e. by the class structure of society.[10]

In practice pluralist democracy sets limits to dissent and diversity: 'Freedom of speech and assembly was granted even to the radical enemies of society, provided they did not make the transition from word to deed, from speech to action'.[11] Marcuse does not completely reject the idea of tolerance: 'Such indiscriminate tolerance is justified in harmless debates, in conversation, in academic discussion; it is indispensable in the scientific enterprise, in private religion'.[12]

Despite his assessment of the ways liberal capitalism can assimilate and defuse dissent, Marcuse supported participation in free speech movements and civil rights crusades because they enabled the participants to see the limits to dissent and the ways in which society prevented change. Marcuse was committed to programmes of action and believed that he should associate himself with the various radical movements of the 1960s that attempted to disrupt the one-dimensionality of American society by their advocacy of alternative models of liberation. This is an important dimension to his work in which he both supported and critically evaluated the various strategies of liberation that the counter-culture developed. A main source for this aspect of Marcuse's work is 'An Essay on Liberation' (1969), in which he describes various potential sources and strategies of liberation.

One basic model of liberation is provided by certain forms of artistic practice. The discussions on this theme in 'An Essay on Liberation' are an expansion and revision of the ideas of a 1937 essay 'The Affirmative Nature of Culture'. In this earlier essay Marcuse had commented on the tendency of the great humanist art of the past to create sublimated fantasy worlds which: 'raised pain and sorrow, desperation and loneliness, to the level of metaphysical powers'.[13] Marcuse sees redemptive value in this fantasy world because it contains: 'not only the justification of the established form of existence, but also the pain of its establishment: not only quiescence about what is, but also remembrance of what could be'.[14] Beethoven's 'Ode to Joy' in this formulation has a contradictory power. The sublime and spiritual qualities in the music create a temporary release from 'the facile resignation of everyday life'.[15] However, the real materialist world is not transformed by the music, only temporarily transcended, and the listener eventually returns to that materialist world. As has been shown earlier Freud described this experience as one of narcotic therapy. In contrast Marcuse claims a greater value for the sublimated transcendental powers of 'affirmative culture' in that however distorted and temporarily therapeutic these experiences and aspirations are, they are shadows of a liberated and utopian world. In *Eros and Civilization* this ability of art to recover a repressed utopian world is linked to the 'specific function of memory' in man's psychic development that preserves:

> promises and potentialities which are betrayed and even outlawed by the mature, civilized individual, but which had once been fulfilled in his dim past and which are never entirely forgotten. (pp. 18–19)

Though Marcuse values the products of affirmative culture, the costs have been high in terms of repression particularly in the ways the sublimations of affirmative culture have led to the 'subjection of sensuality to the domination of the soul', and 'the spiritualisation of sensuality'.[16] This process of spiritualisation is similar to the process by which the 'performance principle . . . achieves the necessary desexualisation of the body' (*EC*, p. 48). The accumulative effects of affirmative culture have been to deny and repress a whole range of man's instincts and potentialities. There are marginal areas in the culture that have escaped this deadening, distorting process, and provide 'the first glimmer of a new culture'[17] in which the body reclaims its full instinctual potential. One of Marcuse's images of this 'new culture' is derived from popular culture:

> The artistry of the beautiful body, its effortless agility and relaxation, which can be displayed today only in the circus, vaudeville, and burlesque, herald the joy to which men will attain in being liberated from the ideal . . .[18]

The basic positions established in 'The Affirmative Nature of Culture' recognised that 'great bourgeois art' was ideologically tied to the needs and frustrations of the bourgeoisie and was therefore a very distorted fragile basis for a revolutionary culture of liberation. In this respect Marcuse is in a mainstream Marxist tradition in which the arts, like all other products under capitalism, are seen as being under the repressive control of a ruling class. Marx formulated this idea of ideological dominance in the following way:

> The ideas of the ruling class are in every epoch the ruling ideas, i.e. the class which is the ruling material force of society is at the same time its ruling intellectual force. The class which has the means of material production at its disposal, has control at the same time over the means of mental production, so that generally speaking, the ideas of those who lack the means of mental production are subject to it.[19]

Marcuse modifies the deterministic severity of this Marxist description of the monolithic power of ideology with his own description of a number of twentieth-century revolutionary movements of liberation that have the potential to disrupt the status quo. In an 'Essay on Liberation' the three movements that Marcuse describes and analyses are twentieth-century modernism, the counter-culture of the 1960s, and certain aspects of Afro-American culture.

The main quality that links these three movements and enables them to constitute the basis of a revolutionary liberating culture is the degree to which they seek 'a desublimation of culture'.[20] These movements do not seek to create the spiritual compensations of affirmative culture. The modernist movement's role in this process of desublimation is to dissolve the fixed three-dimensional models of the world that affirmative culture created. The deliberate technical demystification of the illusion created by three-dimensional perspective that is a clear feature of Cubism and Surrealism is interpreted by Marcuse as an important challenge not only to the aesthetic status quo but also to the political one. 'Non-objective, abstract painting and sculpture, stream-of-consciousness and formalist literature, twelve-tone composition, blues and jazz' are in Marcuse's formulation not just 'new modes of perception re-orienting and intensifying the old ones'; they rather dissolve the very structure of perception. The formal experimentation of modernism is not just an episode in art history, the 'traditional replacement of one style by another' (*EL*, p. 38), rather it aims to disrupt 'the medium of experience imposed by the established society' that has coagulated 'into a self-sufficient, closed "automatic" system' (*EL*, p. 39). Marcuse links this disruption of traditional aesthetic norms in modernist art to 'the methodical desublimation' that is a strong impetus behind the culture of 'social groups which thus far have remained outside the entire realm of the higher culture, outside its affirmative, sublimating, and justifying magic'. This is the entry point for Marcuse's assessment of the revolutionary quality of Afro-American culture. The 'all too sublimated, segregated, orderly, harmonizing forms' (*EL*, p. 46) of the white masters, 'the sublime sublimations' of Beethoven's 'Ode to Joy' are negated by a 'subversive, dissonant, crying and shouting rhythm, born in the "dark continent", and in the "deep South" of slavery and deprivation'. Afro-American music can give 'art a desublimated, sensuous form of frightening immediacy, moving, electrifying the body, and the soul materialized in the body'. Where Adorno saw a monotonous syncopation in Afro-American music, reflecting the technical rationality of an industrialised entertainments industry, Marcuse sees an important 'elementary negation' (*EL*, p. 47) of the sublimated 'music of the spheres' (*EL*, p. 46) that is purveyed by the privileged higher culture of the dominant white master class.

The same spirit of defiant negation can be traced in the demands of a new counter-culture sensibility that developed in the 'anti-authoritarian rebellion' of the 1960s. Behind the contradictory surface elements of the counter-culture, 'miniskirts against the apparatchiks, rock 'n' roll against Soviet Realism' (*EL*, p. 26),

Marcuse saw a whole landscape of repressed needs struggling towards expression:

> The claims of the human organism, mind and body, for a dimension of fulfilment which can be created only in the struggle against the institutions which, by their very functioning, deny and violate these claims. (*EL*, p. 27)

Marcuse's version of the 1960s has been subjected to endless revisions; the culture of rock 'n' roll and black militancy has been shown to be shot through with sexism, and the popular front, created between feminists, liberals, the new left and black militants, eventually disintegrated as a result of the ideological divisions that emerged from within, and the infiltration into its ranks of CIA-planted *agents provocateurs*. Marcuse anticipated many of these revisions, and his reservations are as important as his celebrations. His main reservations centre on the manifest ability of a society of 'repressive tolerance' to absorb and deflect the revolutionary potential of the movements of liberation. The artworks of modernism have been 'quickly absorbed in the art gallery, within the four walls, in the concert hall', and soon adorn 'the plazas and lobbies of the prospering business establishments' (*EL*, p. 42). The counter-culture's desire to dissolve 'the ego shaped by the established society' with psychedelic drugs only creates 'artificial paradises within the society from which it withdrew' (*EL*, p. 37). The culture created by liberation often only succeeds in dissolving and negating the realities of the repressive status quo. It does not achieve 'the radical reconstruction of experience' (*EL*, p. 45).

Marcuse qualifies these criticisms of a culture of liberation by clearly recognising while limiting its revolutionary possibilities which he defines as: 'The disorderly, uncivil, farcical, artistic desublimation of culture constitutes an essential element of radical politics: of the subverting forces in transition' (*EL*, p. 48). This view of the counter-culture is in dramatic contrast with that of neo-conservatives like Daniel Bell. Bell characterised the 'new sensibility' of the counter-culture as 'the fantasies and sexual demands of childhood acted out during adolescence on a mass scale unprecedented in cultural history' (*CCC*, p. 144). Marcuse characterises the same phenomena as a contradictory but progressive subversion of a repressive society. Slogans such as 'Black is beautiful', 'make love, not war' were part of a 'systematic linguistic rebellion' against a military-industrial Establishment. 'Non-conformist youth' has heroically taken this 'reversal of meaning' to the point of open contradiction: 'giving flowers to the police, "flower power" – the redefinition and very negation of the sense of "power" ' (*EL*, pp. 35–6). This existential agitprop counter-culture of defiance cannot, in Marcuse's view, be dismissed as 'infantile regression'. The demand for a more sensuous, less repressive society is legitimate and needs to be supported, not caricatured.

Having made a commitment to the legitimate demands of the counter-culture, Marcuse felt free to question aspects of its tactics and the aesthetics of its favoured cultural forms. The main problems posed by the happenings and large-scale communal music festivals of the counter-culture are that they often employed the same techniques as the sublimated higher culture. The basic technique that higher and counter-culture forms employs is one in which the audience suspends its disbelief and by a leap of imagination is transported into a fictional world. The audience are offered 'a temporary release from frustration' (*EL*, p. 47) after which they return to the monotonous pain of a repressed civilisation. The alternative set of relationships between audience and performance that Marcuse contrasts with the dominant illusionist aesthetic by which 'we immediately identify ourselves with the actors, experience our familiar sympathies', is that created by the 'Estrangement Effect' (*EL*, p. 47–8) of Brechtian theatre. In order to prevent his audiences experiencing surrogate fulfilment by identifying with heroes and heroines inhabiting a fictional universe, Brecht on occasions disrupted the audience's identification with the fictional world of illusion created on stage by deliberately interrupting the narrative action. Characters stand back from the action and comment on its political meaning, often engaging in discussion with the audience. Brecht's plays do not deny themselves the techniques of traditional illusionist art but his use of the estrangement effect enabled him to challenge the dominance of an illusionist aesthetic convention that separates audience from actors, and art from life. In Marcuse's view illusionist art reinforces a tendency to sublimate into art, the energies that should be channelled into life.

Marcuse's qualified but positive evaluation of 'the new sensibility' is linked to his assessment of the role it would play if the technical and productive apparatus of capitalist society could be directed by an unrepressive socialism. This notion that 'freedom indeed depends largely on technical progress' (*EL*, p. 19) separates Marcuse from the anti-technology arguments of such counter-culture theoreticians as Theodor Roszak, ideas that he advanced in his influential analysis, *The Making of a Counter-Culture* (1969). Marcuse believes in a socialist technology:

> in which the growing mechanization of labor enables an ever larger part of . . . instinctual energy . . . to return to its original form . . . to be changed back into energy of the life instincts.[21]

Marcuse, unlike Adorno and Horkheimer, permitted himself a degree of utopian speculation and imagined a future society in which science and technology were:

> reconstructed in accord with a new sensibility . . . Then one could speak of a technology of liberation, product of a scientific imagination free to project and design the forms of a human universe without exploitation and toil. (*EL*, p. 19)

Marcuse took great care to show how an unrepressive society could evolve out of the existing social order and his cultural criticism, developed to meet the conditions of advanced industrial society, remains an impressive set of theoretical entrances, not only to the repressive nature of that society, but also to potential sources of liberation. It is a dialectical form of analysis in which liberation is always endangered by new forms of repressive social control.

There were, however, other investigators of the interaction between personality and culture who were less pessimistic than the Frankfurt School about the impact of culture upon individual development. Erich Fromm, a founder member of the Frankfurt School, joined with such American sociologists as Robert Park and anthropologists such as Margaret Mead to form a distinct school within the culture and personality debate. This group toned down the bleak pessimism of Adorno and Horkheimer. Stuart Hughes has described this more positive tendency as marking a departure from Freud's scepticism of mankind's capacities for improvement. Hughes argues that, for such figures as Fromm, Freud's pessimism:

> no longer sufficed; in the ideologically open and welcoming atmosphere of the United States, they became militant optimists.

Emotional suffering, they began to imply, was not integral to the human condition; beyond Freud's modest goal of alleviating psychic misery gleamed the vision of maximising man's potentialities in a re-ordered society.[22]

This more liberal division of opinion suggested that the impact of society and culture upon the individual could be beneficial and that a liberal democracy like America could offer the individual a diverse range of creative models and value systems. This liberal tradition stresses the individual's ability to choose a value system that can fulfil and nurture his or her own particular temperament. Instead of concentrating on the damage wrought on the individual by repressive social systems, this version of the interaction between self and society argued that:

> Human personality, in its development, structure, and continued functioning, is dependent upon the social groups of which it is a significant member. Social influence is positive, formative, supportive. The child who grows to manhood outside a social group becomes an animal, without language, knowledge, the capacity to reason, or even the ability to love and hate as other men do.[23]

This affirming revaluation of the process by which individuals through cultural conditioning were socialised into human individuality could only take place once the nineteenth-century idea that character and culture were racially and genetically determined had been dethroned by the new anthropological idea of culture rather than race being the main source of learned behaviour and human creativity. The new anthropology as developed by Franz Boas and his students Margaret Mead and Ruth Benedict created a climate of opinion in which a hierarchical ranking of cultures and peoples based on biologically determined ideas of race gave way to a more open account of the interaction between the individual and social systems. An important impact of this new culture concept was the revaluation of supposed inferior primitive societies. In *Coming of Age in Samoa* (1928) Margaret Mead described how the increasingly psychologically stressful experience of adolescence in western societies was imaginatively and sensitively eased in Samoan society by a whole range of culturally conditioned techniques.[24] This appeal to diversity, flexibility and cultural relativism reached a wide audience through

Ruth Benedict's *Patterns of Culture* (1934). Benedict saw culture as a complex form of social cement which had 'to be viewed holistically, for none of its specific features could be adequately grasped without reference to the pattern of which they formed a part'.[25] One implication of this anthropological view of culture was clearly that without such a social cement societies became prone to irrational patterns of unity such as those proposed by fascism.

If the new anthropology stressed the idea of cultural diversity, the new sociology as represented by Robert Park's Chicago School offered proposals as to how the different social and ethnic groups within an increasingly metropolitan America could resolve the inevitable conflicts that ensued as the various immigrant groups struggled against one another in economic and political competition. Park created a model for the creative interaction between different competing groups. He described a four-stage race relations cycle. The cycle began with competition followed by conflict, then by accommodation. Out of this three-stage crucible emerged the final stage of assimilation. This final stage achieved the positive liberal kind of cultural unity and patterning, celebrated by the new anthropology. Park's somewhat idealistic description of assimilation is:

> A process of interpretation and fusion in which persons and groups acquire the memories and sentiments and attitudes of other persons and groups, and, by sharing their experience and history, are incorporated with them in a common cultural life.[26]

A mosaic of diversity was the aim rather than a melting pot of WASP conformity. Behind these developments in sociology and anthropology was the search for a critical but positive definition of the characteristic qualities of democratic pluralism. An important and often implicit part of this agenda was the desire to find in American democracy a model that was as dynamic as the ideological appeal of fascism and communism. In the ideological struggles of the 1930s and 1940s American democratic culture was often favourably contrasted with the heady irrationalism of European fascism. The contrast set the terms of the Cold War of the post-war era in which American liberalism fought its mortal enemy, Stalinist communism. This aspect of the debates on culture is captured in the manifesto of a Council for Democracy organised in the fall of 1940 that announced its purpose as:

To crystallize and instill in the minds of Americans the meaning, value, and workability of democracy as a dynamic, vital creed – just as Nazism, Fascism, and Communism are to their adherents.[27]

In contrast to the views expressed in *The Authoritarian Personality* that certain socio-economic groups within liberal democratic capitalist systems were organically disposed to fascist prejudices, the apologists for democratic pluralism attempted to revitalise a democratic creed that in Europe had proved no ideological match for the heady formulations of fascism. The problem was that democratic values embodied in such concepts as tolerance, cultural diversity and progress did not seem to have the binding mass appeal of other ideologies. The openness and vulnerability of liberalism is captured in Lionel Trilling's affirmation of its value system that appeared in his 1943 study of E. M. Forster. Trilling speaks of 'that loose body of middle class opinion which includes such ideas as progress, collectivism and humanitarianism'.[28] It could be argued that the ethnocentrism and cultural nationalism of fascist ideologies were closer to the spirit of the new liberal anthropology's culture concept of a self-contained cohesive ensemble of values and norms than were the loosely organised diversities of democratic pluralism. This contradiction was matched by others. The publication of Gunnar Myrdal's monumental study of the political and socio-economic status of American blacks, *An American Dilemma* (1944), revealed a deep contradiction between 'the American Creed' of egalitarianism and an American racial practice that condemned a section of its population to miserable segregated ghettoes. The whole debate on the interaction between culture and personality and the effects of mass society that social scientists and anthropologists were engaged in in the 1930s and 1940s provided many of the terms that defined the discussion of mass society among literary and cultural critics that continued after the war. Two figures who addressed what Daniel Bell called 'the pervasive cultural theme of the era . . . the depersonalisation of the individual and the atomisation of society' (*CCC*, p. 42), were Lionel Trilling and David Riesman. Their work can provide examples of the ways the complicated intellectual legacy of the 1930s and 1940s influenced a sociologist and a literary critic in their analyses of American culture.

10. The Lonely Crowd: David Riesman and American Society

THE Lonely Crowd: A Study of the Changing American Character, was published in 1950. It belongs to a particular genre of sociological investigation that aimed to describe and predict the future shape and ideology of post-war America. Looking back at the book in 1961, David Riesman questioned a major assumption of the book that 'took for granted an economy of abundance, however sustained'.[1] This assumption coloured a whole range of investigations into the ideology of what was seen as the post- or advanced industrial civilisation that was taking shape in America. The distinctive characteristics of a post-industrial society included an increasing automation of labour, the shift of jobs and productivity from declining manufacturing industries to an increasingly dominant sector of service industries such as computers and insurance, from blue-collar to white-collar occupations. A corollary of this thesis was that the main problem for such a society that was relieving man from the necessities of crude physical work was how to occupy oneself in a society that was creating more time for leisure than for work. The post-industrial thesis was subjected to a whole range of revisionary critiques from Paul Goodman's *Growing up Absurd* (1960), that examined the psychological costs of a world without meaningful work, to C. Wright Mill's analysis in *The Power Elite* (1956), of how power in a post-industrial society would pass into the hands of three linked groups: corporation capitalists, militarists and politicians. Despite the accuracy of many of the predictions of the post-industrial prophets, the economic circumstances of the 1980s, recession, stagflation and rising levels of unemployment, have revealed the inadequacies of a thesis that was based on the idea of an economy of abundance. The post-industrial thesis failed to recognise that many groups in a time of recession would be denied access to the world of post-industrial leisure, creating a whole range of new inequities. It is in this critical context that the immensely influential themes and metaphors of *The Lonely Crowd* will be placed.

The investigations that were presented in *The Lonely Crowd* began life as a study sponsored by Yale University's Committee on National Policy, funded by the Carnegie Corporation. The research team that carried out the interviews and constructed the theoretical models was headed by David Riesman but included the important contributions of Renel Denney in the area of teenage culture and of Nathan Glazer in the area of 'the relation between politics and character structure' (*LC*, 1961 Preface, p. lvii). However, the decisive influence is that of Erich Fromm with whom Riesman had studied. This can be clearly seen in the emphasis that the study places on social character rather than individual personality. This was an emphasis that redressed what Riesman felt was a myopic tendency in Freudianism to fix 'man's fate too early in assuming it to be solely the playing out of psychosexual experiences mastered or suffered in the early years of childhood' (*LC*, pp. xxiv–xxv). Riesman's model, derived from the culture and personality school, liberated the study of the interaction between self and society from the closed-circuit of childhood and directed attention towards a whole range of agencies that did not just reinforce the traumas of childhood but played an important role in the socialisation of individuals into creative roles in society. Riesman specifically aligned himself with the revisionist neo-Freudians and defined the nature of social character with the following quotation from Erich Fromm. Socialisation is seen as a potentially positive process:

> In order that any society may function well, its members must acquire the kind of character which makes them *want* to act in the way they *have* to act as members of the society or of a special class within it. They have to desire what objectively is *necessary* for them to do. *Outer force* is replaced by *inner compulsion*, and by the particular kind of human energy which is channeled into character traits. (*LC*, p. 5)

The contradiction that emerges in Riesman's application of this methodology is that the findings and critical reception of *The Lonely*

Crowd seemed to suggest that the agencies he described as mediating social character in a post-industrial civilisation such as the corporation and the mass-media were as opposed to individual gratification as the Freudian traumas of childhood. This perspective of a basically repressive conservative American culture flows from Riesman's recognition that:

> Contrary to current opinion on both the Right and the Left, liberalism has not dominated American society but has been a minority tradition in the face of historic, unideological conservatism. (*LC*, 1969 Preface, p. xii)

What Riesman wishes to preserve and promote are the classic liberal demands of diversity and personal fulfilment, but he gives equal if not greater importance to the role of social character and its agencies as important protectors and harnesses of personal development: 'It is one of the ambiguities of human existence, as it is of art, that personal life flourishes within the forms provided for it by tradition and necessity' (*LC*, pp. 5–6).

Riesman's specific description of the ideology and social character of post-industrial America is prefaced by an analysis of the ideology and social character of earlier periods of history. He characterises feudal society as being organised around a 'tradition-directed' (*LC*, pp. 11–13) social character, which is then replaced at the Renaissance period by the rise of an 'inner-directed' social character that coincides with the rise of a society: 'characterised by increased personal mobility, by a rapid accumulation of capital (teamed with devastating technological shifts), and by an almost constant expansion' (*LC*, pp. 14–15). Riesman's assessment of this shift from feudal to capitalist is based on the performance and behaviour of upwardly mobile elites, a perspective he continues when he comes to his third social character, 'the other-directed' behaviour of a particular socio-economic group visible in post-war America: 'In the upper middle class of our larger cities: more prominent in New York than in Boston, in Los Angeles than in Spokane, in Cincinnati than in Chillicothe' (*LC*, p. 19). Riesman focuses his enquiry on: 'Those components of personality that also play the principal role in the maintenance of social forms that are *learned* in the lifelong process of socialisation' (*LC*, p. 4). Viewed from this perspective the tradition-directed social character of medieval society is transmitted and absorbed by a process of osmosis. In such societies all values are communal, since there is no concept of the individual operating within the web of communal values: 'ritual, routine and religion' serve 'to occupy and to orient everyone' (*LC*, p. 11). In tradition-directed static societies 'only to a limited extent is there any concept of progress for the group' (*LC*, p. 12). This kind of social character becomes counter-productive once the spirit of capitalism begins to break up feudal structures. In order to survive and take advantage of the new conditions, the new inner-directed bourgeois individual has to possess a 'greater degree of flexibility in adapting himself to ever changing requirements and in return requires more from his environment'. Parents are still crucial to this new individual for they must implant in their progeny 'a new psychological mechanism appropriate to the more open society'. Riesman employs the metaphor of a 'psychological gyroscope' to describe this process that enables the individual 'to receive and utilize certain signals from the outside, provided that they can be reconciled with the limited maneuverability that his gyroscope permits him. His pilot is not quite automatic' (*LC*, pp. 16–17). The main psychological differences between tradition and inner direction are that the former internalises its values through shame while the latter relies on guilt or conscience. Having established his thesis within a chronology of western civilisation, Riesman then devotes the major part of the book to the other-directed mode of conformity and its specific agencies of mediation.

The main agencies of 'other-directed' post-industrial social character are the culture of school, of the peer group, of the mass media and of corporate bureaucracy. These have replaced such primary agencies of inner direction as the family, parents, the governess and the family firm. The major requirements of post-industrial society mediated by its chosen agencies are the skills of co-operation, adaptability and flexibility: 'the problem for people in America today is other people' (*LC*, 1961 Preface, p. xxx). In the former inner-directed society: 'While the frontiersman co-operated with his sparse neighbours in mutual self-help activities, such as housebuilding or politics, his main pre-occupation was with physical, not with human nature' (*LC*, p. 116). In the new, highly bureaucratised post-industrial society with an expanding service economy of white-collar workers, productivity and social control are 'increasingly dependent on manipulation of people' (*LC*, p. 134). The new professional managerial elite must combine enough 'technological knowledge to talk to the technical men, with enough social skills to sense the wants of the variety of publics that may affect or be affected by their decisions' (*LC*, p. 135). In order to blur an over-determined model of one social character replacing another in a neat evolutionary design, Riesman finds the post-industrial type anticipated in the nineteenth-century character of Stepan Arkadyevitch Oblonsky in Tolstoy's *Anna Karenina*. Stepan possessed the following synthesis of other-directed social and political skills:

> Stepan Arkadyevitch took in and read a liberal newspaper, not an extreme one, but one advocating the views held by the majority. And in spite of the fact that science, art, and politics had no special interest for him, he firmly held those views on all subjects which were held by the majority and by his paper, and he only changed them when the majority changed them – or, more strictly speaking, he did not change them, but they imperceptibly changed of themselves within him. (*LC*, p. 23).

The new metaphor to describe how post-industrial skills are functionally internalised is that of 'a radar' and: 'As against guilt-and-shame controls, though of course these survive, one prime psychological lever of the other-directed person is a diffuse anxiety' (*LC*, p. 26). Riesman describes this process in terms of the way the signals and values of peer group cultural commentary are conveyed by the marginal differentiations of consumer commodities. In post-industrial society:

> The consumer trainee has a lot more to learn than in the early days of industrialization. To take one example, the foreigner who visits America is likely to think that sales-girls, society ladies, and movie actresses all dress alike, as compared with the clear status differences in Europe. But the American knows – has to know if he is to get along in life and love – that this is simply an error – that one must look for small qualitative differences that signify style and status, to observe for instance the strained casualness sometimes found in upper-class dress as against the strained formality of working-class dress. (*LC*, p. 74)

The implicit discriminations of connoisseurship replace the explicit rules of etiquette.

The same emphasis on taste and social skills can be seen in the schools that train the new elite. In contrast to inner-directed schooling where: 'The sexes are segregated from each other' and 'the focus is on intellectual content that for most children has little emotional bite' (*LC*, p. 58), the role of other-directed education, through its teachers and curriculum is to spread 'the messages concerning taste that come from the progressive urban centers'. These agencies of other-direction convey to the children that: 'What matters is not their industry or learning as such but their adjustment in the group, their co-operation, their (carefully stylised and limited) initiative and leadership' (*LC*, p. 62). In this cultural climate the children 'will probably conclude that to be unco-operative is about the worst thing one can be' (*LC*, p. 63). The same pressures are exerted on the child by 'the will of the peer group' which seems to exert a mesmeric totalitarian control over values and attitudes:

> All 'knobby' or idiosyncratic qualities are more or less eliminated or repressed. And judgements of others by peer group members are so clearly matters of taste that their expression has to resort to the vaguest phrases, constantly changed: cute, lousy, square, darling, good guy, honey, swell, bitch (without precise meaning), etc. (*LC*, p. 71)

The relationship between peer groups and the mass media is conceived as follows:

> The peer group accepts a substantial responsibility in the flow of modern communications. It stands midway between the individuals of whom each group is composed and the messages which flow to the group's opinion leaders from the mass media. The mass media are the wholesalers; the peer groups, the retailers of the communications industry. (*LC*, p. 85)

Riesman goes on to detail these trends with an analysis of comics and children's books (television as a mass form did not exist at the time of Riesman's research). Riesman's investigations convince him that: 'The American peer group . . . cannot be matched for power throughout the middle class world' (*LC*, p. 69).

A major impact of Riesman's investigations was to reinforce the image of post-war America as a society fast achieving alarming proportions of conformity. His master metaphor of a 'lonely crowd' had overtones of totalitarianism, a quality that was often noted in the public debate that followed the book's publication. Arthur Brodbeck Jr fleshed out the implications of Riesman's master metaphor as follows:

> A 'crowd' is a group of people without continuity with past or future, a throng acting upon the temporary stimulant of the moment. It conveys a portrait of men turned animals, and running in a herd, pushing and crowding against each other blindly, taking direction from whatever sudden frightening or comforting event is accidentally encountered.[2]

Riesman's conclusions brought to a head one of the major issues within the debates on the effects of mass industrial society: not only whether individualism was being liquidated by such a mass society, but also whether the traditional liberal celebration of personal freedom, identity, choice, and autonomy had not become redundant and counter-productive. Margaret Mead took issue with Riesman's portrait on the grounds that it was:

> essentially a negative one in which the function of character formation is to establish conformity . . . significantly he discusses only negative sanctions – shame but not pride, guilt but not the sense of initiative, anxiety but not identity.[3]

Riesman's liberalism does not include the kind of positive evaluation of individualism that Margaret Mead calls for. Such classic components of liberalism as freedom of choice constitute in Riesman's view a distorted view of how human creativity is guaranteed and achieved. A process of socialisation on the model of Fromm's definition of social character is more important to Riesman than romantic assessments of individualism. A finely tuned social character has the important role of:

> foreclosing some of the otherwise limitless behaviour choices of human beings . . . Since life is too short for such overworked elaboration of choice, the social character permits it to be lived in some sort of working harness. (*LC*, p. 6)

A major contributor to these competing versions of the correct balance between the claims of individualism and those of communal tradition and social character was the literary critic Lionel Trilling. The recently published collected works enables the shape of Trilling's contribution to be effectively traced.

Lionel Trilling's collected literary criticism like Dwight Macdonald's is the product of a lifelong concern with what he called 'the politics of culture'.[4] In 'Some Notes for an Autobiographical Lecture' on which he was working at the time of his death in 1975, he recalled the main influences on his ideas: 'Upon my work in criticism, upon my intellectual life in general, the systems of Marx and Freud had, I have never doubted, a decisive influence' (LD, p. 237). In the same way that Marxist and Freudian techniques of analysis revealed the hidden laws of economic and psychological development, Trilling's literary criticism saw literature as a major agency of a radical and 'programmatic rejection of the settled institutionalized conception of reality' (LD, p. 236). Like psycho-analysis, literature was a means of unmasking 'the falsehood of the established order' (LD, p. 240). The main twist in Trilling's argument is that, in his perception, the literary equivalents of Marx and Freud are not necessarily to be found in avowedly Marxist or Freudian writers. The main figures in the particular 'unmasking tradition' that Trilling constructs would not be the first names to be brought forward as candidates for a radical socialist avant-garde. Jane Austen, Henry James, Kafka and Matthew Arnold, in whose works Trilling sees a radical unmasking critique of western society, were often attacked by Marxist critics for being bourgeois and elitist.

Trilling began his career in the 1930s and quickly encountered that whole set of hard-line Marxist literary judgements that for example dismissed Dickens as a sentimentalising bourgeois moralist,[5] and found the complexities of T. S. Eliot an affront to the working class whose revolutionary sympathies needed to be aroused by explicit agitprop ideology.[6] Trilling consciously set himself against this 'dull repressive tendency of opinion' (LD, p. 141) that throughout his career he described as Stalinism. In Trilling's view the basic premise of Stalinism (itself an impure 'degraded version of Marxism') was: 'a belief that the Soviet Union had resolved all social and political contradictions and was well on its way toward realizing the highest possibilities of human life' (LD, p. 140). Instead of engaging in 'the

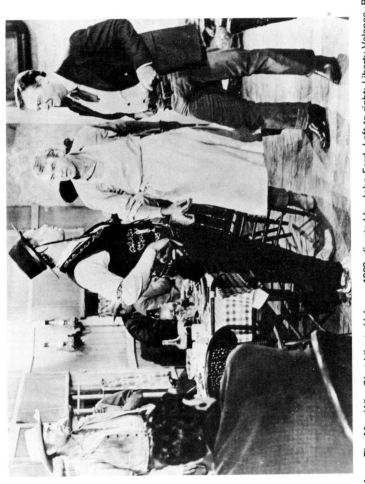

1. Still from *The Man Who Shot Liberty Valance*, 1962, directed by John Ford. Left to right: Liberty Valance, Ransom Stoddard, Tom Doniphon. Notice how Valance's black gear and whip, Stoddard's apron, and Doniphon's stance, announce their character and values.

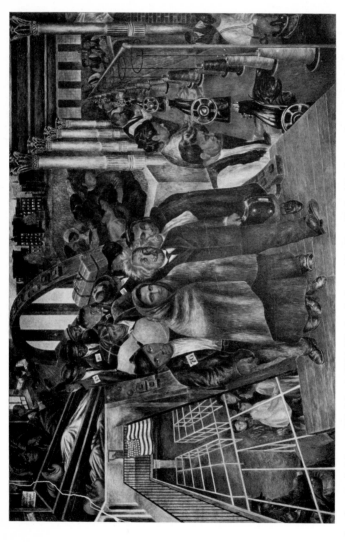

2. *Immigrants Arriving at Ellis Island*, 1937—38, detail of mural by Ben Shahn. For former Community Centre of Jersey Homesteads, Roosevelt, New Jersey. The man carrying the violin is Albert Einstein. Despite the mural's projection of an affirmative image of America as a refuge, the bleak cages of Ellis Island and the production lines of sewing machines qualify the affirmation.

3. *Jackson Pollock at Work*, 1951.

4. *Going Westward*, oil, ca. 1934—38, by Jackson Pollock.

5. *Isaiah* by Michel Angelo. Detail from the Sistine Chapel.

6. *Rosie the Riveter* by Norman Rockwell. *Saturday Evening Post* cover, May 29th, 1943. Norman Rockwell openly acknowledged his borrowings from other artists' designs. I am indebted to Bill Stott for this and many other examples.

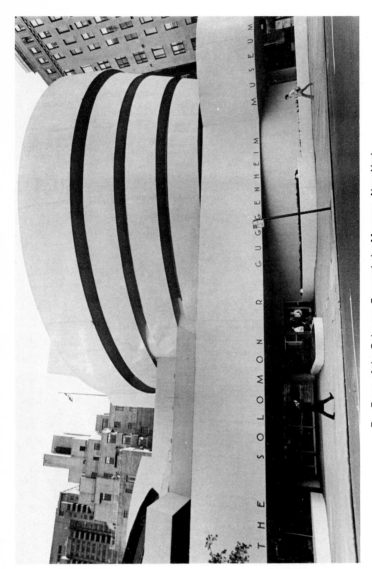

7. Front of the Solomon Guggenheim Museum, New York.

8. *George Gudger, Southern Share Cropper* by Walker Evans, 1936. This photograph was included in *Let Us Now Praise Famous Men* by James Agee and Walker Evans, 1941.

9. *A Jewish Giant at home with his Parents in the Bronx, New York, 1970* by Diane Arbus.

particular acts of will which are needed to meet the many, often clashing requirements of democratic society', Stalinists delegated their individual rights to 'an imposed monolithic government' which created a collective consciousness in which 'the exertions of our individual wills' become redundant. Stalinist ideology came to replace 'the old ethos of liberal enlightenment' (LD, p. 141) as the major creed for 'a large segment of the intelligentsia of the West' (LD, p. 140). Faced with this shift towards an authoritarian intellectual culture of official party lines and denial of individuality, Trilling increasingly campaigned for an alternative ideology of democratic pluralism: 'A political position that affirmed the value of individual existence in all its variousness, complexity, and difficulty'. The role of literature in this campaign was crucial in that: 'Literature, especially the novel, is the human activity that takes the fullest and most precise account of variousness, complexity, difficulty – and possibility' (LD, p. 141). The natural home for such opinions in the late 1930s and 1940s was Partisan Review, where like-minded critics such as Robert Warshow were attempting to redeem cultural debate from crude Stalinist sloganeering. Trilling shared Warshow's analysis that Stalinism had effected: 'A disastrous vulgarization of intellectual life, in which the character of American liberalism and radicalism was decisively – and perhaps permanently corrupted' (IE, p. 33). This gathering of Trotskyites, liberals and other anti-Stalinist groups created a particular mood in American intellectual life that 'after the Moscow Trials and the Soviet-Nazi pact' became 'disenchanted and reflective'. Trilling's literary criticism was a primary source for the new post-revolutionary scepticism in which 'the key terms' were 'irony, paradox, ambiguity, and complexity'.[7] The main features of the Stalinist tendencies this group of critics set themselves against have already been described in terms of Dwight Macdonald's career. Stalinism involved a rejection of experimental modernism and bourgeois high culture on the grounds that they were often negative, elitist, and too complex for a mass popular audience. The favoured revolutionary style, promoted by Stalinist communist parties throughout the world, was Socialist Realism, in which the heroic labours of industrial and agricultural workers were celebrated with a bold, documentary rhetoric. Abstraction and experimental avant-gardism became associated with counter-revolutionary indi-vidualism and were suppressed. Trilling's critical animus was not only directed against Stalinist dogmas. He also attacked some of the orthodoxies of liberal criticism that often uncritically praised the explicit social critiques of writers such as Theodore Dreiser and Sherwood Anderson and condemned Henry James and Faulkner for writing in an evasive anti-democratic style that could only appeal to a small minority. Liberal critics were often too populist in attitude, too prone to find virtue in large abstractions like 'the spirit of the American people'. The future for literary criticism as far as Trilling was concerned lay in not evaluating a writer according to a predetermined ideological grid. His own critical essays claimed that modern society had as much to gain from the insights of an expatriate Boston Brahmin like Henry James or of an English governess like Jane Austen as from the explicit ideological messages of Socialist Realism.

A major intention of Trilling's first published book, a study of Matthew Arnold, was to rehabilitate the radical democratic value of a whole range of nineteenth-century writers whose social critiques had been relegated to insignificance by Stalinist ideology. The critique of industrial democracy that Matthew Arnold makes in *Culture and Anarchy* is a valuable reforming interpretation as are the views of a heterogeneous group of writers who pointed out the inequities of an industrial society from a variety of ideological positions. This group includes 'Chartists, Owenite Socialists, Dr Arnold, Carlyle, the Saint-Simonians, not a few enlightened Tories, the revolutionists of the Continent, among them Marx and Engels'.[8] Trilling is prepared to override the clear contradictions and divisions within nineteenth-century thinking in favour of a generalised culture of humanism that links the disparate traditions. This assessment of the links between Marxism and other traditions of social criticism is a formulation that appears in a lecture given by Trilling in 1970 which reviews and refines a position first established in 1939 in the book on Arnold. In reading Marx's *Economic and Philosophic Manuscripts* (written in 1844 but not published until 1932) Trilling in common with many critics finds that 'the young Marx is more humanistic'.[9] Trilling quotes the end of the section on money: 'Let us assume man to be man, and his relation to the world a human one. Then love can only be exchanged for love, trust for trust, etc.' The fear that Marx expresses here that human relationships have been supplanted by commodity relationships and exchange values is a perception shared by 'the bourgeois moralists of the age'. Matthew Arnold's view that 'culture is not a having but a being and a becoming', and Oscar Wilde's belief from his essay 'The Soul of Man Under Socialism', that 'the true perfection of man lies not in what man has but what man is'[10] should, in Trilling's view, be included in any history of radical social analysis. Marxism did not have a monopoly on radicalism.

Another aspect of Trilling's reconstruction of a usable radical past was his rehabilitation of Romanticism. A number of Marxist and liberal critics had seen Romanticism as one of the sources of Nazi ideology. Trilling in his study of E. M. Forster published in 1943 commented on the 'futile accusations' that 'Romanticism – by which they mean undisciplined emotion – is to blame for the Nazi ideology' (p. 135). Trilling did share the view that the whole tradition of European humanism had been dramatically called into question by Nazism: 'The great psychological fact of our time which we all observe with baffled wonder and shame is that there is no possible way of responding to Belsen and Buchenwald.'[11] This reaction echoes that of Adorno that: 'to write poetry after Auschwitz is barbaric'.[12] But Trilling, the first Jew to be appointed to the English faculty of Columbia University, did not endorse the view that the diseased roots of European fascism resided in a romantic idealisation of individual, nature and nation. In Trilling's literary and cultural criticism Romanticism is one of the primary sources of an ideology that seeks: 'to liberate the individual from the tyranny of his culture in the environmental sense and to permit him to stand beyond it in an autonomy of perception and judgement.'[13] Raymond Williams has commented on the appearance in the historical period of Romanticism, the end of the eighteenth century and the first part of the nineteenth century, of a series of new definitions and claims on behalf of individual inventiveness. The artist in this period became 'a special kind of person', a unique individual medium and instrument of intense perceptions that could break through the tyranny of environmental appearances. Through this process of individuation the artist created the idea of art as a superior reality. The medium of this superior reality was the imagination through which the individual could escape a deadening external world. Among the theoreticians of Romanticism, Coleridge and Shelley provided definitions of the ways an individual artist could create an imaginative world to rival and transcend the constrictions of reality. In *Biographia Literaria*, Coleridge claims: 'The Primary IMAGINATION I hold to be the living Power and prime Agent of all human perception, and as a repetition in the finite mind of the eternal act of creation'. Shelley, in his *Defence of Poetry*, had no doubts about the potential powers of the individual artistic imagination:

> All things exist as they are perceived; at least in relation to the percipient. 'The mind is its own place, and of itself can make a Heaven of Hell, a Hell of Heaven.' But poetry defeats the curse which binds us to be subjected to the accident of surrounding impressions.[14]

For Trilling, Romanticism provided a guarantee of both individual perception and diversity. However, unlike many interpreters of Romanticism who see poetry as the supreme romantic and personal medium, Trilling saw the novel, in the realist tradition of Jane Austen and James, as the most comprehensive fulfilment of the promises of Romanticism. The novel in Trilling's criticism becomes: 'the human activity that takes the fullest and most precise account of variousness, complexity, difficulty – and possibility' (*LD*, p. 141).

Many critics have commented on the degree to which the realist novel, particularly in the hands of Daniel Defoe, coincided with the rise of bourgeois economic individualism and a middle-class reading public.[15] This idea of the developmental individual, Riesman's inner-directed innovator, is central to Trilling's whole programme of criticism, and is in sharp contrast to the Frankfurt School's assessment that though bourgeois individualism had been progressive in its time, the ideology of individualism was anachronistic in the mass society of twentieth-century monopoly capitalism. Trilling has no such reservations about his basic model of a democratic society which guarantees individual creativity. His model is close to that of one of his acknowledged mentors, I. A. Richards, who sees the mind as a plural system of interests which 'must come into play and remain in play with as little conflict among themselves as possible'.[16] Poetry constructed on these principles creates a 'fine organisation of the mind',[17] offering models of a world of diversity in which conflicts are resolved by conciliation.

Throughout his career Trilling refined his commitment to these ideas of individualism and diversity. In 1970 he described the origins of this ideology that dates from the Renaissance, was powerfully reinforced by the great figures of Romanticism in such works as Rousseau's *Confessions*, and cannot be repudiated by the twentieth century. Drawing on this set of ideas, on the insights of the French psychoanalyst Jacques Lacan and of the English historian Christopher Hill, Trilling details the process by which: 'at a certain point in history men become individuals'.[18] Rembrandt's self-portraits, the increased use of mirrors, the growth of autobiography, and the use of 'the word "self" not as a mere reflexive or intensive, but as an autonomous noun',[19] are all signs of a crucial liberating extrication of the individual from the external environment, from feudalism and anonymity. This tradition is then continued and expanded by a number of novelists who chart the fortunes of individuals seeking to preserve their identities in the face of industrial urban society that threatens to overwhelm them. A master metaphor for this interaction is created by 'the frequency with which the image of the prison appears in the imaginative works of the nineteenth century'. Dickens is an important register of this consciousness: 'The modern self, like Little Dorrit, was born in a prison'.[20]

The images and allegories of imprisonment that Dickens employs in his novels are not difficult to relate to twentieth-century consciousness. Jane Austen's novels, set in the world of the landed gentry and concerned with the intricacies of courtship and marriage, seem unpromising territory for Trilling's thesis of the opposing self. In Austen's rigidly conventional society the very idea of individual personality is alien. However, in Austen's themes of appropriate economic marriages and correct behaviour, Trilling sees a model of how susceptible to pressures of conformity the individual has become in modern middle-class society. The sense in which individuals in an Austen novel either succeed or fail to join a 'secular-spiritual elect' is very close to the ways individual quirkiness is suppressed and weeded out in the post-industrial class that Riesman describes in *The Lonely Crowd*. Jane Austen's codes of taste, of sense and sensibility, are portraits of modern forms of social control in the making: 'We learn from her what our lives should be and by what subtle and fierce criteria they will be judged, and how to pass upon the lives of our friends and fellows' (*OS*, p. 201). The marginal differentiations in wealth, birth and breeding that can mean the difference between failure and success in Jane Austen's world have become the standard procedures of a mass consumer society. Jane Austen has a highly developed awareness of how the individual is manipulated in such social systems, and Trilling uses *Mansfield Park* (1814) to illustrate how social conformity can exert an iron control over romantic ideas of individual freedom.

Mansfield Park describes the development and resolution of a crisis in social behaviour that occurs when, in the absence of Sir Thomas Bertram, the owner of Mansfield Park, his family and guests decide to mount an amateur drama production. A dramatic performance involves the impersonation and playing of fictional roles. In the hieratic society over which Sir Thomas Bertram presides, the choice of a profession as lawyer, banker or priest, 'is a commitment which fixes the nature of the self' (*OS*, p. 193). Therefore the adoption of a false self in a play is a calculated transgression of a hieratic society's ideology. The guardian of this ideology is Sir Thomas Bertram: 'It is he who identifies the objection to the theatricals as being specifically that of impersonation. His own self is an integer and he instinctively resists the diversification of the self that is implied by the assumption of roles'. The neo-classic harmony of a country house set amidst the carefully landscaped naturalness of gardens and park is an architectural version of the social code of the owners. The house 'exists to front life and repel life's mutabilities' (*OS*, p. 197). Trilling argues that Austen's sympathetic portrait of Sir Thomas Bertram's conservatism and 'the militant categorical certitude with which *Mansfield Park* discriminates between right and wrong'[21] are unusual in a Jane Austen novel. Her more usual 'method of comprehension' is an ironic one which 'perceives the world through an awareness of its contradictions, paradoxes, and anomalies' (*OS*, p. 181). No single view is allowed to predominate as is the case in *Mansfield Park*. No single group has a monopoly over truth. The only American novelist who consistently creates this kind of plural, diverse world that Trilling's literary criticism seeks to promote is Henry James.

Behind Trilling's promotion of James is a supporting theory of how writers mediate the culture whose values their works express and analyse. In an analysis of V. L. Parrington's *Main Currents in American Thought* (1927–30), Trilling questions the validity of Parrington's metaphor of culture as a flowing current and provides the following alternative metaphor:

A culture is not a flow, nor even a confluence; the form of its existence is struggle, or at least debate – it is nothing if not a dialectic. And in any culture there are likely to be certain artists who contain a large part of the dialectic within themselves, their meaning and power lying in their contradictions; they contain within themselves, it may be said, the very essence of the culture, and the sign of this is that they do not submit to serve the ends of any one ideological group or tendency. (*LI*, p. 9)

Henry James, whose novels convey an awareness of 'tragedy, irony and multitudinous distinctions' (*LI*, p. 10) is, like Jane Austen, a model of what Trilling calls 'the dialectical mode of apprehending reality'.[22] The source for Trilling's idea of a dialectic is Friedrich Engels. In his study of Matthew Arnold Trilling italicises the following passage from Friedrich Engels' book on Ludwig Feuerbach as a basic definition of the dialectical process. It is a process in which:

> That which is recognised now as true has also its latent false side which will later manifest itself, just as that which is now regarded as false has also its true side by virtue of which it could previously have been regarded as true.[23]

Arnold's perception that at one stage of history bourgeois capitalism and individualism had been progressive forces, extending the franchise and economic opportunity, but by the 1880s had become the agents of a repressive status quo, is a dialectical one. Trilling's version of this 'dialectical mode of apprehending reality', which enables the artist to escape and transcend 'the partisan aims of any one ideological group or tendency', is clearly part of his campaign in the 1940s to create a more flexible liberal alternative to the hard line dogmas of Stalinism.

Trilling's conception of how Henry James embodies this dialectical process can be seen in his essay on *The Bostonians*, published in 1953. At the centre of the novel, published in 1886, is a dialectical conflict between 'two principles of which one is radical, the other conservative' (*OS*, p. 95). The radical, reforming impulse analysed in the novel is represented by the militant feminism of Olive Chancellor. The opposing conservatism is represented by Olive's cousin, Basil Ransom. This personalised conflict is also a regional, sectional one, in that Basil's homeland is the South, a traditional home of conservatism, whereas Olive is a product of the abolitionist, reforming North. The novel is, in the main, set in Boston, the traditional home of high-minded American ideas of moral reform. As the novel develops, James creates a complex evaluation of the claims and nature of the two rival principles, a process in which the flaws and virtues of both sides are revealed. Despite this dialectical process in which neither principle is seen as in absolute possession of enlightenment, both Trilling and James seem more attracted to the romantic conservatism of Basil Ransom who, though he is often portrayed as a penniless and archaic figure, is also far more humanly and sympathetically depicted than his antagonist, Olive Chancellor, with her relentless 'abstract intellectuality' (OS, p. 100). Having established James as his model of excellence, Trilling has a critical perspective from which to make an assessment of other American writers.

Trilling's assessment of the main characteristic of other classical American writers of the nineteenth century such as Cooper, Poe and Melville is as follows: 'The great characters of American fiction, such, say as Captain Ahab and Natty Bumppo, tend to be mythic' (LI, p. 246). Unlike James, who 'was alone in knowing that to scale the moral and aesthetic heights one has to use the ladder of social observation (LI, p. 200), writers like Poe tend to substitute metaphysical and psychological concerns for the complex social worlds created by European fiction. Trilling argues that in America:

> The real basis of the novel has never existed – that is, the tension between a middle class and an aristocracy which brings manners into observable relief as the living representation of ideals and the living comment on ideas. (LI, p. 245)

James is again excepted from this charge in that many of his novels have an international theme and context in which a pragmatic democratising America encounters a sophisticated, aristocratic Europe. In contrast to Trilling's reservations about the inadequacy of a national literature based on myth and psychology, several of his fellow American critics celebrated exactly this mythic strain as a uniquely American quality and resource. Harry Levin's *The Power of Blackness*, and Leslie Fiedler's *Love and Death in the American Novel*, are relevant examples of this school of mythic criticism that was largely initiated by D. H. Lawrence's *Studies in Classic American Literature*. Trilling, however, remained unrepentant in his view that Henry James represented the central model, and that twentieth-century American fiction had failed to develop since James. In 1948 he offered the following report on the state of the American novel:

> So far as the novel touches social and political questions it permits itself to choose only between a cheery or a sour democratism; it is

questionable whether any American novel since *Babbitt* has told us a new thing about our social life. In psychology the novel relies either on a mechanical or a clinical use of psychiatry or on the insights that were established by the novelists of fifty years ago. (*LI*, p. 247)

This failure to add to or improve upon the tradition of analysis established by James is in part due to the failure of modern liberalism to stimulate a great literature in which the particular issues and crises of liberalism could be critically examined. By modern liberalism, Trilling means: 'a ready if mild suspiciousness of the profit motive, a belief in progress, science, social legislation, planning, and international co-operation' (*LI*, p. 93). Trilling goes on to claim that: 'Not a single first-rate writer has emerged to deal with these ideas, and the emotions that are consonant with them, in a great literary way'. This poverty of modern liberal culture is contrasted with the great wealth of insights generated by such 'monumental figures of our time' as 'Proust, Joyce, Lawrence, Eliot, Yeats, Mann (in his creative work), Kafka, Rilke, Gide' to whom 'liberal ideology has been at best a matter of indifference' (*LI*, p. 94). The kind of analysis that modern liberalism has produced and recognised is typified, in Trilling's view, by the Kinsey Report, a sociological study of sexual behaviour in American society, published in 1947. The main intention of the book is to habituate 'its readers to sexuality in all its manifestations; it wants to establish, as it were, a democratic pluralism of sexuality' (*LI*, p. 227). There is no dialectic in the report's analysis, no tragic or spiritual awareness. All values are adjusted to a supposed norm of a healthy natural paganism, which though potentially liberating for hitherto repressed sexual minorities, is ultimately a dehumanising and reductive view of mankind.

In Trilling's review of modern culture, the Kinsey Report's tendency to see human individuals as biological units without any sacred or spiritual qualities has also appeared in two other, more literary, movements in contemporary culture, the novelists and theorists of the French *nouveau roman*, and the structuralist school of criticism. Both movements seek to disestablish the idea of the individual self that is central to Trilling's whole practice as a literary and cultural critic. In his reply to Robert Scholes' book of structuralist criticism which by its very title, *The Illiberal Imagination*, took issue with Trilling's position, Trilling defended the way 'the novel in its traditional form confirmed the liberal ethos by its loving and enthusiastic account of individual characters'. In contrast to this view, Scholes sees the individual and 'personal intention' as 'but one of several formal elements' within the technical repertoire of the novel. Novelists such as Iris Murdoch, Barth, Pynchon, Fowles and Coover 'are no longer interested in individual fates'. Scholes sees the individual as an arbitrary capricious element, certainly not a component on which to build a whole theory or fictional world. Structuralism gives greater emphasis to 'the universal and systematic at the expense of the individual and idiosyncratic' (*LD*, p. 142). Individual characters are only one element within the novel which depends as much on such devices as plot and narrative as on what Trilling calls 'a loving and enthusiastic account of individual characters' and Scholes calls 'individual quirkiness'. Trilling sees the same indifference to the idea of individual characters in the theories and practice of the *nouveau roman*, which views 'the introduction of psychology into the novel' as 'a corruption of the genre's purity'. For Trilling the idea of the self and psychology are interdependent: 'We know we have psyches because they make trouble for us – our most constant and reliable awareness of selfhood derives from the experience of that trouble.'[24] Trilling notes with despair how the idea of the self in such novels as Philip Roth's *Portnoy's Complaint* has become an absurd comic liability. A recent study of post-war American fiction takes as its dominant theme this sadly contracted status of the individual and notes that the Rousseauistic glorification of the unsocialised, uncultured noble savage can be seen as a source, not only of liberal democracy, but of totalitarianism, 'of Stalin's police state'.[25] This decline in the status of the individual is, in Trilling's view, part of an attempt to dispense with the conflict between individual wills that is basic to democratic culture. He describes these attacks on individualism as a revival of Stalinism.

Trilling's definition of selfhood also determined his responses to the counter-culture and student radicalism of the 1960s. In contrast to the view expressed by Professor Archibald Cox that: 'The present generation of young people in our universities are the best informed, the most intelligent, and the most idealistic this country has ever known' (*LD*, p. 173), Trilling diagnosed the culture of student radicalism as a degraded form of narcissism that has distorted the historic and legitimate demands of individualism. Instead of a commitment to an organic process of self-development that by its very nature involves a selection of certain qualities to the exclusion of others, this new culture of narcissism seeks to short-circuit all restraints and demands 'a limitlessness in our personal perspective . . . a multiplicity of options' (*LD*, p. 175). Trilling finds a direct image of this perversion of the historic culture of individualism in the aesthetics of the favoured art-forms of the counter-culture. His guide to this area is Harold Rosenberg, the art critic who along with Clement Greenberg was an important theoretician for the generation of American avant-garde painters such as Jackson Pollock and his fellow abstract expressionists, who came to international prominence in the late 1940s and 1950s. Rosenberg contributed a paper to a symposium *Art and Confrontation*, occasioned by the student uprising in Paris in the spring of 1968, in which he argued that the artist should remain firmly within the whole tradition of personal development in that art is 'the one vocation that keeps a space open for the individual to realize himself by knowing himself' (*LD*, p. 138). This conception of the artist heroically creating self-contained, individual master-pieces is rejected by the students, who favour a culture of happenings and participation that seeks to eliminate 'the distance between audience and art-object or art-event'. Rosenberg characterises this aesthetic as a movement that wants to 'dispense with ego-values' (*LD*, p. 143). For Trilling, the ego is a crucial source of perception that enables the individual mind to become 'separate from its environment' (*LD*, p. 144). To Marshall Mcluhan, the subject of the next chapter, such ego-based individualism is a distinct liability.

11. Marshall Mcluhan: The Modernism of the Mass Media

In his profile of Mcluhan, called 'What if he is right?', Tom Wolfe examines the process by which Mcluhan, a hitherto unknown professor of English literature, became by the mid-1960s an internationally celebrated expert on the effects of the mass media, a consultant to 'IBM, General Electric, Bell Telephone'.[1] In return for his promotion of the electronic media, a number of multinational corporations began to subsidise Mcluhan's Centre for Culture and Technology at the University of Toronto. The immense popular and academic purchase of Mcluhan's ideas and in particular his two catch phrases 'the medium is the message' and the world as 'global village' is just one symptom of a craze for Mcluhan's theories in his heyday that one critic has called 'Mcluhanacy'.[2] Mcluhan's ideas, so influential in the creation of post-war attitudes towards the electronic media, particularly television, need to be taken out of the world of corporate public relations, where they once found a temporary fashionable home, and returned to their original context as part of the debate on the effects of mass culture.

Mcluhan's positive attitude towards the electronic media is based on an historical view of how changes in technology have affected the central nervous system. He believed that humans only function at their full potential if the cultural and technological environment with which they interact caters for all the five senses of sight, hearing, touch, smell and taste. From this model of sensory balance between the five senses, he goes on to argue that since the invention of the technology of the printing press by Gutenberg in the middle years of the fifteenth century, western culture has been slavishly dominated by the printed word which is an extension of only one part of the sensorium, sight. Television, so often denigrated by print-dominated literary intellectuals, offers, in Mcluhan's view, a possible release from the fetish of the printed book into a richer world of interaction between man's nervous system and the environment.

Mcluhan's case against the dominance of the printed book is not just on the grounds that print excludes other kinds of sensory awareness and training. He also argues that the social and political system ushered in by the invention of printing destroyed the communal values of medieval feudalism, and replaced them with a highly individualistic ideology. The introduction of mechanical linear typography was responsible for the rise of:

> Nationalism, the Reformation, the Industrial Revolution, the whole concept of causality, Cartesian and Newtonian concepts of the universe, perspective in art, narrative chronology in literature and a psychological mode of introspection or inner direction that greatly intensified the tendencies towards individualism and specialization.[3]

It is interesting to compare Trilling's celebration of a protestant culture of autobiography, mirrors and self-conscious individuals with Mcluhan's reservations about Renaissance individualism whose 'specialist intensity burst the bonds of medieval corporate guilds and monasteries, creating extreme individualist patterns of enterprise and monopoly'.[4] The invention of movable type becomes the symptomatic model for how work and experience have since been organised in western industrial society until the advent of post-industrial society, in which the electronic media of television and computers are more important than print. The printing press of the fifteenth century initiated principles of mechanisation and scientific management that reached their high point in Henry Ford's moving assembly line, principles that Mcluhan summarises as follows: 'The breaking up of every kind of experience into uniform units in order to produce faster action and change of form' (UM, p. 85). The long sway of these principles that created an industrial goods-producing society is now being challenged by a new technology and social system as disruptive as the printing press was in its period. The post-industrial society of the second half of the twentieth century is a society in which services and information, not manufactured goods, are the crucial commodities. The computer is ushering in a paperless revolution that will change society as radically as Gutenberg's printing press did. The printed book and the industrial society it supports will vanish as rapidly as the medieval illuminated manuscript and scribe who in 1333, before the advent of the printing press, took six months to make one two-hundred-and-seventy-eight-page copy of the New Testament. Mcluhan's commitment to the post-industrial thesis is complete and euphoric:

> Today computers hold out the promise of a means of instant translation of any code or language into any other code or language. The computer, in short, promises by technology a Pentecostal condition of universal understanding. The next logical step would seem to be, not to translate, but to by-pass languages in favour of a general cosmic consciousness. (*UM*, p. 80)

Out of the divisive individualistic chaos of an obsolescent industrial society will rise wired cities linked by cable and satellites. Post-industrial society will become, in Mcluhan's famous phrase, 'a global village'.

Mcluhan's hot gospel praise of electronic technology is an instructive part of that shift among literary critics of his generation, like John Crowe Ransom, towards a more scientific attitude. His emergence as a post-industrial prophet could not have been predicted on the basis of his ideological position in the 1930s and 1940s. In this period, under the influence of F. R. Leavis and John Crowe Ransom, Mcluhan had supported an anti-technology agrarian system of values, in which he took a stand on behalf of an organic American South against the devouring industrialism of the North. In an essay published in 1947 in the *Sewanee Review*, Mcluhan celebrated the organicism of the Southern writer who:

> shares most of his experience with the majority of Southerners, who never have heard of him – there is not the split between educated and 'uneducated' which occurs in an atomized industrial community . . . there is not the familiar head-heart split of the North.[5]

Jonathan Miller in his excellent critique of Mcluhan's ideas assesses Mcluhan's ideological position at this period as follows:

Up to this point in his career [the beginning of the 1940s] Mcluhan seems to have stagnated into a well-recognised form of cultural nostalgia. The familiar themes of conservative Agrarianism repeat themselves like a monotonous fugue in the essays he published during the forties.[6]

Like John Crowe Ransom, Mcluhan was to abandon this anti-technological bias but with a careful distinction between good and bad, old and new technology. The new post-industrial technology of television and computers that has its origins in such developments as electricity and the telephone at the end of the nineteenth century has the potential to create a qualitatively different society from that created by the printing press and the goods-producing technologies of the first industrial revolution. At first sight this seems an illogical reversal of Mcluhan's conservative Agrarianism, but a closer inspection reveals a distinct resemblance between his vision of the organic, tribal, face-to-face communities of the pre-industrial, pre-Gutenberg era of the agrarian South and the interconnected 'global village' of post-industrial society. Mcluhan's real quarrel is with the industrial society, founded upon print and protestantism, that intervened between pre- and post-industrial society. This industrial era 'elimi-nated nearly all the emotional and corporate family feeling' (*UM*, p. 82) that had characterised society. The electronic media and the multinational corporations that control them, can, in Mcluhan's view, become the new, benign agencies of a collective consciousness, like the Roman Catholic church in the feudal period. Mcluhan's positive evaluation of the benefits of the new post-industrial society of mass communications and information is a striking reversal of the orthodoxy of rejection that was a characteristic response among conservative, liberal and Marxist commentators.

Mcluhan's ideas, generated out of a view of how changes in technology affect the nervous system, became the basis for a whole series of what he called 'probes' into the history of western culture. At the heart of his particular view of western culture that ranges in time and subject matter from an analysis of prehistoric cave paintings to the iconography of commercial advertising, is a belief that the culture of the West contains a series of artistic developments and movements such as Cubism, which can form the basis of a richer sensory awareness than that provided by the printed book. Mcluhan then links these artistic developments to the culture of the electronic media to form an alternative way of perceiving the world to that provided by a literary culture of print. Before looking at this alternative culture, it is important to isolate the main elements of Mcluhan's sensory quarrel with the dominant industrial culture of print and protestantism.

First of all, the coming of print devalues and often destroys complex oral systems of communication. The whole range of rich non-verbal skills and faculties developed in the process of human evolution are set aside in the relentless drive to acquire western literacy. This diminution of the oral in favour of the machine-produced printed text includes the devaluation of the literary achievements and forms of handcrafted texts. The rich sensory combination of iconographic and hand-scripted skills that produced the medieval illuminated manuscripts is no longer practised once the printed book takes over as society's main medium of developmental education and training. This shift from hand to machine, from oral to literary, not only signals a reduction in sensory awareness, it fixes man in a highly alienated 'typographical spell'. The individual reader who buries himself in that classic product of the new culture of print and protestantism, the realist novel, becomes a silent atom of sensory deprivation, marooned in a private island of introspection:

> Man in a literate and homogenized society ceases to be sensitive to the diverse and discontinuous life of forms. He acquires the illusion of the third dimension and the 'private point of view' as part of his Narcissus fixation. (*UM*, p. 19)

Not only does a culture dominated by the printed book encourage excessive introspection, it also reduces the level of active participation by the silent consumer. Whereas the illuminated medieval manuscript employed an allegorical, iconographic aesthetic in which words and images are imaginative entrances to a fictional world that the reader can colour and enlarge with his own speculations, the realist novel overwhelms the reader with a highly detailed exhaustive account of man in society. Mcluhan develops a shorthand code of terms to illustrate his thesis that different media promote different levels of participation. A cool medium, whether the spoken word or the illuminated manuscript or TV, leaves much more for the listener or user to do than a hot medium: 'If the medium is of high definition, participation is low. If the medium is of low intensity, the participation is high. Perhaps this is why lovers mumble so' (*UM*, p. 319). According to this code, the realist novel would be a hot, high-definition medium. Mcluhan's aesthetic of participation was one of the reasons for his great popularity among a 1960s generation that demanded a more activist, less consumer-oriented culture. Armed with these definitions, Mcluhan reconstructed a personal history of western culture in terms of a contrast between hot and cool media, between art forms that reinforced the individualistic sensory poverty of print and those that offer means of releasing the individual from the restricted fields of awareness imposed by print.

A major source of this richer alternative to print is avant-garde culture, represented by Cubism in particular and modernism in general. In Mcluhan's history of western painting, the visual equivalent of the reductive aesthetic of the printed book is the dominance of three-dimensional perspective in European painting. The techniques of perspective developed by Florentine artists in the same fifteenth century that saw the emergence of Gutenberg's printing press, arbitrarily, in Mcluhan's view, fixed the technical conventions that have controlled the stylistic evolution of western painting until the various impressionist and Cubist innovations of Cézanne and Picasso. Under realism's arbitrary rules of composition and pictorial geometry, the artist created naturalistic three-dimensional models of reality from a flat canvas. Objects have to diminish in size as they recede into the distance. These techniques of perspective fix and control the terms on which a viewer experiences the illusory world created on the canvas. The viewer is permitted to peer, from a fixed position, through the open window of the framed picture and gaze upon a ready-made, essentially static world. This kind of naturalistic painting does not, like a Cubist painting, allow the spectator to shift perspective and explore the world from other dimensions and planes. Cubism disrupts this rigid three-dimensional system of visual organisation that has been central to western painting since the fifteenth century. Cubism:

> by giving the middle and outside, the top, bottom, back, and front and the rest, in two dimensions, drops the illusion of perspective in favor of instant sensory awareness of the whole. Cubism, by seizing on instant total awareness, suddenly announced that the medium is the message. (*UM*, p. 13)

Mcluhan's concept of Cubism's multifaceted wholeness and his delight in the nature of the medium as opposed to content parallel Ransom's move to an idea of 'fulness', sustained by technical virtuosity.

Mcluhan's attacks on the sensory poverty of realist painting and the printed book are characteristically used to support his theory of community. In the same way that the global village created by the electronic media is a welcome return to the organic tribal consciousness of pre-industrial society, Cubist painting is a 'recovery of the world of the cave paintings'.[7] The shallow surfaces and iconographic masks of primitive painting so often recalled by Picasso's faces are, like illuminated medieval manuscripts, and the electronic media, cool, low-definition forms and environments which invite the spectator to participate rather than passively consume. The main purpose of Mcluhan's 'probes' into art history is to establish this aesthetic and sensory connection between primitive painting, avant-garde modernism, and the electronic media. The key connection is the ability of these three forms to create a sensory wholeness of response and experience. They are all media that have the potential to reintegrate that famous 'dissociation of sensibility', that separation between head and heart, between mind and body, between the intellectual and physical, that T. S. Eliot and a host of others had announced as the prime source of modern alienation. Mcluhan's analysis of the problem includes a cure:

> Synesthesia, or unified sense and imaginative life, had long seemed an unattainable dream to Western poets, painters, and artists in general. They had looked with sorrow and dismay on the fragmented and impoverished imaginative life of Western literate man in the eighteenth century and later. Such was the message of Blake and Pater, Yeats and D. H. Lawrence, and a host of other great figures. They were not prepared to have their dreams realized in everyday life by the esthetic action of radio and television. Yet these massive extensions of our central nervous systems have enveloped Western man in a daily session of synesthesia. (UM, p. 315)

Mcluhan's model of a new synesthetic awareness is not only based on the arts. He also argues that avant-garde science in the shape of Einstein and Relativity Theory had discarded that same fixed three-dimensional world whose illusory solidity Cubism exposed: 'Relativity Theory in 1905 announced the dissolution of uniform Newtonian space as an illusion or fiction' (*UM*, p. 163). No longer could the scientist construct models of the universe and its behaviour that, like the realist novel, split the world into logically connected sequences. Einstein's speculations challenged the hypothesis that the scientist could isolate a single phenomenon or object for scrutiny and analysis. Relativity Theory, like Cubism, created portraits of the world in which the fluid relationships between objects was as important as the objects themselves. This synthesis of an avant-garde art and science whose perceptions could be realised in a global village of post-industrial inter-connectedness was an attractive combination to societies whose intelligentsia were often maintaining a contradictory hostility towards the mass cultural values of the electronic media. Mcluhan's argument that mass and avant-garde culture were not diametrically opposed to one another and that mass culture was conveying important artistic and sociological messages was for many a disconcerting entry into the debate on mass culture and its effects. For others, it helped to ease their transition from liberal humanist anxiety about mass communications to post-industrial belief in the educational potential of the electronic media. Instead of the historical antagonism between high and mass culture, Mcluhan constructed a continuum in which comics, Cubism and Relativity Theory occupied the same aesthetic space: 'Einstein pronounced the doom of continuous or "rational" space, and the way was made clear for Picasso and the Marx Brothers and MAD' (*UM*, p. 163). A good example of the ways Mcluhan attempted to subvert the rigid discriminations between high and low, avant-garde and pop, so sedulously maintained by Dwight Macdonald, is his *The Mechanical Bride: Folklore of Industrial Man* (1951).

The format of the book places pages of newspapers, advertising copy, film posters, cartoons, and the illustrated covers of pulp fiction adjacent to Mcluhan's written analysis of the artistic qualities and social messages conveyed by this popular, commercial folk art. The first text he analyses is the 20 April 1950 front page of the *New York Times*. The lay-out of the page, in which a whole range of disconnected stories and features simultaneously seek the attention of the reader, creates the same kind of landscape as that envisioned by avant-garde painting and science. The 'front page Cubism' of the *New York Times* makes it hard for the reader to fix on one story at a time and follow its narrative through. On the contrary, the reader is invited to scan the page like a symbolist painting in which there is no fixed point of view or clear narrative of beginning, middle and end. This 'mosaic' format of the *New York Times*, in which no single voice predominates, is reminiscent of 'the literary techniques of James Joyce'. *Ulysses*, like the *New York Times*, tries to capture reality through a multiplicity of voices and points of view. The whole drive of Mcluhan's analysis is to show how in both mass and avant-garde culture 'the medium is the message'. The mosaic 'front page Cubism' of the *New York Times* is a medium which by its very nature argues against the idea that the world can be viewed from a single point of view. The *New York Times* is pasted up like a collage, and thereby offers 'an Arabian Nights entertainment in which a thousand and one astonishing tales are being told'. Newspapers should not be read like nineteenth-century novels; they should be listened to like a jazz improvisation, for their 'ragtime discontinuity'.[8]

Having established the artistic pedigree of mass-culture forms, Mcluhan then analyses the social messages within mass culture. As examples of the ways the stereotypes and conventions of mass culture comment on the values of modern society, Mcluhan takes two forms of popular culture, the masculine frontier world of the Hollywood Western, and the home town domesticity of the melodramatic world of TV soap operas. His entrance to the Western is via a publicity poster for John Ford's 1949 Western, starring John Wayne, *She Wore a Yellow Ribbon*. The world of the Western, or horse opera as Mcluhan calls it, offers: 'Equestrian dash and characters of ruthless and exuberant individualism to a population bedraggled by mechanical routine . . .'[9] It is also: 'Like the sports page . . . A man's world, free from the problems of domesticity'. By contrast: 'Soap opera is a woman's world, laden with personal problems'.[10] Mcluhan's argument is that mass-culture forms such as horse opera and soap opera are, like the myths of ancient Greece, expressions of a society's ideology and anxieties. This same mythic awareness is present in the images and stereotypes created by advertising agencies:

> With very large budgets the commercial artists have tended to develop the ad into an icon, and icons are not specialist fragments or aspects but unified and compressed images of a complex kind. They focus a large region of experience in tiny compass. (*UM*, p. 226)

This process of compression in the techniques of modern advertising creates mythic archetypes of a society's utopian dreams and anxieties. For Mcluhan, this process in which mass culture acts as a binding standardising agency is wholly benign. For his critics, it is symptomatic of 'a cybernetic drive to program the world'.[11]

Mcluhan's thesis that the electronic media of post-industrial society can be the instruments of 'a pentecostal condition of universal understanding' (*UM*, p. 80) had geo-political implications that were not lost on either the American government, who supported the research that led to *Understanding Media*, or the multinational producers of information technology, who subsidised Mcluhan's Centre for Culture and Technology at the University of Toronto. This support helped to generate a model of how to stabilise and integrate the diverse cultures and political systems of the world into one linked system. Mcluhan's image of a global village joined by a single universal technology of electric circuitry chimed in with America's world role in reconstructing and maintaining the world economic and political system after the chaos of the Second World War. If Mcluhan was right, the new systems of information technology could be the basis for a new world order. In the same way that the new criticism assimilated individual quirkiness, Mcluhan's theories aimed to integrate the diversity and individuality of the world's cultures into cybernetic unity. Mcluhan's image of a benign electronic universalism can be tilted to produce a less flattering view of American aspirations. Herbert Schiller, in *Mass Communications and American Empire*, sees Mcluhan's electronic global village as an international exportable extension of a domestic American system that had the following characteristics:

Domestically, the realm is governed confidently by a propertied managerial industrial corps, instructing a consumer community stratified by income and race. A combination of media supply the primary ideological ingredient of the affluent society; the concept of the good life.[12]

12. Tom Wolfe and the New Journalism

If Mcluhan's thesis challenged the orthodox denigration of mass culture that dominated liberal, conservative and Marxist theorising, the writings of new journalists such as Tom Wolfe brushed aside the rigid moral and sociological categories of high, middle and low, and sought to reveal the myriad and differing behaviour patterns, styles, and subcultures that he believed were the actual stuff of mass culture. Instead of mass culture and behaviour appearing as monolithic, increasingly standardised consumer responses, firmly controlled and manipulated by the culture industries, an alternative model and image of America began to emerge. Dwight Macdonald had anticipated this alternative model when revising his initial rejection of mass culture. This revision 'is a compromise between the conservative and liberal proposals' as to how to preserve artistic quality in a mass society. Macdonald's optimistic revision is based:

> on the recent discovery – since 1945 – that there is not One Big Audience but rather a number of smaller, more specialised audiences that may be commercially profitable ... The mass audience is divisible, we have discovered – and the more it is divided, the better. (*AAG*, p. 73)

The range of subcultures and specialised activities that appear in Tom Wolfe's own writings and those of a number of writers he included in his anthology *The New Journalism* mirrors Macdonald's model of an energetic cultural pluralism. Tom Wolfe's writings move through a kaleidoscopic world of diversity that includes the milieux of *Playboy* chief Hugh Hefner in 'King of the Status Dropouts', of Southern stock-car racer Junior Johnson in 'The Last American Hero', of the New York art world in *The Painted Word*, and the hermetic world of NASA's astronauts in *The Right Stuff*. The selection of writings anthologised in *The New Journalism* explores a mass society that offers a bewildering cornucopia of diversity. Instead of standardised sameness, America as a mass society seems to exult in creative and exotic displays of individualism; from Hunter S. Thompson's study of the Hell's Angels, to Terry Southern's portrait of Southern baton twirling and culture, and Gary Wills' meditation on Martin Luther King's funeral and the gospel rhetoric of Southern evangelism. The main aim of these writings is to reveal the inner workings of subcultural codes and styles, to document as accurately as possible events and manners, not to structure them according to predetermined sociological categories.

One of the major preoccupations of this form of investigative journalism became the criminal mind and its acts. In Truman Capote's account of the murder of a Kansas farm family, *In Cold Blood*, Ed Sanders' account of the Charles Manson murders, *The Family*, and Norman Mailer's retelling of Gary Gilmore's story, *The Executioner's Song*, the aim is literal documentation, not moral evaluation. Despite Tom Wolfe's attempt to exclude what he feels are the moralising analytic techniques of high culture from *The New Journalism*, individual journalists in practice often had to abandon this non-commital attitude. Hunter S. Thompson, for example, often framed his responses to a particular subculture or milieu in terms of a mixture of 'fear and loathing'. After 18 months spent in the close company of the Hell's Angels, Thompson: 'Pushed his luck a little too far and got badly stomped by four or five Angels, who seemed to feel I was taking advantage of them'.[1] This incident disrupts the non-committal documentary stance of the new journalism, and Thompson inserts a quotation from Joseph Conrad's study of the contradictory encounter between Savagery and Civilization, *Heart of Darkness*, to indicate his reactions: 'The horror! The horror! . . . Exterminate all the brutes!'[2]

The cultural pluralism of the new journalism that came to prominence in the 1960s became the official national ideology as affluence created the economic basis for diversity and individualism. The rigid orthodoxies of the Cold War and the effort to maintain consensus were increasingly difficult to sustain in face of the economic and political demands of the 1960s. This shift of American ideology towards an acceptance of a complex pluralism of styles, values and behaviour can be clearly traced in the decline of consensus magazines like *Life*, and the enhanced circulations of specialist journals and magazines, like *Harper's*, *Esquire*, the *New Yorker* and the *New York Review of Books*. The majority of the writings that Tom Wolfe gathered in his anthology of *The New Journalism* first appeared as features in these pluralist magazines. The aspirations of *Life* to present core definitions of centralising norms that sought to transcend class and create universal consensus were succinctly summarised by Dwight Macdonald. *Life* was, for Macdonald, the supreme example of Masscult:

> *Life* is a typical homogenized magazine, appearing on the mahogany library tables of the rich, the glass cocktail tables of the middle class, and the oil cloth kitchen tables of the poor. Its contents are as thoroughly homogenized as its circulation. The same issue will present a serious exposition of atomic energy followed by a disquisition on Rita Hayworth's love life. (*AAG*, p. 12)

Somewhat ironically, Thomas R. Shepherd Jr, the publisher of *Look*, a similar consensus-seeking mass-circulation magazine, proudly delineated in 1970 the features of a format and strategy that contributed to the magazine's demise a little more than a year later:

> The power of *Look* is that it spans the universe of interests. It is a platform for all Americans to turn to, to learn about the basic issues, the real gut issues of the day . . . It is information and entertainment for the whole family.[3]

The format that was proving more successful than the consensus design was described in 1971 by a former *Life* editor, Chris Welles:

> The most financially successful magazines of the past ten years have been designed to appeal to highly particularised intellectual, vocational, and avocational interests and are run by editors who know exactly what they are saying, and to whom they are saying it.[4]

These specialist magazines included Hugh Hefner's *Playboy*, and Helen Gurley Brown's *Cosmopolitan*, founded in 1965 to offer advice not only on such time-honoured topics as home-making hints and beauty tips but also on the more personal sexual and psychological aspects of a contemporary woman's life. It also aimed, in the words of its editor, to help the modern woman 'get through the night'.

The mass-society norms of the 1950s fragmented in the 1960s into a burgeoning proliferation of special interest groups. Most Americans sought:

> To be something more than a single person but clearly less than the common mass. We are young, middle-aged, or old. Many of us find an attachment to a racial or ethnic minority more important than a status as an American. We are Easterners or Southerners or Westerners or Texans or Californians and proud of it. We are environmentalists, women's libbers, a part of the counter-culture, Jesus freaks, skiers, sports car enthusiasts, concerned parents, swinging singles; we collect stamps and coins and beer cans and model trains and antique cars and nostalgia items; we ski, surf, hike, climb mountains, scuba dive, sail, camp, fish, hunt, bowl, golf, ice skate, and swim.[5]

The new journalism was part of this phenomenon, catering for the more up-market sections of the pluralist audience. Established magazines such as *Esquire* and *Harper's*, and the 1960s newcomer *Rolling Stone*, gave generous space to the new journalists whose muckraking documentary aesthetic made a direct appeal to the reform-minded, college-educated middle class of the 1960s. *Harper's* defined this 1960s aesthetic as follows:

> Somewhere west of journalism and this side of history . . . there is a place where reporting becomes literature. There are those – namely one million readers – who think *Harper's* magazine is the place.
>
> For *Harper's* magazine is dedicated to the idea that fine writing need not buckle under the pressure of a deadline, nor should literature be solely confined to the dim distant past or the recent inventions of a novelist's mind. It can deal with now – with the angers of our time, the beautiful beginnings of a changed society and the sad vestiges of a violent past . . .[6]

Although Tom Wolfe concentrated more on the styles and manners of the 1960s than its politics, his studies of modern American painting and architecture, *The Painted Word*, and *From Bauhaus to Our House*, typify the narrative format and style of the new journalist magazine article that keeps the audience in the know and up to date in cultural trends. *The Painted Word* began life in *Harper's*, April 1975, and *From Bauhaus to Our House* appeared in the June and July issues of *Harper's* in 1981. Instead of confronting the reader with the complex language of scholarly journals, Wolfe's strategy is to involve him or her in the hermetic world of post-modernism as an intimate debunking participant. There are no footnotes to delay the reader in needless complexity as the world of high culture is revealed as more a clash of autocratic personalities than of aesthetic ideas. Wolfe's attitude to high culture is muckraking, investigative and debunking.

The Painted Word opens on a Sunday morning with Wolfe in company with most culture-conscious New Yorkers immersing himself in the leisure section of the *Sunday New York Times*: 'People don't read the morning newspaper, Marshall Mcluhan once said, they slip into it like a warm bath'.[7] A review by art critic Hilton Kramer catches his attention and in particular a passage that reads:

> Realism does not lack its partisans, but it does rather conspicuously lack a persuasive theory. And given the nature of our intellectual commerce with works of art, to lack a persuasive theory is to lack something crucial – the means by which our experience of individual works is joined to our understanding of the values they signify.

Wolfe then experiences what he calls the aha! phenomenon, the debunking moment when a high-culture activity gives its conspiratorial nature away by a seemingly innocent statement in parenthesis. Kramer's 'seemingly innocuous obiter dicta ... give the game away'.[8] The game is the promotion and control of New York avant-garde painting by an incestuous magic circle of critics, dealers and *nouveau riche* 'culturati' who cannot develop their own taste, and buy only on advice. The result of this process is the promotion of a highly arbitrary selection of artists whose works then constitute the dominant avant-garde. The same picture of a high-culture activity manipulated by an autocratic elite emerges in Wolfe's view of modern architecture in America. Wolfe's thesis in *From Bauhaus to Our House* is that corporate America has promoted an architecture, imported from Europe, that it secretly loathes. The glass and steel boxes that line the Avenue of the Americas in New York are seen by Wolfe as: 'row after Mies van der row of glass boxes. Worker housing pitched up fifty stories high'.[9] Corporate America that in the nineteenth century used to delight in all kinds of baroque, neo-classic and gothic decoration has deferred to the functional aesthetic of émigré socialist European theoreticians such as Walter Gropius, who became head of the School of Architecture at Harvard. American architects such as Philip Johnson side-stepped the politics of the Bauhaus, but appropriated the aesthetics of this socialist stream of modernism and built according to 'the now inviolable theory of the flat roof and the sheer facade'. The functionalism of the Bauhaus aesthetic combined with the new industrial materials of concrete, glass and steel to offer an egalitarian architecture, as an alternative to the class-conscious styles of traditional bourgeois architecture since: 'It had been decided in the battle of theories, that pitched roofs and cornices represented the "crowns" of the old nobility which the bourgeoisie spent most of its time imitating'.[10]

Wolfe's debunking of high-culture modernism includes an attack on what he felt was the literary equivalent of post-modernist painting and architecture, the anti-realist experimental novel. In the same way that the Bauhaus attacked bourgeois decoration, experimental novelists such as John Barth, Richard Brautigan and Robert Coover have either dismissed or parodied the bourgeois realism of the traditional novel. In the experimental novel the formal devices and qualities of the realist novel are set aside:

> The characters have no background, no personal history, are identified with no social class, ethnic group or even nationality, and act out their fates in a locale that has no place name, often some timeless and elemental terrain such as forest, swamp, desert, mountain or sea.[11]

Wolfe's theoretical defence of realism and his celebration of the new journalism as an important modern development within the tradition of the novel appears in an essay and appendix that preface *The New Journalism*. Wolfe asserts that the realism that transformed the novel in the works of Defoe, Dickens and Balzac, had an effect:

> like the introduction of electricity into machine technology. It was not just another device. It raised the state of the art to a new magnitude. The effect of realism on the emotions was something that had never been conceived of before. (*NJ*, p. 49)

Since the heyday of realism in the eighteenth and nineteenth centuries a whole range of high-culture devices have corrupted the practices of realism. Instead of 'réalisme pour le réalisme', novelists like James have tried to make the novel 'deep, morally serious, cosmic and not too easy to read' (*NJ*, p. 53). Realists like Defoe did not see the novel as a form in which elaborate development of character, complex moral debates, and the clash of ideas should take precedence over the primary role of the writer to create a realistic depiction of man's behaviour in society. Not only has high culture corrupted the novel, it has also created a type of journalist who, like the experimental novelist, has increasingly moved away from an aesthetic that seeks to deliver to the public a direct unmediated apprehension of reality. Wolfe names this type as the 'Literary Gentleman in the Grandstand' who does not soil his genteel sensibilities by entering 'the bailiwick of the people he is writing about' (*NJ*, p. 59). Unlike new journalists, such as Hunter S. Thompson who shared the dangerous subculture of the Hell's Angels, and used his own emotions as a register and entrance into the world he was writing about, the 'Literary Gentleman in the Grandstand' tries to remain aloof, detached and non-committal. The defining characteristic of the literary gentleman's style is neutral understatement:

> You can't imagine what a positive word 'understatement' was among both journalists and literati ten years ago. There is something to be said for the notion of course, but the trouble was that by the early 1960s understatement had become an absolute pall. Readers were bored to tears without understanding why. When they came upon that pale beige tone, it began to signal to them unconsciously, that a well-known bore was here again, 'the journalist', a pedestrian mind, a phlegmatic spirit, a faded personality. . . . (*NJ*, p. 31)

It is Wolfe's thesis that the new journalism transformed the status of the journalist by sweeping aside the high-culture intrusions that had corrupted an ideology of 'réalisme pour le réalisme'. He isolates four devices that the new journalists have recovered from the golden age of documentary realism. The basic one is: 'Scene-by-scene construction, telling the story by moving from scene to scene and resorting as little as possible to sheer historical narrative'. The second is the: 'Recording of the dialogue in full', since: 'Realistic dialogue involves the reader more completely than any other simple device'. The third device is:

> The so-called third-person point of view, the technique of presenting every scene to the reader through the eyes of a particular character, giving the reader the feeling of being inside the character's mind and experiencing the emotional reality of the scene as he experiences it. (*NJ*, p. 46)

The particular way that this third device was adapted by the new journalist was through the interview format in which the interviewee free-associated in response to questions. Wolfe points to his record of Ken Kesey's psychedelic subculture in *The Electric Kool-Aid Acid Test* as an example of the interview format. The fourth device is the one that Wolfe in particular extensively used: 'The recording of everyday gestures, habits, manners, customs, styles of furniture, clothing, decoration, styles of traveling, eating, keeping house'. These social and personal surfaces are: 'Symbolic, generally, of people's status life, using that term in the broad sense of the entire pattern of behavior through which people express their position in the world or what they think it is or what they hope it to be' (*NJ*, p. 47). Throughout his definition of the new journalist aesthetic, Wolfe stresses technique and professionalism: 'The proof of one's technical mastery as a writer becomes paramount and the demonstration of moral points becomes secondary' (*NJ*, p. 66). Wolfe sees ideology as yet another high-culture device and intrusion.

Armed with this vision of investigative journalism as a form of technology, Wolfe gathers in his anthology a range of pieces that illustrate his thesis. He also reviews the extant tradition of the new journalism genre, that includes Truman Capote's *In Cold Blood*, and Norman Mailer's *Armies of the Night, The Novel as History: History as the Novel*. In the twentieth century, George Orwell's *Down and Out in Paris and in London*, the radical reportage of the 1930s, centred on Joseph North's magazine *New Masses*, and *Let Us Now Praise Famous Men*, a portrait of Southern tenant farmers, text by James Agee and photographs by Walker Evans, have preceded the achievements of the 1960s. Wolfe's quarrel with parts of this historical tradition is either ideological or aesthetic. The Marxist reportage of *New Masses* 'degenerated into propaganda of a not very complex sort' (*NJ*, p. 61), and James Agee's writing is flawed by unnecessary ' "poetic" descriptions and is very short on dialogue' (*NJ*, p. 60).

Running through Wolfe's theorising is a behaviourist model of reality that perceives the external surface as a direct unmediated reflection of the internal personal world. Indeed, Wolfe's writings suggest that there is no disjunction between the public and the personal, the visible and invisible: people and events are simply one. The essential nature of the Black Panthers and their liberal sympathisers can be clearly gleaned at Leonard Bernstein's party that Wolfe describes in 'Radical Chic and Mau-Mauing the Flak Catchers', the dress, behaviour and languages of Phil Spector, the record producer whom Wolfe described in 'The First Tycoon of Teen', are direct, unmediated essences of their character and role in the culture. There are no mysteries in the hermetic world of the NASA astronauts; they are a clearly identifiable subculture driven by the desire to attain and display the mixture of professionalism and macho daring known as 'The Right Stuff'. Linked to this perception that Wolfe calls 'the physiology of realism' is a theory of history: 'The sixties was one of the most extra-ordinary decades in American history in terms of Manners and morals. Manners and morals were the history of the sixties' (*NJ*, p. 44). This thesis may downgrade the role of the serious political struggles, civil rights and liberation movements of the 1960s, but is nevertheless an accurate reflection of the ways in which cultural diversity and differentiation rather than rigid Cold War norms and consensus values became the dominant cultural ideology of the period.

Although Wolfe's politics often seem to consist of maverick populist attacks on high-culture elitism and the insincerities of radical chic, other exponents of the new journalism became the engaged investigative instruments of the counter-culture. These more politically minded journalists such as Tom Wicker were also confronted by 'one of the most extra-ordinary decades in American history', not in terms of 'manners and morals', but in terms of political events. Larry King, looking back at the political history of the 1960s that included President Johnson's declining to run for a second term and the rise of an anti-war crusade led by Senator Eugene McCarthy, questioned whether even a major novelist let alone a journalist could document this decade:

The America of 1968, with its assassinations, torched ghettos, campus wars, crime waves, alienations, deposed kings and crazed pretenders, almost seems too much for a single book. Offered as a novel, it might be rejected even by the lowliest of publishing house readers. . . . Nor does it seem reasonable that a power-driven and proud President could be so easily forced from office by a handful of disgruntled Eastern intellectuals and legions of dedicated college kids rallying around a half-mystic Mid-Western Senator who alternately dabbles in poetry and sarcasm.[12]

The investigative stream within the new journalism of the 1960s that sought to expose social and political abuse could draw on a well-established muckraking tradition inherited from the reformist ideology of the Progressive Movement at the turn of the century. *The Selling of the President*, Joe McGuinniss' revelations about the way Nixon was successfully packaged by his media advisers in the 1968 Presidential elections, could fit neatly into Herbert Gans' model of the basic professional ideology of practising journalists that he derived from extensive interviews with the news-gathering personnel of CBS Evening News, NBC Nightly News, *Newsweek* and *Time*:

In reality, the news is not so much conservative or liberal as it is reformist; indeed, the enduring values are very much like the values of the Progressive Movement of the early twentieth century. The resemblance is often uncanny, as in the common advocacy of honest, meritocratic, and anti-bureaucratic government, and in the shared antipathy to political machines and demagogues, particularly of populist bent. Altruistic democracy is, in other words, close to the Progressive ideal of government. The notion of responsible capitalism is also to be found in Progressivism, as is the dislike of bigness, the preference for craftsmanship over technology, the defense of nature, and the celebration of anti-urban pastoral society.[13]

Many of these characteristics feature in 1960s investigative new journalism, but other elements, developed in response to the counter-culture, were grafted on to this model. *Rolling Stone* magazine, founded in November 1967, is a good example of this adaptation and extension of the muckraking formula.

Rolling Stone was the inspiration of Jann Wenner, a young unemployed radical journalist. It quickly found a readership of more than a million readers of median age 21 years and 9 months. Its original content covered the whole range of counter-cultural interests with an emphasis on rock music. This was later expanded to include 20,000 word pieces on politics by its National Affairs Editor, Dr Hunter S. Thompson, and a series of star interviews, such as Andy Warhol in conversation with William Burroughs or Truman Capote, or vice versa. *Rolling Stone*'s mixture of investigative journalism, the counter-culture and a belief that 'Rock 'n Roll is more than just music', has proved an enduring successful formula. Such was Jann Wenner's belief in Rock 'n Roll that he spent $75,000 to proclaim its virtues in a full-page advert in the *New York Times* in 1969.[14] Although the new journalism celebrated the polymorphous plural energies of the counter-culture and challenged the aesthetic discriminations that had traditionally banished a whole range of mass and subcultural activities to a banal kitsch wasteland, writers such as Ed Sanders in *The Family*, and Hunter S. Thompson in his apocalyptic vision of America, *Fear and Loathing in Las Vegas*, used the form to reveal the brute horrors of mass America. Charles Manson and Las Vegas seemed to have more in common with an air-conditioned nightmare than an attractive cultural pluralism.

Although the distinctions between high culture and mass culture survived the 1960s and are still actively asserted, the economy of abundance that was a key feature of the era supported a wide range of multifarious subcultures within a mass culture. These subcultural codes were quite capable of functioning as social or personal value systems in the minds of whatever particular socio-economic or cultural group espoused them. The humanist dream of making a high culture of 'the best that has been thought and said', available on a mass basis, still remained a constant theme in American liberalism but the actual cultural practice of significant groups of Americans showed clear signs of being indifferent to such grand designs. When culture, in an age of affluence, becomes overwhelmingly a commodity, the purchase of a rock and roll album, a Van Gogh reproduction, a ticket to an Ingmar Bergman film at an art house cinema, or the espousal of a subculture like that of the Hell's Angels become equally valid expressions of cultural values; the enthusiast of the aesthetic and intellectual values of Abstract Expressionist painting is separate from but equal to the devotee of Country and Western music. Value judgements become spurious and redundant in a world of cultural relativism and official pluralism. Instead of a conflict model in which high culture is engaged in a mortal struggle with mass culture, the proponents of subcultural diversity accept the cultural stratifications of a class-based society as the signs of a healthy pluralism, preferable to the elitism of the defenders of high culture, who seek to impose their standards on the rest of society. Herbert Gans gives the following description of cultural pluralism and its advantages that have developed alongside American capitalism:

> Homogeneous societies offer little cultural diversity; they generally develop only a single concept of beauty, one style of art (often religious), and one way of home furnishing. American society, with its pervasive division of labor and heterogeneity, includes varieties of art ranging from pinups to abstract expressionism, types of music ranging from the latest rock hit to electronic chamber music, and most important, an equally large number of aesthetic standards to determine the choices people make from the available content.[15]

This vision of a healthily proliferating diversity has been challenged by a whole range of cultural critics who have denied that the seeming heterogeneousness of pluralism is the result of any genuine process of choice or individuality. A representative version of this indictment of the cultural pluralism model offered by Gans can be found in Stanley Aronowitz's *False Promises: The Shaping of American Working Class Consciousness* (1973).

Aronowitz, drawing on theoretical models derived from Marcuse and the Frankfurt School, sees the apparent pluralism of modern mass culture as entirely superficial in that: 'Mass art is a one-way communication and thus takes on the character of domination'.[16] The consumer recipients of this one-way process are largely powerless to develop cultural activities and institutions as alternatives to those retailed to them as commodities. Mass culture generates a common stereotypical image of the good life, transmitted to all groups regardless of socio-economic status, race or culture. Even groups who by any criteria have been consistently denied access to the ladder of upward mobility, up which the individual can climb into the good life, are subjected to this false promise:

> The mass media flood the ghetto with images of affluence, which

negroes absorb without absorbing the ethic of disciplined self-denial and postponement of gratification that has traditionally been a central component of the materialist ethic.[17]

Aronowitz argues that this phase of monopoly capitalism seeks to liquidate all alternatives and integrate the individual into what Adorno and Horkheimer called 'a civilization of employees'.

Aronowitz gives a number of examples of how this process can be seen in the culture of post-war America. Elia Kazan's 1954 film *On the Waterfront* charts the struggle of its working-class hero, Terry Malloy, to break away from a whole range of groups and loyalties that, in Aronowitz's view, have traditionally represented and defended working-class interests against government and big business. Group solidarity against government and big business is replaced by Terry's commitment to American individualism. The labour union depicted in the film is corrupt and in the hands of the mob. Terry's individualism also involves the rejection of class and ethnic loyalties. His transition from a world of group values to individualism is eased with the help of: 'a socially marginal liberal catholic priest and his upwardly mobile lover, a longshoreman's daughter who attends college to escape the fate of her father'. The film is: 'about the validity of private goals, the ephemeral quality of communal values and social ties, the legitimacy of the individual against the mob'. In contrast with the standard liberal analysis of the film in which Terry Malloy's progress is an heroic one, Aronowitz sees it as a tragic betrayal. Significantly, Terry's individualism leads him away from the heart of the city towards the classic home of the good life, suburbia. As he makes this progress he has to shed a whole set of mediating agencies between himself and society. His significant others do not include any class or ethnic dimension. They have been reduced to 'the immediate family, particularly one's mate'. The film telescopes what Aronowitz sees as a pernicious historical process in which individuals are spun away from any organic or group identity and become individual atoms, subject and prey to the false promises of a mass society: 'the message of the working class movies of the fifties is, "You're on your own, young man" '.[18]

Elia Kazan, the director of the film, clearly intended the film to be an allegory of heroic individualism. Aronowitz sees the film as a further attempt to erode working-class institutions and traditions that might challenge the one-way process of culture and ideology in a mass society. A whole tradition of Marxist history and cultural analysis in America has argued that Aronowitz's model of working-class culture is not a nostalgic myth of a golden age; it is as recent as the late nineteenth century. Herbert Gutman, for example, has reconstructed the range of institutions and culture-making activities that characterised immigrant industrial communities in late nineteenth-century America, as follows:

> A model sub-culture included friendly and benevolent societies as well as friendly local politicians, community-wide holiday celebrations, an occasional library (the Baltimore Journeymen Bricklayers' Union taxed members one dollar a year in the 1880s to sustain a library that included the collected works of William Shakespeare and Sir Walter Scott's Waverley novels), participant sports, churches sometimes headed by a sympathetic clergy, saloons, beer gardens, and concert halls and, depending upon circumstances, trade unionists, labor reformers, and radicals.[19]

Gutman's portrait suggests a world where dialectical relationships exist between groups; culture is not conceived as a process of 'one-way communication'. When one turns from Gutman's portrait to Aronowitz's portrait of post-industrial culture, dialectical relationships have disappeared:

> In the cities, secretaries, saleswomen, and the male professionals and supervisors need no longer spend evenings alone in front of a television set. The growth of 'singles' bars, housing developments equipped with recreational facilities, social clubs, sports groups, and encounter groups directed specifically at the white collar 'market' resonates to the emotional starvation that is the product of the atomisation of large portions of the American public. The need for community among this stratum supports the transformation of social life into a commodity. The desperation with which the search for human contact is pursued by those isolated in the commercial centers of our country has generated a flourishing industry that has stimulated the expansion of civilian airlines, the clothing industry, important consumer goods manufacturing, and a large share of the proliferation of service industries generally creating and satisfying the demand for leisure.[20]

Aronowitz's apprehension that all cultural activities are being transformed into leisure and entertainment commodities on the model of a Disneyworld theme park is a further version of the kitsch nightmare imagined by Dwight Macdonald in which all audience reactions are programmed and built-in. This mass culture of one-way communication in which consumer reactions are carefully anticipated and controlled recalls Adorno's characterisation of Tin Pan Alley commercial music: 'The composition hears for the listener'.[21] Aronowitz, like Marcuse, does find some exceptions to this uniform standardisation such as: 'The world of high culture . . . where the relationship of the artist to the audience is dialectical, at least potentially'[22] and Bob Dylan's: 'existential ballad "Like a Rolling Stone", which addresses the inevitable separation of children from their families and the agony of individuation in a hostile culture'.[23] However, these more analytic cultural forms are marginal within a society increasingly dominated by a one-dimensional culture of commodities and are easily absorbed and defused. The main tendency in mass culture that Aronowitz described in *On the Waterfront*, namely the separation out of the atomic individual from any mediating social network that might interfere with or filter the blandishments of the good life of material consumption, has continued unabated. Since the publication of Aronowitz's book such films as the phenomenally successful *Saturday Night Fever* (1976), have further glamourised an ethic of individualism and personal consumption. The hero of the film, played by John Travolta, can only escape from the confinement of a crude blue-collar culture via the magical world of disco music and the youth subculture that the music has created. Although the film includes subplots concerning ethnic rivalry and the dream of Travolta's aspiring dancing partner to 'make it' into the world of advertising in up-town Manhattan, the film concentrates on the hero's virtuoso individualistic dancing brilliance. Disco music becomes a transcendent force of youth culture that enables young people to break away from destructive inhibiting social environments. The film is a classic example of the supreme mass-cultural production in that it combined two closely connected markets, film and popular music. The highly orchestrated music provided by the Bee Gees was a key marketing factor that enabled the film to hit the centre of the major American and international record-buying and film-going market, the 16 to 25 year-old consumer.

Increasingly, cultural products are designed to meet the needs and tastes of this particular socio-economic and age group.

Despite various attempts to reconstruct and redeem ethnic and working-class culture in such films as *The Deerhunter* (1978), *Godfather Part I* (1972) and *Part II* (1974), and *Blue Collar* (1978), Hollywood films and in particular TV serials have tended to employ hero figures who are upwardly mobile, and represent middle-class professionalism. Their ideological message is clear: don't be caught in blue-collar culture, escape either into a discrete subculture or upwards into the post-industrial world of the professions. TV serials psychologically condition their audiences to this upward imperative: 'Young doctors shown as giving "service" to patients and young lawyers struggling for social justice . . . prepare large numbers of new workers for these roles'.[24] Even the non-conformist rebels against the norms of middle-class professionalism and institutions, from James Dean in *Rebel Without a Cause* (1955) to Jack Nicholson in *One Flew Over the Cuckoo's Nest* (1975), rebel in the name of an individualism that in Aronowitz's view leaves them dangerously isolated and vulnerable to assimilation by a mass society. Aronowitz's view of a post-war America increasingly dominated by one-way processes of communication is a powerful antidote to Tom Wolfe's image of the same society as rich in populist behavioural diversity. The subject of the next chapter, Norman Mailer, employs many of the techniques associated with the new journalism, not to advocate populist pluralism like Tom Wolfe, but to document the paranoias of a disintegrating society.

13. Norman Mailer and Mass America

NORMAN Mailer's career as a writer and political activist is a personal index of American history since the Second World War. Throughout this period he has sustained a record of social analysis through a variety of literary forms: six novels, short stories, films like *Maidstone*, and a whole range of journalism or non-fiction works that has included coverage of heavyweight boxing, successive Presidential party conventions since 1960, and of the Apollo manned moon-shot. His work has appeared in a diverse range of publications, that straddle mass and minority culture; from radical journals like *Dissent*, and *Village Voice*, which he co-founded in 1954, to the middle brow world of *Harper's*, *Esquire* and *Playboy*. His political activism has included forays into institutional party politics and participation in mass street action. In 1952, as the Cold War intensified, he publicly defended the promise of socialism against the attacks of Dwight Macdonald at Mt Holyoake College; in 1967 he marched on the Pentagon in protest against the Vietnam War, and was arrested, and in 1969 he sought the Democratic nomination for Mayor of New York. In recent years his main form of commentary on American culture has been non-fiction that has included two photo-journalistic biographies of Marilyn Monroe, and most recently a life of Gary Gilmore, a convicted multiple murderer who demanded to be executed rather than pardoned. Although he has never repudiated a somewhat contradictory commitment to socialist ideology, he has completely distanced himself from his early support of communism and the Soviet Union. He views both America and Russia as totalitarian societies, and has therefore taken as a major theme the destruction and warping of individual energies by mass society.

His first treatment of a mass society inexorably submitting to totalitarianism was in his war novel, *The Naked and the Dead* (1948).

The action of the novel, set in the Pacific war against the Japanese, charts the destruction of liberalism, symbolised by the humane Lieutenant Hearn. Hearn is manipulated and finally destroyed by two proto-fascists, General Cummings and Sergeant Croft. The American working class, represented by the GIs in the reconnaissance platoon that Hearn commands, are depicted as a contradictory, volatile mixture of racism, degraded sexuality, and brutality, occasionally redeemed by passages of stoic endurance and temporary camaraderie in the face of mutual danger. Such a mixture is clearly no match for the military professionalism and authoritarianism of General Cummings and Sergeant Croft. Everyone in this military society which is 'a preview of the future' is monitored and controlled by a hieratic ladder of fear. General Cummings tells Hearn that:

> The only morality of the future is a power morality, and a man who cannot find his adjustment to it is doomed. There's one thing about power. It can flow only from the top down. When there are little surges of resistance at the middle levels, it merely calls for more power to be directed downward, to burn it out.[1]

The eclipse of individual freedom by an authoritarian militarism is conveyed in the final scene of the novel not by the jack boot but by an image of a triumphant mediocre bureaucracy that serves the warrior fascists. The novel closes with a scene in which a desk officer, Major Dalleson, exults in the recognition he may gain by introducing a new method of map reading. In future Major Dalleson proposes to:

> Jazz up the map reading class by having a full-size color photograph of Betty Grable in a bathing suit, with the co-ordinate grid system laid over it. The instructor could point to different parts of her and say, 'Give me the co-ordinates'. Goddam, what an idea![2]

Mailer's next novel, *Barbary Shore* (1951), reduced the broad epic structure and sweep of *The Naked and the Dead* to the narrow claustrophobic world of a drab Brooklyn boarding house. Diana Trilling interprets this shift in scale as an ideological one:

> The great battle of history is now fought out, not on the wide 'proletarian' front where his first novel had located it, but on the intellectual left flank where Mailer had been isolated by his inability to maintain his trust in Stalin's revolution.[3]

Barbary Shore certainly documents the marginality and despair of ex-communists in the shape of an ex-government employee, Macleod, who is no longer a participant in history, but spends his time intensively analysing Marxist theory. Not only has Macleod been betrayed by ideology and history, he is sexually betrayed by his wife Guinevere. The novel domesticates and internalises the theme of worldwide political struggle into a squalid tale of sexual and political duplicity. The action of the novel also includes the tracking down and investigation of Macleod by a robot-like FBI agent called Hollings-worth, who, like Major Dalleson in *The Naked and the Dead*, is a mediocre bureaucrat. Macleod has stolen a 'little object' from the State Department which contains the remnants of revolutionary socialism. Macleod passes this legacy on to another inmate of the boarding house, Lovett, an amnesiac young writer, an intellectual through whose eyes the action and characters are viewed, but not before Mailer has comprehensively depicted Macleod's political and personal defeat. Macleod, like Soviet-style communism, is 'the God that failed'; he is no longer at the potential centre of history. He is, like Lovett, an alienated marginal radical. Macleod loses his wife to Hollingsworth and commits suicide. *Barbary Shore*, like *The Naked and the Dead*, ends on a note of ironic absurdity: Lovett, a man with no memory, inherits the task of preserving future socialism.

Mailer's third novel, *The Deer Park* (1955), reproduces the same psychological landscape of alienation and depersonalisation. The locale is not the subculture of a marginal intelligentsia, but that of a Hollywood movie colony who control the culture industry that manufactures the American mass sexual dream. Mailer's portrait of this movie culture of sex and monopoly capitalism (so often imagined as a world of liberation, not subject to middle-class respectability) reveals a society as defeated and anxiety-ridden as the left-wing circles in *Barbary Shore*: 'The inhabitants of Mailer's Hollywood are wracked by a fever without cure; in their freedom from conventional sexual restraint sounds the rattling of the chains of a bondage as awful as that of the Army'.[4] The master of ceremonies in this world is a predatory agent figure called Marion Faye, whose character of sadistic amorality gives him a manipulative control over other people's needs and anxieties. Hollywood is constructed according to an ideology that Mailer defined in his following commentary on Marx's *Das Kapital*: 'That first of the major psychologies to approach the mystery of social cruelty so simply and practically as to say that we are a collective body of humans whose life-energy is wasted, displaced and procedurally stolen as it passes from one of us to another'.[5] In a world in which everything is being transformed into a commodity, Marion Faye and Hollywood are major agents and refiners of this process. Mailer, in common with the Frankfurt School, became increasingly aware that modern mass industrial societies were, regardless of their ideological promises and programmes, liquidating any idea of individual creativity. Mailer uses the term totalitarian to describe a process of dehumanisation that was as evident in the culture of American capitalism as in that of Soviet Russia. Before looking at Mailer's account of totalitarianism in America and the possible sources of resistance to such an ideology, it is important to place the debate in America on totalitarianism in its historical context.

H. Stuart Hughes has described the course of the post-Second World War debate on totalitarianism as follows:

> In retrospect it seems clear that the vogue of 'totalitarian' explanations, more particularly in the United States, was a by-product of the Cold War. In the late 1940s and early 1950s, the term served to ease the shock of emotional readjustment for Americans or Englishmen – or émigrés – who had just defeated one enemy and were now called upon by their governments to confront another. If it could be proved that Nazism and Communism were very much the same thing, then the Cold War against the late ally could be justified by the rhetoric that had proved so effective against the late enemy.[6]

Mailer's contribution to this debate is summarised in an article he wrote for *Esquire* in August 1963, collected in *The Presidential Papers*. In the article he declares that: 'Totalitarianism has been the continuing preoccupation of this book'.[7] He is at pains to distinguish the particular signs of a culture of totalitarianism that are visible in America. Totalitarianism is a force that: 'beheads individuality, variety, dissent, extreme possibility, romantic faith, it blinds vision, deadens instinct' (*PP*, p. 201). Its deadening operations can be found in: 'the image of the commercials on television which use phallic and vaginal symbols to sell products which are otherwise useless for sex'. Modern architecture, which: 'began with the desire to use the building materials of the twentieth century – steel, glass, reinforced concrete . . . to increase the sculptural beauty of buildings' (*PP*, p. 200), has succumbed to totalitarianism by making all public build-ings look alike: 'factories look like college campuses or mental hospitals' (*PP*, p. 201). Taking his cue from Yeats's poem 'The Second Coming', Mailer sees totalitarianism as a 'rough beast' of transformation that obliterates all distinctions. America since the 1930s has been converted in this process from a contradictory mixture of:

> Bigotry, initiative, strife, social justice and social injustice, into a vast central swamp of tasteless, toneless authority whose depend-able heroes were drawn from FBI men, doctors, television enter-tainers, corporation executives, and athletes who could cooperate with public-relations men. (*PP*, p. 199)

Mailer, like his contemporary Hannah Arendt in *The Origins of Totalitarianism* (1951), sought to show how mass industrial society could create a pervasive psychology and culture of totalitarianism, as it relentlessly eroded class, family and individual identity. Having charted the triumph of a totalitarianism that had come to America 'with no concentration camps' (*PP*, p. 200), and the demise of the possibility of world socialist revolution led by the Soviet Union, Mailer began to develop a thesis that saw a form of resistance against conformity in the calculated transgressions against the social norms demanded by mass society, that various criminal subcultures com-mitted.

The most controversial of these forms of resistance is defined in his 1957 essay 'The White Negro'. The essay celebrates a new kind of rebel against society, who has no conscious political programme. The energies of this figure are the product of the interaction of three subcultures: 'In such places as Greenwich Village, a *ménage-à-trois* was completed – the bohemian and the juvenile delinquent came face-to-face with the Negro, and the hipster was a fact in American life'.[8] The resulting amalgam of dissent is the existential figure of the 'white Negro', who is revolutionary because he has never had a stake in the society of which he is a marginal alienated member. Mailer's celebration of the revolutionary potential of the criminal mind and culture is part of a whole literature that includes Jean Genet's homosexual thieves and the equation that Malcolm X made between his early life as a pimp and street hustler and his later political radicalism. This model of liberation is a contradictory one: 'the hipster is equally a candidate for the most reactionary and most radical movements'.[9] With this formulation, Mailer connects the politically ambivalent energies of the existential hipster with those of characters like Sergeant Croft and Marion Faye. Mailer is interested only in a contradictory dialectic of extreme left and extreme right. There is no room for liberal reformism in his diagram of a revolutionary social analysis. Mailer's own position at this period in the mid-1950s is defined in an interview he gave in 1955 to Lyle Stuart, a magazine editor.

In reply to a question as to how his 'social ken' had changed since *The Naked and the Dead*, Mailer replied:

> I was an anarchist then, and I'm an anarchist today. In between I belonged to the Progressive Party during the Wallace Campaign, and then broke off rather abruptly at the time of the Waldorf Peace Conference in 1949 . . . today I'm a Marxian anarchist which is a contradiction in terms, but a not unprofitable contradiction for trying to do some original thinking. I suppose part of the change in my 'social ken' is that politics as politics interests me less today than politics as a part of everything else in life.[10]

The impact of the idea contained in the last part of this statement, that the machinations between and within political parties whether communist or republican were no longer the main focus of his attention, can be seen in the themes and subject matter of his next major book, *The Presidential Papers* (1963). Two pieces in particular reflect this changed appreciation of how and where politics and ideology reveal themselves in a mass society; an essay entitled 'Superman Comes to the Supermarket', on the personality and media magnetism of John F. Kennedy; and an account of the first Floyd Patterson versus Sonny Liston heavyweight championship fight, which is part of the Eleventh Presidential Paper, entitled 'Death'. Both pieces in Mailer's mind anticipate the dramatic existential quality of politics and history in the 1960s. Mailer, in a new preface, added in 1976, described the book as:

> a paradigm of the prodigious anxiety which attached to politics in the early sixties. In the fifties, every subliminal political sense was ready to tell us that the country was being run by the corporations,

the FBI, the CIA and the Mafia. . . . In the sixties, that cancer seal
began to crack – Kennedy's election was the hairline split in the
American totalitarianism of the fifties. (*PP*, pp. 7–8)

Mailer, like many of the new journalists, responded to this split that
promised release from the iron conformities of the 1950s by making
his own self and reactions to events the main agencies and channels of
social analysis. Instead of the fictional allegories of his early novels,
Mailer presents his own public and private persona and experiences
as a reflecting mirror of American history. The claims he advances on
behalf of this set of non-fiction techniques and the view of America
that emerges from a position in which 'politics as politics interests me
less today than politics as part of everything else in life' are basic to an
understanding of his non-fiction work. The following analysis of *The
Presidential Papers* (1963), *Armies of the Night* and *Miami and the Siege of
Chicago* (1968), and *The Executioner's Song* (1979), examines these
claims. 'You know,' said Lowell in his fondest voice, 'Elizabeth and I
really think you're the finest journalist in America.'[11] Mailer's
chagrin that Robert Lowell, a leading contender in the stakes for
America's finest poet, did not call him America's best writer, should
not obscure his total commitment to the new journalist aesthetic.
What need to be stressed are the various departures that Mailer's
journalism makes from the ideological model proposed by Herbert
Gans. Instead of the picture of dignified investigative latter day
progressives that Gans paints, Mailer sees journalists as a group who
help to 'keep America slightly insane'. While paying lip-service to
freedom of information, journalists in reality have to pander to a
repressive silent majority: 'The more readers he owns, the less he can
say. He is forbidden by a hundred censors, most of them inside
himself, to communicate notions, which are not conformistically
simple, simple like plastic is simple, that is to say, monotonous' (*PP*, p.
236). Instead of exhibiting the dignity of middle-class professionals,
the journalists who gather to cover presidential conventions or
heavyweight boxing matches are pictured by Mailer as follows: 'Two
hundred reporters and photographers congregated for a press
conference are as void of dignity, even stuffed-up, stodgy, middle class
dignity, as a slew of monkeys tearing through the brush' (*PP*, p. 234).
Journalism has also succumbed to the general malaise that has
afflicted post-war America; it has become a 'captive of the welfare
state' (*PP*, p. 238). In the same way that former socialists such as

Daniel Bell have turned into liberal apologists for an affluent, supposedly conflict-free society, journalists have been absorbed into this liberal mainstream where all their expenses are paid. Mailer's critique of the ways conflict and dissent have been defused and assimilated is basic to his view of post-war America.

The main elements to the idea that America was no longer a society characterised by divisive class, economic and cultural conflicts have already been described in Daniel Bell's 'end of ideology' thesis and the various definitions of post-industrial society. Mailer sees this process by which models of co-operation replaced models of conflict and new alliances were forged between labour and business, between intellectuals and government, as the product of an 'infatuation with the economy of abundance'. The new culture of co-operation that post-industrial society prophets like David Riesman detected in America is an artificial one: 'to be sheared at a stroke because the economy of abundance is artificial, grown from a war economy and subject either to crisis in the event of no war, or subject to war itself for continuing health'.[12] Riesman's theorising leaves no room for any idea of class or economic conflict: 'Competitive strife begins to disappear and is replaced by the co-operative jockeying for position of the other-directed types who are essentially more anxious to meet approval than to succeed at any cost'.[13] The clear implication of the co-operative model was that the Marxist model of the historic revolutionary role of an oppressed working class has become redundant. The theoreticians of this new post-industrial America saw no need for revolutionary socialism in an affluent society in which Marx's: 'law of increasing misery was refuted by the tremendous advances of technology'.[14] This version of post-war America is described in Daniel Bell's *End of Ideology*:

> It is in the advanced industrial countries, principally the United States, Britain, and North Western Europe, where national income has been rising, where mass expectations of an equitable share in that increase are relatively fulfilled, and where social mobility affects ever greater numbers, that extremist politics have the least hold.[15]

The cultural values that are within the grasp of this expanding democratising economy of abundance are those of classic post-war American liberalism, as articulated by writers like Lionel Trilling: a high degree of individual freedom, variousness, complexity and diversity. Mailer's quarrel with this liberalism adopted by such former socialists as Daniel Bell, Dwight Macdonald and Lionel Trilling, is that it blurs the very real class and economic conflicts within American society. The consequences of the lack of any radical critique of the successive promises of Roosevelt's 'New Deal', Truman's 'Fair Deal' or Johnson's 'Great Society' has been the wholesale absorption of intellectuals into a treacherous: 'Liberal center of America, where most of the action was, building contracts, federal money for super-highways, youth programs for the slums, wars against poverty, bigotry, violence and hate'. The absence of any radical scrutiny of the liberal ideology of abundance has led to 'a war in Vietnam, and a permanent state of police alert in the cities in the summer'.[16] The Welfare State had become the Warfare State. Mailer's attempts to challenge this ideological paralysis and transform the nature of political journalism are announced in his essay on Kennedy's campaign style in 1960, 'Superman comes to the Supermarket'.

Kennedy's presidential campaign throws into sharp relief the degree to which politicians in a mass media society have become products to be marketed like the stars of Hollywood: 'The Democrats were going to nominate a man who, no matter how serious his political dedication might be, was indisputably and willy-nilly going to be seen as a great box-office actor' (*PP*, p. 51). From this essay on Kennedy to his biography of Gary Gilmore, the process by which a single event, via the media, becomes a mass event, is one of Mailer's central concerns. Not only is a demystification of this process central to an understanding of mass society, it prompts Mailer to develop a whole range of fictional and documentary techniques in order to uncover the nature of history in a mass society. Kennedy's appeal is based on his ability, through the mass media, to evoke powerful images of America's individualistic frontier past: 'a country which had grown by the leap of one hero past another'. Yet this heroic appeal is made in the midst of a mass manufacturing system dedicated to a contrary levelling purpose, 'the creation of men as interchangeable as commodities, their extremes of personality singed out of existence' (*PP*, p. 52). This structural contradiction between the mass, and the myth of the individual has led to a schizophrenia in the American imagination:

Since the First World War Americans have been leading a double life, and our history has moved on two rivers, one visible, the other underground; there has been the history of politics which is concrete, factual, practical and unbelievably dull . . ., and there is a subterranean river of untapped ferocious lonely and romantic desires, that concentration of ecstasy and violence which is the dream life of the nation. (*PP*, p. 51)

In the same way that Sonny Liston, an ex-convict, is an existential ideological threat to the civil rights liberalism of Floyd Patterson when they step into the boxing ring, Kennedy challenges the Eisenhower legacy of 'false security in the power and panacea of organised religion, family, and the FBI' (*PP*, p. 57). Kennedy's presidency touches the 'subterranean river', he is the 'existential hero' who in his own phrase 'will get America moving again'. This version of the Kennedy promise has been subjected to the full force of revisionism that now sees Kennedy as a cold warrior and the initiator of a war in Vietnam, rather than the herald of a new liberal existential order. Mailer is keenly aware of Kennedy's deficiencies:

He does not have the kind of mind which can see a new solution to an old problem. Rather he manipulates the best single elements in the old solutions, and applies his political craft to composing a package with new consumer interests. (*PP*, pp. 13–14)

Kennedy's failure to halt the invasion of Cuba implicates him in what Mailer calls 'one of the meanest blunders in our history'. It also brings him into sharp contrast with Fidel Castro, whom Mailer describes as the authentic embodiment of his country: 'The man is the country, revolutionary, tyrannical . . . hysterical . . . brave as the best of animals, doomed perhaps to end in tragedy, but one of the great figures of the twentieth century' (*PP*, pp. 103–4). Mailer's qualified support for Kennedy rests on the idea that he represents the only alternative to an intensified totalitarianism in American society. America needs an 'existential politics . . . rooted in the concept of the hero' (*PP*, p. 16) to break the rigid conservative mould of post-war America. Kennedy represents this promise in a number of contradictory ways that includes: 'The fact that he was Catholic would shiver a first existential vibration of consciousness into the mind of the White Protestant' (*PP*, p. 63).

The essay on Kennedy established the basic format for Mailer's psycho-historical accounts of presidential party conventions that culminated in his coverage of the 1968 Democratic and Republican Conventions, *Miami and the Siege of Chicago*. Mailer was not alone in making documentary political journalism a major genre in post-war America. His contributions need to be placed within the general context of the rise of public fascination in a new political culture, largely made up of what Daniel Boorstin called 'pseudo-events'. Boorstin anatomised the pseudo-event as follows:

(1) It is not spontaneous, but comes about because someone has planned, planted or incited it. Typically it is not a train wreck or an earthquake but an interview.

(2) It is planted primarily (not always exclusively) for the immediate purpose of being reported or reproduced. Therefore, its occurrence is arranged for the convenience of the reporting or reproducing media.[17]

Politicians in particular employ these techniques. Boorstin cites Joseph McCarthy who 'invented the morning press conference called for the purpose of announcing an afternoon press conference'.[18] The media event, the President addressing the nation at prime time, becomes a crucial weapon in the manipulation of public opinion. As well as the pseudo-event, the personalities of Presidencies and the culture of political activity became objects of mass interest. Theodore White's encyclopaedic day-by-day, meal-by-meal, accounts of Presidential campaigns mark this trend and denoted, by their titles, the idea of a manufactured political commodity: *The Making of the President*. In this genre the reader is a witness of history in the making. Not only did journalists who were attached to the Presidential campaigns adopt this genre, it was increasingly typical for Presidential aides and advisers to contribute their own eye witness accounts of Presidential political culture. Arthur Schlesinger Jr's memoir of Kennedy's Presidency, *A Thousand Days* (1965), exemplifies the more deferential school. The tone is intimate, a mix of domesticity and world crises. Schlesinger is a master of a form which makes the reader privy to political·high life:

We sat in the living-room and except for Kennedy, sipped Bloody Marys while we chatted about the election. Jackie said, 'I cast only one vote – for Jack. It is a rare thing to be able to vote for one's husband for President of the United States, and I didn't want to dilute it by voting for anyone else'.[19]

Instead of adopting the impersonality of the reported speech of the third person historian, Schlesinger himself becomes the mediator between the personal world of the President and the public political events which surround him. Schlesinger is an accountable intimate agent rather than a detached analyst. The use of such novelistic techniques became standard in this genre, enhancing the sheer factual power of documentary memoir. As Tom Wolfe pointed out:

> The result is a form that is not merely like a novel. It consumes devices that happen to have originated with the novel and mixes them with every other device known to prose. And all the while, quite beyond matters of technique, it enjoys an advantage so obvious, so built-in one almost forgets what a power it has: the simple fact that the reader knows all this actually happened. (NJ, pp. 48–9)

Eventually the genre expanded to include total coverage of all aspects of the campaign trail. This recognition that the Presidency was a major source of media culture dates from Franklin Roosevelt. In Hoover's last year as President in 1932, at a time of deepening economic crisis 'he held only twelve press conferences and handed out twenty-six statements'.[20] Roosevelt, in contrast, 'promised reporters two press conferences a week and, with astonishing regularity, he held to that: 337 in his first term, 374 in the second, 279 in the third'.[21] Roosevelt, like Nixon, used his powers of media access to by-pass the press and Congress, and speak directly to the nation: 'In the 1936 Presidential campaign, more than 80 per cent of the press opposed Roosevelt, and he won by the highest percentage ever'.[22] One of the ways Roosevelt achieved this hold over public opinion was through his hearthside chats:

> He ad-libbed in the days before ad-libbing was allowed. During a 1933 broadcast he interrupted his talk to ask for a glass of water, paused while it was brought, took a swallow audible in living rooms across the country, and then told the listeners: 'My friends, it's very hot here in Washington tonight.' His simple gesture drew thousands of sympathetic letters.[23]

One consequence of the rise of this new political culture was a parallel rise in the status of the political correspondent, who often became a less than critical member of the world of the White House, dependent on the President and his press secretary for inside interviews and information. This somewhat cosy relationship was rudely shattered by Hunter S. Thompson's coverage of the 1972 campaigns, *Fear and Loathing on the Campaign Trail '72*. Thompson bucked at the unwritten rules of political journalism. Thompson, an open partisan of McGovern's cause, asserted his own code:

> As far as I was concerned, there was no such thing as 'off the record'. The most consistent and ultimately damaging failure of political journalism in America has its roots in the clubby cocktail personal relationships that inevitably develop between politicians and journalists.[24]

Thompson invented his own rules and became: 'the first journalist in Christendom to go on record comparing Nixon to Adolph Hitler'.[25] The next development in the genre was to look at the journalists themselves, which Timothy Crouse did for *Rolling Stone* in *The Boys on the Bus* (1972). The form is still massively alive and entered its mega stage with Jules Witcover's 656-page account of the 1976 Presidential campaigns, appropriately titled *Marathon*. Despite all this increased coverage of politics, political participation is not significantly higher as a result. A key to this anomaly can be seen in the role of primaries, which have become classic instances of this new politics of media events. Primaries were devised in the early twentieth century during the reformist Progressive era as a way to take power from corrupt party bosses and make politics more democratic. However, recent statistics show that the 31 state primaries in 1976 spectacularly failed to achieve this effect:

> Only about 25 per cent of the voting age population voted in primaries. Of these about two-thirds voted Democratic. This means that Carter won the Democratic nomination with the support of roughly 7 per cent of the voting age population in primary states – or about 5 per cent of the entire voting age population.[26]

The real importance of the primary in modern politics is that, early in the Presidential election year, vote-seeking candidates descend on the scarcely populated state of New Hampshire that traditionally holds the first Presidential primary, in order to gain exposure and publicity. The pollsters rarely refrain from predicting trends even though they are based on such miniscule returns. It is in this context of media politics and pseudo events that Mailer's two most extended accounts of American politics in action during the 1960s, *Armies of the Night* and *Miami and the Siege of Chicago*, should be placed, in that both books are as concerned with the formal problems involved in creating an accurate version of a mass event as with the historical import and political meaning of those events. The two issues have become indivisible.

Mailer's investigations of the reliability of facts and evidence in a mass society are not unique; they are part of a whole process in modern literature that has questioned both the subject-centred approach and the perspective so often characteristic of the nineteenth-century novel in which the author stands above the action, distributing morality and understanding. David Lodge's description of this process, by which the old narrative certainties have been replaced by the more sceptical strategies of modern fiction, is very close to the techniques employed in *Armies of the Night*:

> Modern fiction eschews the straight chronological ordering of its material, and the use of a reliable, omniscient and intrusive narrator. It employs, instead, either a single, limited point of view, or multiple viewpoints, all more or less limited and fallible; and it tends towards a complex or fluid handling of time, involving much cross reference back and forward across the temporal span of the action.[27]

As early as *The Naked and the Dead*, which continually switches viewpoints, Mailer was involved in this modernist disruption of traditional narrative techniques. He adds a particular slant to these investigations in that in *Miami and the Siege of Chicago* and even more in *Armies of the Night*, Mailer, the narrator of events, becomes their protagonist. In *Armies of the Night* his participation in the march on the Pentagon carries him to the point of arrest and imprisonment. In *Miami and the Siege of Chicago* the reader follows the action through the eyes of a persona called 'the reporter' which is Mailer the professional journalist. This stance, by which Mailer the personality is to a certain extent made subject to the professional code of a journalist, is ultimately defeated when Mailer the reporter becomes embroiled as a protagonist. While seeking to carry out his legitimate enquiries as an accredited journalist, his freedom is restricted by a National Guard officer, and the following dialogue takes place:

> 'You'll have to step back.'
> 'Why?'
> 'Just step back.'
> 'I'm a reporter for *Harper's* magazine and I wish to be able to describe the barbed wire on that jeep.'[28]

Mailer, like many journalists during the 1968 Democratic Convention, discovered that the investigative rights of journalists were not sacred in the eyes of the police and National Guard, who attacked and clubbed both protestors and journalists, in an action that was later officially described as 'a police riot'. Although Mailer adopts the role of reporter, he is fairly cynical about journalism's claims to represent freedom of speech. Throughout *Armies of the Night* the complex perspectives of Mailer's account of events are directly compared to the poverty of those offered by *Time* magazine and the *New York Times*. James Reston's version in the *New York Times* of the issues and interactions between protestors and the guardians of the Pentagon is a classic example of the moralising stance of what Tom Wolfe called 'the Literary Gentleman in the Grandstand'. Reston reduces the complexities of the event to the following formula:

> It is difficult to report publicly the ugly and vulgar provocation of many of the militants. They spat on some of the soldiers in the front line at the Pentagon and goaded them with most vicious personal slander. (*AN*, p. 297)

Unlike the new journalism, Reston does not try to see the action from a number of perspectives that includes the view of the protestors. Instead, he pontificates in what Sir Walter Scott called the 'big Bow-Wow strain', a tone which newspaper editorial columns invariably assume when seeking to speak on behalf of an imagined national consensus. The half-truths that masqueraded as the whole truth in Reston's prose are in Mailer's coinage 'factoids':

That is, facts which have no existence before appearing in a magazine or newspaper, creations which are not so much lies as a product to manipulate emotion in the Silent Majority. (It is possible, for example, that Richard Nixon has spoken in nothing but factoids during his public life.)[29]

The factoids and pseudo-events created by the mass media surrounded the march on the Pentagon with 'a forest of inaccuracies which would blind the efforts of an historian' (*AN*, p. 231). *Armies of the Night* is a model of the techniques through which a writer can rescue the complex nature of an event from the simplifications of the mass media.

In order to do literary justice to the event, Norman Mailer divides his account of the 1967 anti-Vietnam war protest march on the Pentagon into two parts; in the first part, called 'History as a Novel', the reader has access to the event through Mailer's own experience and reactions, in the second part, called 'The Novel as History', the rich personality and solo existentialism of Mailer, the protagonist of the first part, are submerged in a well-researched investigation of the march. The second part has the benefit of hindsight and access to a number of other accounts. Although a different version of the event emerges from the separate parts, Mailer does not ask the reader to arbitrate between the two versions. By offering these two perspectives, the experience of an individual, and a comparative distilled assessment of the versions of the march offered by 'all newspaper accounts, eyewitness reports, and historic inductions available' (*AN*, pp. 267–8), Mailer seeks to achieve a fullness of response that will throw into sharp relief the inadequacies of the versions handed down by the mass media and James Reston. Although both parts and both sets of techniques are necessary, Mailer finds that only the techniques of the novel can explore the interior history of the event. The form of 'the novel' enables the writer to imagine the consciousness beneath the helmeted heads of the military police and: 'unashamedly enter that world of strange lights and intuitive speculation which is the novel' (*AN*, p. 268). In the first part of the book this freedom to speculate, to penetrate into this interior world, has only one channel, the consciousness of the single contradictory figure of Mailer himself. Mailer leaves the reader in no doubt as to the quixotic temperament of this narrator:

Mailer is a figure of monumental disproportions and so serves willy-nilly as the bridge – many will say the *pons asinorum* – into the crazy house, the crazy mansion, of that historic moment when a mass of the citizenry – not much more than a mob – marched on a bastion which symbolized the military might of the Republic. (*AN*, pp. 64–5)

Mailer places himself in the long line of slightly marginal figures employed by novelists to provide a set of entrances into history. Like Pierre Bezuhkov wandering amidst the chaos of the Battle of Borodino in Tolstoy's *War and Peace*, or the Good Soldier Schweyk, Mailer's perspective on the march is not that of a central political organiser 'like David Dellinger or Jerry Rubin' (*AN*, p. 64), but that of a man at the fringe of the main events, which he reveals only as far as they impinge on his experience. The overall effect of Mailer's stripping bare of the techniques of the novelist and the historian is a heightening of the reader's sense of participation. The reader develops a critical dialectical relationship with the text, becomes enmeshed in the open technology of the book, and has to be continually alert to the changes in gear from novel to history, and back again. Through these techniques, Mailer constructs a portrait of American society in which a whole series of tensions and conflicts have erupted to the surface. The ideological and sociological implications of the march are central to Mailer's portrait.

The protestors are in the main drawn from:

The urban middle class . . . who always feel most uprooted, most alienated from America itself, and so instinctively most critical of America, for neither do they work with their hands nor wield real power. (*AN*, p. 270)

Within this broad category of class, the protestors divide into a contradictory alliance between black militants, old leftists, Students for a Democratic Society, pacifists and moderate middle-class liberals. This heterogeneous amalgam is confronted by the blue-collar police and soldiers, the defenders of patriotism, authoritarianism, and the war in Vietnam. In the eyes of the defenders of the Pentagon, the protestors are 'a pullulating unwashed orgiastic Communist-inspired wave of flesh' (*AN*, p. 270). Mailer's portrait gives the lie to any idea of America as a pluralist society in which co-operation has replaced conflict. The immediate cause of this revival of radicalism and mass protest is the Vietnam war, and Eugene McCarthy's 1968 Presidential campaign against Lyndon Johnson 'a movement whose strength was in the suburbs and the academy'[30] becomes its focus. Although Mailer is clearly in broad sympathy with the protestors, his own ideological position creates a certain distance between himself and the counter-culture that has become a major factor in American society. In the chapter of *Armies of the Night* called 'Why are we in Vietnam?', Mailer defines his own politics as follows: 'Mailer was a left Conservative. So he had his own point of view. To himself he could suggest that he tried to think in the style of Marx in order to attain certain values suggested by Edmund Burke' (*AN*, p. 196). Edmund Burke, the conservative defender of organic tradition, might appear at first sight an unlikely influence on Mailer. Burke sought to defend the progressive stabilising elements of tradition at a time when the French Revolution threatened to destroy the whole fabric of society. Mailer sees the 1960s as a similar age of revolution and uses Burke's organicism to reject the extremism that is always a possibility in a period of civil disturbance. Mailer's coverage of Barry Goldwater's nomination for Republican Presidential candidate in 1964, included in *Cannibals and Christians*, continually uses quotations from Burke to point up Goldwater's extremism. This passage from Burke's *Reflections on the Revolution in France*;

> They should not think it amongst their rights to cut off the entail, or commit waste on the inheritance by destroying at their pleasure the whole original fabric of their society; hazarding to leave to those who come after them a ruin instead of a habitation,

is positioned immediately before a newspaper report containing Goldwater's speculations on possible military options in Vietnam:

> There have been several suggestions made. I don't think we would use any of them. But defoliation of the forests by low-yield atomic weapons could well be done. When you remove the foliage, you remove the cover.[31]

The point of the contrast is clear: Goldwater has no respect for nature or the future. As Mailer documents the violence of the 1967 march on the Pentagon and Mayor Daley's abuses at the 1968 Democratic

Convention in Chicago, he is as conscious of apocalyptic chaos as of revolutionary change. Nevertheless, he throws in his political fortunes with the new radical army that marches against the Pentagon, a constituency that is a cross between 'a citizen's army' and 'the legions of Sgt Pepper's Bank ... assembled from all the intersections between history and the comic books, between legend and television' (*AN*, pp. 102–3).

The literary devices and ideological positions that Mailer developed in *The Armies of the Night* and *Miami and the Siege of Chicago* were responses to the dramatic upheavals of the 1960s. In his most recent large-scale work of non-fiction, *The Executioner's Song* (1979), his focus is not on the mass events of politics and history but on the complexities of mediation, interpretation and documentation that occur when a single event becomes a mass event. Gary Gilmore, a convicted murderer, became an overnight sensation when he insisted on his right to be executed, rejecting the liberal Christian ethic that commutes death into life imprisonment. Mailer's interest in this event is threefold: what is the history of the man who demands such rights? how do the various agencies of law and order react to such a demand? and what do the mass media, the merchants of 'factoids', make of the story? The first of these enquiries is in the beginning of the book, called 'Western Voices', which describes Gary's personality, upbringing and the events leading up to his conviction for the murder of two men. The other two concerns offer a portrait of the genuflections in attitude that occur in society as a result of Gilmore's demand that the judge's death sentence be carried out. These are explored in the second half of the book, called 'Eastern Voices'.

Mailer's overarching metaphor of East and West provides a cultural landscape in which his interpretation is placed. The East in the shape of the Supreme Court, is the supreme arbiter of events that take place in the West. The East is the centre of national interpretation, the base for the great media monopolies of CBS, NBC, *Time* and *Newsweek*. It is also the liberal home of the American Civil Liberties Union that tries to prevent Gilmore's execution. Amongst liberals, Gilmore's demands constitute an excessive abuse of the idea of individual personal rights. Alongside these regionally constructed values and institutions are mobile mavericks like Larry Schiller, a one-eyed former *Life* photographer, who becomes Gary Gilmore's literary executor. Schiller eventually succeeds in buying up the rights to Gilmore's story, and becomes the master of ceremonies for the event as it develops into an absurd circus. Schiller's imagination becomes the filter and source of the diverse scenarios and mass media formulae into which the Gilmore saga can be endlessly transformed. In order to ensure total control, Schiller needs to buy up the rights of all the protagonists including those of Gilmore's girlfriend, Nicole, and of his cousin, Brenda. At one point, Schiller has not firmly contracted any of the main characters, but his grasp of the popular imagination is so acute and flexible that a best-seller is still possible:

> On the other hand, said Schiller, if they got the girl, but couldn't succeed in signing up Gilmore, they might do an interesting struggle of two sisters both in love with the same criminal. They'd have to substitute a fictionalised criminal, but could still explore the triangle. Or they could focus completely on Nicole . . . Play down the murders but emphasize the romantic difficulties of trying to live with a man that society does not trust.[32]

Despite Mailer's comprehensive treatment of the relevant socio-logical and psychological background to Gilmore's personality and motivations, Gilmore seems to remain a collection of elliptically played roles rather than a fully rounded character. The temptation to see Gilmore as a type of existential criminal rebel, a version of 'the white Negro', is firmly resisted. Instead, we are offered a whole series of documentary assessments of Gilmore. His official psychiatric report sees him as: 'An individual who is very hostile, socially deviant, currently unhappy with his life . . . he has a high hostility component towards the establishment.' The report concludes that during the commission of the murders 'he knew what he was doing'.[33] When Gilmore is transformed into a mass media event, new qualities and contradictions in his personality emerge. One of the scriptwriters employed by Schiller to write up Gilmore's story is provoked into the following assessment of Gilmore when a twenty-year-old man asks to have Gilmore's eyes after his execution:

> By God, was Gary like Harry Truman, mediocrity enlarged by history? Christ, he had even become the owner of a cottage industry: the precise remains of Gary Gilmore. . . . Gilmore, he thought, had a total contempt for life, his life, your life, anyone's life. Waved his own away because it was a boss thing to do, show down shit, pure pathology that came out of long years of playing

chicken with prison authorities. Yet, now, overnight new celebrity, movie star without portfolio, Gilmore was responding humanely to all the attention, actually functioning like a decent man.[34]

Though Gilmore is the centre of the book, he is also part of a whole series of multiple parallel narratives and biographies that Mailer constructs in his 1019-page book in order to reveal the intricate workings behind the production of a mass event. The narrative structure is similar to that used by John Steinbeck in *The Grapes of Wrath*. A panorama of American society from Gary's arthritic mother, marooned in a trailer home, to the hermetic Mormon world of Salt Lake City, opens up as the life histories and involvements with Gilmore of lawyers, blood relations, journalists, and his murder victims are alternately set into narrative motion, suspended and reactivated in sequence. In contrast to his participant reportage of the 1960s, Mailer does not intrude himself into the narrative as a protagonist. He relies on interviews, court proceedings and Schiller's materials to construct his documentary. The sheer density of biographical, psychological and cultural information that Mailer orchestrates in the book makes it one of the major reports on modern mass society.

14. Coming to Terms with Hollywood: From Mass to Auteur Theory

FROM the 1930s onwards (with surprisingly few periods of recession considering the potential risks of investment) the Hollywood studio system provided a mass audience with a stream of Westerns, musicals, gangster thrillers, comedies, social problem pictures, and a host of generic variations and cross-breedings. In many ways, this particular system of industrialised mass entertainment has passed its hegemonic heyday, with the rise of television and the record industry. Nevertheless, the aesthetic status of Hollywood and all its works has been such a central issue in the debate on mass culture, in the development of American Studies, and within the history of world cinema, that it constitutes an important case-study of arguments and attitudes.

Some of the major problems posed by Hollywood are raised by Peter Wollen in his influential *Signs and Meanings in the Cinema*:

The main stumbling block for film aesthetics, however, has not been Eisenstein, but Hollywood. Eisenstein, as we have seen, was part of a general movement which included not only film directors, but also poets, painters and architects. It is relatively easy to assimilate the Russian cinema of the 1920s into the normal frame of reference of art history. Hollywood, on the other hand, is a completely different kind of phenomenon. . . . There is no difficulty in talking about Eisenstein in the same breath as a poet like Mayakovsky, a painter like Malevich, or a theatre director like Stanislavsky. But John Ford or Raoul Walsh? The initial reaction, as we well know, was to damn Hollywood completely, to see it as a threat to civilised values and sensibilities.[1]

The problem of Hollywood in Wollen's assessment is that it does not possess a recognisable high-culture avant-garde such as sustained Russian cinema in the 1920s. Hollywood's neglect or rejection of experimental avant-garde practice has been a crucial component in the various critical approaches to Hollywood cinema. As we have seen, Dwight Macdonald did isolate a phase of high culture in America's classic 'silent' directors. However, these individual imaginations were swept aside by the coming of sound and the dominance of the studio system. In Macdonald's view, Hollywood mass-culture production then dominated world cinema until 1955 when a number of European directors such as Ingmar Bergman and Antonioni, and French new wave directors such as Truffaut and Godard, revived individual avant-garde traditions. A more recent contribution to the idea of an avant-garde appears in a long article by Andrew Sarris called 'Avant-garde Films are More Boring Than Ever'. Sarris questions the artistic claims of a privileged avant-garde and defends his own preference for mainstream Hollywood narrative cinema in the following terms:

> The narrative film is too rich and varied to be encompassed in the seamless prose of a closed system comparable to that of the avant-garde. . . . It just growed and growed so that today it has attracted the serious attention of some of the best minds throughout the world. At best, the avant-garde cinema is an eccentric reaction to the narrative cinema.[2]

Sarris, unlike Macdonald, does not accept the divine right of the avant-garde to be the sole source of artistic excellence in cinema and the arts generally. Sarris has devoted most of his critical activity to the rehabilitation and defence of Hollywood cinema, admittedly in terms of selected directors, but with a firm rejection of Macdonald's wholesale denigration of Hollywood. The exact nature of Sarris' rehabilitation of Hollywood cinema will be explored later, but his main position vis-à-vis the 'problem' of Hollywood is succinctly put in a collection of essays called *The Primal Screen*:

> . . . film for film, director for director, the American cinema has been consistently superior to that of the rest of the world from 1915 thro' 1962 . . . [it is] . . . the only cinema in the world worth exploring in depth beneath the frosting of a few great directors at the top.[3]

He dismisses the dominant high-culture thesis about Hollywood production as a crude conspiracy theory: 'Somewhere on the western shores of the United States, a group of men have gathered to rob the cinema of its birthright'.[4] In Sarris' view, the movie moguls created in Hollywood one of the greatest concentrations of technical, human and economic resources ever assembled for the purposes of cultural production. Though this system attracted its fair share of mediocre hacks, it also attracted a number of directors who managed to impose their own highly creative personal style on the studio system:

> These are the directors who have transcended their technical problems with a personal vision of the world. To speak of any of their names is to evoke a self-contained world with its own laws and landscapes. They were also fortunate enough to find the proper conditions and collaborators for the full expression of their talent.[5]

Sarris did not singlehandedly create the new critical assessment of Hollywood. He was part of a revaluation that had a number of features. For example, Robert Warshow's work on genre had established that the Western and the gangster possessed conventions that were as complex as those of 'Elizabethan revenge tragedy and Restoration comedy'.[6] In many respects this genre and conventions approach applies to cinema a methodology derived from Aristotelian literary criticism. Instead of seeing Hollywood production as an undifferentiated cultural nightmare, Warshow and others showed that in the same way that ancient tragedy and comedy possessed distinctive conventions, characters and social themes, Hollywood production also had a range of constituent genres: screwball comedy, the Western, the gangster film. This genre and conventions approach raised the whole status of Hollywood's artistic potential. John Ford's Westerns were really modern versions of Homeric epic, the satirical brilliance of comedies like *Bringing Up Baby* by Howard Hawks was on a par with that of Aristophanes or Restoration Comedy.[7] Alongside this genre and conventions approach emerged a fine-arts-based criticism that sought to establish the pictorial virtues of film as a complex system of visual signs. Film, like painting, was a medium in which character, social milieu and physical place could be created through the use of iconographic and colour codes. Dialogue was relegated to secondary status. Ed Buscombe's article on 'The Idea of

Genre in the American Cinema' and the Western in particular gives the following examples of cinematic pictorialism:

> There are also certain clothes for specialist occupations: boot-lace ties for gamblers, black gloves for psychopathic hired guns; a man who wears a watch-chain is often a judge, and a black hat can denote a preacher; a bowler, a newspaperman. For women, there are usually only two sorts of clothes: wide full skirts and tight bodices, or the more tomboyish jeans and shirt. (There is a third costume usually reserved for the Mexican girl or prostitute – often synonymous – in which the bodice is looser and the neckline appreciably lower.)[8]

The reconciliation between high and mass culture that these various revaluations of Hollywood's artistic status sought to establish had been anticipated in Hollywood's own mythology. In Walt Disney's 1940 production of *Fantasia* Mickey Mouse mounts the sacred podium of the classical music conductor and shakes hands with Leopold Stokowski. Andrew Sarris' route to an unequivocal celebration of the artistic glories within Hollywood cinema was more circuitous. He had to go to Paris and absorb the teachings of a group of French critics and film-makers before he could proclaim 'the sacred importance of the cinema'[9] in such works as *The American Cinema: Directors and Directions 1929–1968*.

As resident film critic for *Village Voice*, Sarris belongs to the world of minority journals of opinion that have played such a significant role in mediating cultural attitudes to an audience largely composed of college-educated Americans. The contradiction in his approach is that he has used a minority journal to proclaim the artistic values of mass culture. In his writings film directors such as John Ford, Howard Hawks, Fritz Lang and Jean Renoir, emerge as self-conscious artists whose films should be evaluated in the same terms as the novels of Henry James or the plays of Shakespeare. At the centre of his critical method is the auteur theory, which makes the same artistic claims on behalf of directors working within the commercial studio system as Romanticism makes on behalf of the individual creativity of the single artist. In the same way that a poem by Wordsworth exhibits a set of 'Wordsworthian' characteristics, revealed in certain stylistic qualities, images and recurring thematic preoccupations, such as nature, childhood and memory, Hollywood film directors can achieve similar effects over a series of films. In order to achieve auteur status, that high degree of artistic control over all the various technical elements within cinematic production, directors must fulfil the following conditions:

> Over a group of films a director must exhibit certain recurring characteristics of style which serve as his signature. Because so much of the American cinema is commissioned, a director is forced to express his personality through the visual treatment of the material, rather than through the literary content of the material.[10]

In his reworking of the aesthetic of Romanticism, the personal vision of the director is a dominant though repressed force that in the main shows itself in 'the visual treatment of the material' rather than in the content of the story line. In Sarris' view, the Hollywood system places all kinds of controls over the content of a film, forcing the auteur director to express himself in the look of a film, its visual style. This Hollywood system of controls and permissions has almost by default created a rich repertoire of visual styles. Sarris is happy with this fortunate accident in that he has always favoured an aesthetic in which there is 'a preoccupation with form for its own sake'. As a result he does not see film as a medium that has successfully lent itself to sociological or political statement. His spirit is formalist and romantic, an approach he summarised as follows:

> It would seem that my strongest instincts are Christian rather than Marxist and that I believe more in personal redemption than social revolution. . . . The ascending and descending staircases of Hitchcock are more meaningful than all the Odessa steps.[11]

This emphasis on the ability of the auteur director to create both a personal visual style and an individual vision of the world, despite the controls over individual initiative with which the Hollywood studio system surrounds the director, is at the heart of the hieratic ranking of directors that is basic to Sarris' criticism. A film by John Ford or Alfred Hitchcock is immediately recognisable not only through its visual style but through the recurrence of certain thematic preoccupations, pictorially conveyed. John Ford's concern with community and family is as characteristic of his films as Hitchcock's morality is of his. Hitchcock insists: 'almost intolerantly, upon a moral reckoning for

his characters and for his audience. We can violate the Command-
ments at our own psychic peril, but we must pay the price in guilt at
the end.'[12] By a whole range of stylistic and thematic cues the auteur
director reminds the audience of the whole range of his work. In
Hitchcock we wait for and expect the moment when he will make a
fleeting walk-on appearance. In Ford, we expect and speculate about
the nature of the variation upon the theme of community that a
particular film will execute. The visual style in which these thematic
preoccupations are explored is probably, in Sarris' view, the clearest
indication of the director's 'personal signature'. Hitchcock's mastery
of style is described as follows:

> His films abound with objects as visual correlatives – the missing
> finger in 'The 39 Steps', the crashing cymbals (not symbols) in both
> versions (1935 and 1956) of 'The Man Who Knew Too Much', the
> milk chocolates on the assembly line in 'Secret Agent' . . . these
> objects embody the feelings and fears of characters as object and
> character interact with each other in dramas within dramas.[13]

Visual style is therefore paramount in auteur directors, whose
qualities Sarris summarised as follows: 'These are the directors who
have transcended their technical problems with a personal vision of
the world. To speak of any of their names is to evoke a self-contained
world with its own laws and landscapes.'[14]

The broad detail of the way Sarris constructed his model of artistic
achievement in Hollywood appears in *The American Cinema: Directors
and Directions 1929–1968* (1968). Topping his pyramid are the auteur
directors who constitute a pantheon of excellence by which all other
directors are judged. Other categories (in descending order of merit)
are 'The Far Side of Paradise', 'Expressive Esoterica', 'Fringe
Benefits', 'Less Than Meets the Eye', and 'Strained Seriousness'.
This personal hierarchy has powerfully influenced the critical
assessment of mainstream Hollywood cinema from the 1930s to the
1960s when the film-making careers of many of the directors he placed
at the top of his cinematic pyramid came to an end. Sarris'
judgements owe much to the revaluations of Hollywood that were
made by French critics and film-makers. The critical reputations of
Howard Hawks, Nicholas Ray, Douglas Sirk, Samuel Fuller and
Alfred Hitchcock were powerfully enhanced by the support they
received from leading French directors such as Truffaut and Godard,

whose films often paid direct homage to Hollywood genres like the thriller, and culminated in guest appearances in their films by these aging directors and American actors like Jack Palance.[15] Out of this network of revaluations two distinct features emerge in Sarris' own preferences: firstly a high estimate of émigré European directors such as Fritz Lang and Douglas Sirk who brought into the Hollywood repertoire the full range of high-romantic, melodramatic, expressionist techniques of German cinema in particular; and secondly an equally high estimate of the action-oriented formulae of such home-grown American directors as Howard Hawks, and John Ford, who practise a 'good, clean, direct, functional cinema, perhaps the most distinctively American cinema of all'.[16]

This reassessment of Hollywood cinema is not, as has been often suggested, the inverted snobbery of new wave film-makers and critics deliberately seeming to outrage conventional opinion by praising the frankly commercial products of Hollywood. On the contrary, it is quite clear from Sarris' ranking procedures that there is a clear discrepancy between his view of Hollywood excellence and the popular or commercial view. If one compares Sarris' assessments mediated through minority journals of opinion such as *Film Culture* and *Village Voice* with those of such mass circulation magazines as *Newsweek*, a clear difference regarding Hollywood cinema emerges. In its 9 January 1956 survey of the Hollywood scene, *Newsweek* highlighted the imminent release of John Huston's *Moby Dick* as the main event of the year. The article went on to name William Wyler, George Stevens, Fred Zinnemann and Billy Wilder along with Huston as the top five directors in Hollywood. With the exception of George Stevens, who is somewhat grudgingly admitted into Sarris' second-ranking category ('The Far Side of Paradise') only on the basis of his films of the 1930s and 1940s, Sarris relegates the other directors praised by *Newsweek* for their combination of box office success and serious artistic concern to one of his more damning categories, 'Less Than Meets the Eye'. In this category, Sarris puts the directors with reputations in excess of inspirations. 'In retrospect, it always seems that the personal signatures to their films were written with invisible ink.'[17] It is rare for films that are highly rated by Sarris to have figured in the top ten box office successes for any one year. Many of the '25 Most Memorable Art Films', named by Sarris in a *Village Voice* round-up, 18 December 1978, did not meet with popular success but have in the light of Sarris' and other auteur-influenced critical revaluations been rated as highly important. These include *Johnny Guitar* by Nicholas Ray and *Magnificent Obsession* by Douglas Sirk (1954), *The Searchers* by John Ford (1956) and *Touch of Evil* by Orson Welles and *Man of the West* by Anthony Mann (1958). Sometimes, of course, popular and critical assessment coincide as in John Ford's 1936 Academy Award winning version of John Steinbeck's novel, *The Grapes of Wrath*, but in the main Sarris has been engaged in the critical action of rescuing neglected masterpieces: 'A reminder of movies to be resurrected, of genres to be redeemed, or directors to be rediscovered.'[18]

Auteur criticism has not entirely closed the gap between high and mass art, it has created a revisionist 'great tradition' of neglected masterpieces that did not succeed in popular commercial terms. This element of revisionist cult raising is an explicit part of Sarris' strategy of rehabilitating the hidden masterpieces of Hollywood cinema, a tactic he openly devised from a 'fateful year in Paris' in 1961 and his contact with the *Cahiers du Cinéma* group:

> I have never really recovered from the Parisian heresy (in New York eyes) concerning the sacred importance of the cinema. Hence I returned to New York not merely a cultist but a subversive cultist with a foreign ideology.[19]

The function of the cult auteur directors that Sarris establishes, Ford, Hawks, Welles and so on, is to provide, like a modernist avant-garde, critical models of excellence. However, unlike a modernist avant-garde that is in part motivated by the desire for continual formal experimentation, Hollywood auteur directors work within standard mass-culture narrative formulae. Their artistry lies in their ability to insinuate their own personal vision and aesthetic into stereotypical mass-cultural formulae. Thus Sarris praises Hawks for stamping: 'His distinctively bitter view of life on adventure, gangster, and private-eye melodramas, Westerns, musicals, and screwball comedies, the kind of thing Americans do best and appreciate least'.[20] The auteur-influenced critic of Hollywood continually emphasises the ability of certain directors to 'subvert' or 'transcend' mass-culture formulae, to play ironically and ambiguously with the mechanical procedures of melodrama:

> The purpose of criticism becomes therefore to uncover behind the

superficial contrasts of subject and treatment, a structural hard core of basic and often recondite motifs. The pattern formed by these motifs, which may be stylistic or thematic, is what gives an author's work its particular structure, both defining it internally and distinguishing one body of work from another.[21]

The enhanced status of auteur Hollywood directors that Sarris and others have promoted, this ability of a director 'to evoke a self-contained world with its own laws and landscapes' is well conveyed by Philip French's gloss on John Ford:

During the credit titles of 'How the West Was Won' the vast Cinerama screen is filled with the words 'The Civil War directed by John Ford'. The audience invariably laughs, I imagine. Yet at the same time they recognise a certain ironic truth.[22]

In his review of John Ford's 1962 Western, *The Man Who Shot Liberty Valance*, Sarris closed his analysis on the following high note:

'The Man Who Shot Liberty Valance' must be ranked along with 'Lola Montes' and 'Citizen Kane' as one of the enduring masterpieces of that cinema which has chosen to focus on the mystical processes of time.[23]

It is time to explore the validity of such claims on behalf of Hollywood cinema.

In the closing sequence of *The Man Who Shot Liberty Valance*, as the steam train moves towards the East through settled landscape away from the Western town of Shinbone, Senator Ransom Stoddard, played by James Stewart, has the following exchange with his wife Hallie, played by Vera Miles:

STODDARD: Hallie, Hallie, would you be too sorry if, once I get the new irrigation bill through, would you be too sorry if we just up and left Washington? I . . . I sort of have a hankering to come back here to live. Maybe open up a law office.

HALLIE: Ranse. If you knew how often I've dreamed of it. My roots are here. I guess my heart is here. Yes, let's come back. Look at it. It was once a wilderness, now it's a garden. Aren't you proud?

RANSE: Hallie who . . . who put the cactus roses on Tom's coffin?
HALLIE: I did.[24]

In the course of the film so many of the themes, explicitly summarised in this denouement, have affected the main action and individual characterisation that this closing scene can serve as a distillation of the film's treatment of the Western genre. Senator Stoddard is an Eastern symbol of progress and civilisation, turning arid landscape into a fertile garden of Eden with his 'new irrigation Bill'. As a lawyer he is also specifically the bringer of order to Shinbone, a volatile frontier town of violence and anarchy. He is not, however, a totally confident symbol of civilisation, one of the many adjustments that Ford makes to the standard stereotypes employed by the Western. Stoddard exhibits a certain hesitancy and tentativeness, clearly signalled by his habit of pausing and repeating himself in such characteristic phrases as 'I . . . I sort of' and 'Who . . . who put'. This kind of liberal stutter and shuffling hesitancy was a hallmark of Stewart's acting style and is in clear contrast to the bluff decisive persona of the other main male character in the film, Tom Doniphon, played, not surprisingly, and with anachronistic relish, by John Wayne.

At the beginning of the film, Stoddard and his wife have returned to Shinbone for Tom Doniphon's funeral. As the famous senator and assorted human relics of the town's old frontier days gather round Tom Doniphon's starkly simple pauper's coffin, the Senator, prompted by the town's newspapermen, who are nonplussed by the famous Senator's presence at an obscure funeral, explains why he has come. He recalls the life and times of the years preceding 1876 when Shinbone was still a territory, not a state. Through his memories the film unfolds backwards from the present like a reconstructed chronicle. The story that the film enacts has the following elements. Stoddard arrives in Shinbone as a penniless law graduate from the East, hoping to establish the town's first law firm. Just outside Shinbone his stagecoach is held up by outlaws led by a sadistic gunman incongruously called Liberty Valance, played by Lee Marvin. He savagely rejects Stoddard's appeals for fair play and brutally beats him near to death, hurling his law books to the ground in absolute contempt. Tom Doniphon, an independent small ranch-holder, finds Stoddard on the road and brings him to Shinbone, where Stoddard takes a job in a restaurant called Peter's Place, where Hallie works as a waitress. Although Stoddard suffers continual humiliation from both Tom Doniphon and Liberty Valance, particularly for taking a job in the restaurant and wearing an apron to wash dishes, a woman's role, he gradually gains respect from the townspeople, starts a school, and becomes the champion of the farmers and townspeople who wish to transform the unfenced territory into a fully fledged state. These aspirations are directly challenged by Liberty Valance, the hired gunman of the cattle interests who wish to keep the land as an open range. Valance succeeds in terrorising the supporters of statehood to the point where only his removal will enable democracy to succeed. Stoddard becomes the reluctant hero who challenges Valance and surprisingly kills him in a personal shoot-out. The next step on the road that will transform society from raw nature to civilisation is the convention for statehood. Stoddard is the chosen delegate of the townspeople and farmers and is on the verge of winning the ballot when he is denounced as a man with blood on his hands, unfit for public office. He withdraws, only to be taken aside by Doniphon who tells him that he, Doniphon, really killed Valance with a rifle shot from a side alley. Stoddard with a clear conscience goes on to political success and marries Hallie.

As can be deduced from this brief summary of the main action, the morality of Stoddard's behaviour is distinctly flawed, and therefore any interpretation of the film that fails to give a generous space to the whole series of ironic questionings of the moral basis of the progressive civilisation that comes to Shinbone during the course of the film, omits an important revisionary dimension to Ford's treatment of the Western theme. In one sense civilisation is built on an act of shame which is then turned into an heroic legend. The murder of Valance is not the classic equal confrontation between two men. Valance is gunned down by three men, Stoddard, Doniphon and Pompey, Doniphon's black servant. Doniphon is quite clear about the nature of the act when he comments: 'It was cold blooded murder and I can live with it'.[25] Despite Doniphon's pragmatism, the incident unhinges his swaggering certainty and in a state of depression over losing Hallie to Stoddard and the breaking of his code of personal honour by shooting someone from the shadows of a side alley, he sets fire to the ranch-house on to which he had built an extension in preparation for his marriage to Hallie. His apparently implacable will has been so broken by events that were it not for Pompey rescuing him from the fire, the suggestion is that he would have immolated himself in a symbolic blaze of suicidal defeat, hardly the behaviour of the classic Western hero.

What emerges from a close analysis of the action and characterisation of *The Man Who Shot Liberty Valance* is a continual ironic subversion and questioning of the whole range of foundation myths that constitute the ideological core of the majority of Hollywood Westerns. Ford himself had articulated this affirming national mythology in a series of earlier Westerns, like *Wagonmaster* (1950), that celebrated the theme of westward expansion: 'In the work of Ford we see the celebration of a vast panorama of the American past. We see the American dream as it inspired immigrants and pioneers: the dream of an ideal moral community.[26] The two basic creation myths around which so many American values cluster are those of the building of social order and community on the one hand, and the importance of heroic individualism on the other. Ford's Westerns often point up this dualism, but his treatment of these two potentially contradictory elements is particularly inventive and dialectical. The following map of dialectical tensions that runs through *The Man Who Shot Liberty Valance* and many Westerns is instructive:

> Order/anarchy, East/West, Civilisation/Savagery, Stoddard/Valance, train/horse, stagecoach/buckboard, law book/gun, coffee/whiskey, shoes/boots, words/action, fences/open range, statehood/territory, rose/cactus-rose, fame/anonymity, prosperity/poverty, life/death.

The interaction of these basic propositions and conflicts creates the dynamics of the Western form, and although these abstractions can be located in specific time and place, and the West is often lovingly reconstructed in rich documentary detail, the Western form by nature inhabits universal rather than local environments. Such grand conflicts as that between savagery and civilisation cannot be compressed into a single historical moment or afternoon. Therefore, the Western deals in generalised images of history, and mythologies. Scott, the editor of the *Shinbone Star*, to whom Senator Stoddard initially addresses his revisionist tale, pinpoints this quality in the Western, when he rejects the opportunity to publish the real story about the identity of *The Man Who Shot Liberty Valance*, preferring to preserve the platonic fiction: 'This is the West, sir. When the legend becomes fact, print the legend.'

In *The Man Who Shot Liberty Valance* Ford uses the basic pattern of dualistic conflicts in the Western form to create an ironic shifting interplay between appearance and reality. Although the forces of progress are in the ascendant at the end of the film, so many questions have been raised as to the morality of that ascendancy that the price of progress seems high. The pathetic image of Tom Doniphon's crude pauper's coffin, on which a cactus rose is isolated in full frame, symbolises Doniphon's reductive fate, which is out of all proportion to his heroic role in Stoddard's success. Although Doniphon's individualistic skills are anachronistic and redundant in the new civilisation of law and organised community politics that has come to Shinbone, his memory creates guilt and uneasiness among the group who have gathered round the coffin. Ford is clearly chipping away at the foundation myths of American society, myths he himself projected, questioning the whole dynamic of liberal social progress. Ford is also questioning the process by which a society, through myth, deliberately distorts the nature of history in order to promote the forces of progress. The contradictions and ambiguities Ford reveals in the American myth of progress are achieved without sacrificing or collapsing the classic components of the Western genre. In many ways, the genre form lends itself to infinite subtle variations on well-established themes, actions, characters and locations. An audience comes to a Western with certain expectations, some of which may be fulfilled, but this audience can also be led in new directions:

> Hollywood genre production tended both to foreground convention and stereotypicality in order to gain instant audience recognition of its type – this is a Western, a Gangster, a Woman's Picture, etc. – and to institute a type of aesthetic play among the conventions in order to keep them coming back – not 'what is going to happen next?' to which they would already have the answer, but 'how?'[27]

A classic example of this phenomenon is Hollywood's depiction of male heroes at war with the contradictions of their personality. Hollywood cinema provides a whole gallery of these types, in which the demands of society and culture are at odds with a cult of individualism. In *The Man Who Shot Liberty Valance*, these issues are spread over the three characters of Stoddard, Doniphon and Valance. Valance, of course, exhibits no play of contradictions, but his violence is contrasted with the culture and civil order of Stoddard. Doniphon's character is full of contradiction: his swaggering machismo is threatened by the possibility of marriage and domestication, and he is clearly troubled by the new social order that is taming Shinbone's wildness. Stoddard hesitates between violence and a pacifist turning of the cheek (Plate 1). These contradictions are part of a master design in which Ford's obvious relish for the positive qualities of untamed nature and individualism is set against the dominant ideology of culture and social progress. Not only can Ford draw upon the audience's knowledge of his own earlier versions of this dialectic, Hollywood cinema in a number of genres had created a whole series of figures caught in a nature-culture bind. Clark Gable developed the type in a series of films made in the 1930s, but particularly in *Red Dust* (1932) and *China Seas* (1935). In both films Gable plays an expatriate soldier-of-fortune, who, like Huckleberry Finn, flees from civilised society. The films are disguised Westerns, in which colonial imperialism in Asia duplicates the expansion westward across the American continent of the classic Western. Gable's attitude to the idea of social ties emerges strongly in his attitude to his prostitute girlfriend, played by Jean Harlow. In *China Seas*, Gable sets the following clear limits to the relationship: 'Look, Dolly, we've been friends, and there's no question you're the number one girl in the archipelago, but I don't recall making any vows or asking for any'.[28] Despite his desire to remain unentangled by social obligations or personal ties, the characters played by Gable are usually absorbed into society at the end of the film.

Clearly, Hollywood faced both ways on the issue of wildness versus civilisation, as in its depiction of reluctant heroes such as Terry Malloy, the boxer hero of *On the Waterfront*, who can take the world on with his fists, but also tenderly breeds pigeons, or that most celebrated man of divided loyalties, the night club owner hero of *Casablanca*, Rick. Rick conceals his idealism and personal romanticism behind a pragmatic cynical exterior. In conversation with Renault, the Casablanca police chief, Rick carefully links his political idealism to economic self-interest, in order to preserve his apparent freedom from dangerous emotional ties, ideological or personal:

RENAULT: In 1935, you ran guns to Ethiopia.
   In 1936, you fought in Spain on the Loyalist side.
RICK: And got paid well for it on both occasions.

This range of fictional hero types, in which the outlaw stands alongside the law-giver, constitutes a catch-all paradoxical national folklore, whose ideological dynamic Norman Mailer, in an essay occasioned by Kennedy's Presidency, described as follows:

> . . . America was also the country in which the dynamic myth of the Renaissance – that every man was potentially extra-ordinary – knew its most passionate persistence. Simply, America was the land where people still believed in heroes: George Washington; Billy the Kid; Lincoln, Jefferson; Mark Twain, Jack London, Hemingway; Joe Louis, Dempsey. (*PP*, p. 52)

The tensions within a populist pantheon that can include boxers and statesmen prompted Daniel Boorstin to remark: 'Never did a more incongruous pair than Davy Crockett and George Washington live together in a national Valhalla'.[29]

The importance of this theme and debate on the nature of the relationship between social progress and individualism not only constituted a major theme in Hollywood, but surfaced as a major preoccupation in a number of books that laid one of the foundations of American Studies as a discipline. R. W. B. Lewis in his study of the hero in nineteenth-century literature, *The American Adam* (1955), abstracted the following archetype from a range of sources:

> An individual emancipated from history, happily bereft of ancestry, untouched and undefiled by the usual inheritances of family and race; an individual standing alone, self-reliant and self-propelling, ready to confront whatever awaited him with the aid of his own unique and inherent resources.[30]

The similarities between Shane, the reluctant hero of George Stevens' 1953 Western, and Lewis' hero-model are striking. Shane seems to have no past and though during the course of the film he hesitates between separateness and communal obligations, at the end of the film he chooses to ride on alone into the wilderness.

The energies of this Western hero, who succeeds in throwing off the iron laws of environmental and societal conditioning through the myth of self-reliant individualism, were not always seen as productive. In his 1950 study of Western literature and culture, *Virgin Land: The American West as Symbol and Myth*, Henry Nash Smith, while acknowledging the democratic possibilities of the Western myth, also questions the social value of a mythology which:

> Throws the hero back in upon himself and accentuates his terrible and sublime isolation. He is an anarchic and self-contained atom – hardly even a monad – alone in a hostile, or at best a neutral, universe.[31]

John Ford's Westerns, like *The American Adam* and *Virgin Land*, critically examine America's foundation myths of individualism and community.

Ford began to explore the Western theme in the silent era. Lindsay Anderson, in his recent book on Ford, reports these early Westerns as follows: 'He began making Westerns in 1917, when he was twenty-two. "I can't remember much about them, now," he said. "We made about one a week. I directed them and Harry Carey acted them." '[32] A second period of making Westerns began in 1939 with *Stagecoach*, and finished in 1964 with *Cheyenne Autumn*. Like Fenimore Cooper's novels on the West, or Faulkner's on the South, Ford's Westerns are 'inextricably linked in an awesome network of meanings and associations'.[33] What is now clear from the extensive work that has been done on all aspects of Ford's Westerns is the extent to which his view of the West is a revisionary one. The mood constantly changes: 'Compare, for instance, the Wyatt Earp of 'My Darling Clementine' – upright, devout, courageous – with the Wyatt Earp of 'Cheyenne Autumn' – decadent, dissolute and cowardly'.[34] This shifting assessment of character and history is particularly striking if one examines the roles played by John Wayne in successive Westerns by John Ford. From the maverick heroics of the Ringo Kid in *Stagecoach* (1939) through the various inflections of chivalric militarism in the cavalry trilogy *Fort Apache* (1948), *She Wore a Yellow Ribbon* (1949) and *Rio Grande* (1950), to the bitter despair of Ethan Edwards in *The Searchers* (1956), John Wayne has been an index of Ford's transformation of the myth and genre. There are, however, limits to Ford's revisionism that culminated in *Cheyenne Autumn*, his 1964 portrait of the wrongs done to the Indians. If one places Ford's treatment of America's foundation myths alongside Christopher Lasch's analysis of the same historical materials, one can clearly see where Ford's revisionism ends and a more ruthless demystification begins. Lasch sees the heroic myth of the West as a sublimated cultural fig leaf for an unparalleled assault on nature and Indians:

> In the heat of the struggle to win the West, the American pioneer gave full vent to his rapacity and murderous cruelty, but he always envisioned the result – not without misgivings, expressed in a nostalgic cult of lost innocence – as a peaceful, respectable, churchgoing community safe for his women and children. He imagined that his offspring, raised under the morally refining influence of feminine 'culture', would grow up to be sober, law-abiding, domesticated American citizens, and the thought of the advantages they would inherit justified his toil and excused, he thought, his frequent lapses into brutality, sadism, and rape.[35]

15. The Politics and Aesthetics of Modernism

ONE of the major strategies, developed by such critics as Dwight Macdonald, in order to preserve aesthetic quality within mass industrial societies, was an unrepentant defence of an experimental minority avant-garde. Much of the support for this defence of the 'old avant-garde of 1870–1930, from Rimbaud to Picasso' (*AAG*, p. 56) and its successors, is generated out of a comparison between the complex forms and effects of an experimental avant-garde and those of mass culture. Whereas a high-culture avant-garde places 'high value on the careful communication of mood and feeling, on introspection rather than action, and on subtlety, so that much of the culture's content can be perceived and understood on several levels',[1] mass culture has forms and effects that do not involve the audience in analysis and discrimination. Mass culture is full of 'built-in' reactions and is characterised by 'standardisation, stereotypy, conservatism, mendacity, manipulated consumer goods'.[2] Avant-garde culture combines a high degree of innovation and experimentation in form with an inexhaustible fund of possible meanings. Mass culture by contrast is not concerned with ambiguities of meaning, or the technical processes of art; it provides finished 'statements' leaving no room for complexity. Clearly this orthodoxy has been challenged by such figures as Andrew Sarris, who has sought to show how directors like John Ford and Howard Hawks have insinuated complexity of meaning and form into the action-oriented popular cinema. Nevertheless, the myth of an experimental avant-garde became so important in American culture in the late 1940s and 1950s that its incarnation in the work of a highly experimental group of New York painters – Jackson Pollock, Willem de Kooning, Mark Rothko,

Arshile Gorky and others – appeared to confirm the vitality and validity of the theory of an avant-garde, advanced by such critics as Clement Greenberg.

The actual historical record of reactions to an experimental modernistic avant-garde in America is one of hostility, until the period after the Second World War, when the Abstract Expressionist painters of New York became internationally accepted and championed. Since then New York, in particular, has been the patron and source of a highly successful avant-garde that has generated a rapid succession of styles and schools:

> A new style has managed to establish itself there every two or three years, in the rough sequence: abstract expressionism – post-painterly abstraction (hard edge and colour field) – kinetic and op art – pop art and assemblage – environments and happenings – minimalism, conceptualism and documentary art – and photorealism.[3]

This picture of burgeoning creativity and success is a far cry from the almost universal hostility that greeted the first major public show of the non-realistic, non-figurative modernist movement in America, the Armory Show of 1913.[4] Theodore Roosevelt's comment on seeing at the Exhibition Marcel Duchamp's abstract painting 'Nude Descending a Staircase', that it reminded him of a Navajo blanket, was typical of the incomprehension and ridicule that the patron class in America exhibited towards abstract art. Further standard reactions were expressed in 1923 by Royal Cortissoz, art critic for the *New York Tribune*, who saw the dominance of European modernism in the show as a dangerous invasion and adulteration of the white Anglo-Saxon protestant core of American culture. Cortissoz dubbed modernism 'Ellis Island Art' and set his remarks in the context of the debate on immigration quotas that led to restrictive legislation in 1924. He saw the United States as being invaded: 'By aliens, thousands of whom constitute so many acute perils of the body politic. Modernism is of precisely the same heterogeneous alien origin and is imperilling the republic of art in the same way.'[5] With hindsight, it is exactly the dynamic of this interaction between immigrants and great cities that has been seen as a positive creative stimulus to the formation of an avant-garde:

> Certain factors in avant-garde culture, and especially the conscious

breaks from 'traditional' styles, have to be analysed not only in formal terms but within the sociology of metropolitan encounters and associations between immigrants who share no common language but that of the metropolis.[6]

Although the marginality of a self-conscious avant-garde is often seen as an important creative characteristic within minority groups whose art is created out of an antagonism towards mass taste, American modernism was almost pathological in its isolation. This image of marginality can be seen in the small coteries of experiment that gathered around such figures as the photographer Alfred Stieglitz and his Gallery 291 in New York, and Harriet Monroe's magazine *Poetry* in Chicago. The triumphs of experiment in Europe, such as Cubism and Surrealism, intensified the provincial status of American modernism in the 1920s. It was characteristic of this period that American modernism depended on expatriates in Paris or London. Ezra Pound, T. S. Eliot and Ernest Hemingway followed the expatriate road taken by the earlier generation of Henry James, John Singer Sargent, and James Macneil Whistler. It seemed that what happened in Gertrude Stein's sitting room in Paris would always be more important to American avant-garde developments than what might occur in the aesthetically conservative circles of New York, Chicago or even less likely, of Boston.

The cause of modernism in America suffered a further set-back with the coming of the Great Depression in the 1930s. Roosevelt's New Deal included government support for the arts, which in the case of painting isolated large-scale figurative public murals as the major sponsored form. Many of the artists who became the leading figures in the Abstract Expressionist movement after the Second World War – Jackson Pollock, Willem de Kooning, Arshile Gorky and Mark Rothko – participated in the public mural programme. The murals that were produced as decoration for airports, post offices and other public buildings usually celebrated in a realistic style heroic episodes in American history. Scenes of industrial production, technological achievement or healthy sporting activity helped to create an image of affirmative struggle and of America's innate ability to overcome adverse economic conditions (Plate 2). By 1936 there were more than 6000 artists employed by the Works Progress Administration (WPA), each drawing $28 32 cents a week for producing commissioned work for the government. Predictably, many opponents of Roosevelt's

New Deal saw subversive elements in the programme, particularly when, as in San Francisco, the murals celebrated workers and labour struggles. Another kind of criticism of the mural programme was developed with hindsight by supporters of American modernism such as Harold Rosenberg. Rosenberg, who himself served within the WPA writer's group, now sees the period of the mural movement as a disastrous one for the development of American painting. Painters were forced to produce a content-dominated realist art, which mechanically depicted 'pioneer and proletarian totems'.[7] Despite the presence of such expert muralists as the Mexican artist Diego Rivera and Orozoco as advisers, Rosenberg sees no formal inventiveness in the American mural movement, which is a 'debacle of class-conscious art, regional-scene painting, Americana, WPA history and other "communicating modes" '.[8] Public murals, whether commissioned by Stalin in Russia or Roosevelt in America, represent 'an ideological substitute for experience, a Ready-Made, suitable for packaged distribution'.[9] The realistic style favoured by the muralists is admirably suited to convey sentimental messages: 'patriotic and homey scenes of the folk and its heroes'.[10] As a style, WPA art reinforced the content-based sentimentality of the dominant realist tradition in American painting:

> Paintings of the American Scene have a natural appeal to the public and its political leaders, much of which is owing, no doubt, to sentiments aroused by their subjects; from Indians below a waterfall, or Pilgrims in the snow, to boys playing handball in a slum schoolyard.[11]

The role of any experimental avant-garde was thus distinctly marginal and precarious, in the political climate of the 1930s, in all fields of artistic activity. Although there was a modernist non-figurative tradition in American painting, kept alive by such painters as Georgia O'Keefe, Stuart Davis, John Marin and the founding in 1936 of the Association of American Abstract Artists,[12] home-grown modernism in painting never approached the virtuosity and consistent inventiveness of European painting:

> American painting, reluctant to depart from illustration or narrative, held strongly to the third dimension. Perspective was parted with very slowly, and even where it is merely vestigial as in the later

Marin, it is unmistakably there in a horizon line, a depth of sail, a clear array of objects placed one behind each other and separated by definable if not defined distances.[13]

For many critics, the breakthrough by American painters from provincial status to that of an avant-garde that began to lead rather than to follow modernist developments in Europe did not occur until the 'action' paintings of Jackson Pollock in the late 1940s and 1950s. After Pollock there ensued that proliferation of activity that succeeded in making New York rather than Paris the main location of avant-garde activity in world culture. Pollock's status as a model of American modernism and the critical controversies that surround his work and that of the Abstract Expressionists have become critical *causes célèbres* worth exploring in some detail.

In a film of Jackson Pollock at work, made by Hans Namuth in 1951, the soundtrack interleaves an atonal staccato modernist musical score by Morton Feldman with Pollock's own commentary on his working methods and evolution as an artist. Pollock's words offer such a direct entrance into his work that they are worth quoting in full:

My home is in Springs, East Hampton, Long Island. I was born in Cody, Wyoming, thirty-nine years ago. In New York I spent two years at the Art Students League with Tom Benton. He was a strong personality to react against. This was in 1929.

I don't work from drawings or color sketches. My painting is direct. I usually paint on the floor. I enjoy working on a large canvas. I feel more at home, more at ease in a big area. Having the canvas on the floor, I feel nearer, more a part of the painting. This way I can walk around it, work from all four sides, and be in the painting, similar to the Indian sand painters of the West. Sometimes I use a brush but often prefer using a stick. I like to use a dripping, fluid paint. I also use sand, broken glass, pebbles, string, nails and other foreign matter. My method of painting is a natural growth, out of a need. I want to express my feelings, rather than illustrate them. Technique is just a means of arriving at a statement.

When I am painting, I have a general notion as to what I am about. I can control the flow of the paint, there is no accident, just as there is no beginning and no end. Sometimes I lose a painting. But I have no fear of changes, of destroying the image. Because a painting has a life of its own, I try to let it live.

This is the first time I am using glass as a medium. I lost contact with my first painting on glass and I started another one.[14]

During the course of the film, we watch Pollock at work on a painting. He is working in the open air, crouching over and energetically moving around the painting which lies flat on the ground. He first arranges sand, broken glass and string over the sheet of glass. He then drips paint on to the surface in short bursts of controlled flow from a can (Plate 3). The technical and philosophical ideas, so succinctly and vividly expressed in the film, were the basis for Pollock being singled out as the supreme model of the American avant-garde artist who, in the late 1940s and 1950s, was seen to achieve a leading status in world art. As a result of his heroic energies, American painters no longer needed to defer to a superior European avant-garde. No longer need they be metaphorically 'Americans in Paris', since Paris had been dethroned as the major city of modernist culture. Although Pollock was considered the major figure, other painters in Pollock's circle, William de Kooning, Barnett Newman and Mark Rothko, known collectively as the 'Abstract Expressionists', also earned a fame and fortune that in the light of their earlier marginality must have seemed bizarre and arbitrary. The context to this reversal of fortunes has been the subject of endless debate and revision. One school, now led by Tom Wolfe, sees the promotion of these New York painters as an elitist commercial plot hatched by critics such as Clement Greenberg and Harold Rosenberg, who combined with dealers and patrons such as the heiress Peggy Guggenheim to foist their partisan arbitrary tastes on to a critically supine audience.[15] Another school, represented by Max Kozloff, now sees the championing of American abstract art in the 1940s and 1950s as a subtle but sinister reflection of Cold War propaganda: 'How fresh in memory even now is the belief that American art is the sole trustee of the avant-garde "spirit", a belief so reminiscent of the US government's notion of itself as the lone guarantor of capitalist liberty'.[16] The speed with which Pollock moved from the marginal world of minority avant-garde circles to a full-colour spread in the mass circulation magazine *Life*, suggests that there was an uncritical momentum in American culture to find great

American artists. In the 8 August 1949 edition of *Life* a photograph of Pollock is captioned as follows:

> Jackson Pollock: is he the greatest living painter in the United States? Recently a formidable high-brow New York critic hailed the brooding, puzzled-looking man shown above as a major artist of our time and a fine candidate to become 'the greatest American painter of the 20th century'.[17]

Despite Pollock's belief that the idea of a uniquely American painting is as absurd as 'a purely American mathematics or physics',[18] there is no doubt that New York painters of his generation were promoted not only for purely commercial reasons, but also for the ideological ones suggested by Kozloff. Despite these factors, the major retrospective of Pollock's work in Paris at the Centre Charles Pompidou in 1982, and his obvious influence on world painting, demands an interpretation that looks as closely at his paintings as at the motives of his sponsors.

Pollock's contribution to an international modernism can be abstracted from the film of him at work in 1951. Firstly, there is his use of large canvases that not only break away from the tradition of vertical easel painting, but also create visual environments that cannot be taken in by the normal field of human vision. This is not unique to Pollock. Michelangelo's Sistine Chapel, for example, cannot be taken in at a single glance, but Michelangelo's paintings can be read and broken up into historical episodes and small narrative units. Pollock's paintings, particularly in the drip-technique period between 1947 and 1951, are like single fields or environments that cannot be broken up into discrete narrative units, or a visible beginning and end. This particular quality of Pollock's large abstract canvases has been succinctly summarised by Clement Greenberg. Pollock's effects are created: 'By optical rather than pictorial means: by relations of color and shape largely divorced from descriptive connotations, and often by manipulations in which top and bottom, as well as foreground and background, become inter-changeable'.[19] Instead of the certainties of pictorial incidents that tell a story in the tradition of narrative, figurative realism, Pollock's avant-garde modernism signals a disruption of the illusion of three-dimensional space, that goes beyond the disruptions of Cubism. Pollock's paintings cause the eye trouble in 'locating central emphases'. The viewer: 'is more directly compelled to treat the whole of the surface as a single undifferentiated field of interest, and this in turn, compels us to feel and judge the picture more immediately in terms of its over-all unity' (*AC*, p. 137). Pollock's other main contribution to the shape of international modernism is his drip technique, which not only radically extended the repertoire of methods that a painter could employ to apply paint to a surface, but also the kinds of paint other than oil and watercolour that could be used. Pollock used a range of industrial paints, including enamel, and exploited the different viscosity of each paint. He did not pioneer these techniques. In 1938 he had worked alongside David Alfaro Siqueiros, who experimented with spray guns and airbrushes. But Pollock explored the technique to its limit.

What emerges from an analysis of Pollock's techniques and ideas is his ability to take hints from other artists and harness them to his own unique development. His opportunity to experience the methods and ideas of other avant-garde artists was to some extent the result of an accident of history. Many leading European artists, among them Léger, Miro, Mondrian, Lipchitz, Ernst and Breton, found refuge in New York from fascist persecution. As a result, Pollock was exposed to a rich émigré culture of modernism. Picasso's famous painting 'Guernica', which uses Cubist forms to express his horror at the bombing of the ancient Basque capital during the Spanish Civil War, was hung in New York's Museum of Modern Art from 1939. In a number of paintings such as 'Guardians of the Secret' and 'Pasiphae', dating from the early 1940s, Pollock's iconography and style are clearly influenced by Cubist forms and Surrealism's: 'concept of the source of art being the Unconscious'.[20] Pollock's early interest in the mythology of the American Indians of the South-West of the United States and the ritualistic techniques of their sand paintings gave him a direct entrance into a major feature of European avant-garde painting; its use of the masks and iconography of primitive art. Out of this amalgam of interests and influences, he created, between 1947 and 1951, his series of drip paintings, which constitute his major contribution to avant-garde culture.

The basic pattern of Pollock's development is fairly clear. In the 1930s, under the influence of the regionalist painter Thomas Hart Benton, he painted in the mainstream realist, scene-painting style that became the dominant aesthetic within the government-sponsored Mural Programme. Although virtually none of his roughly fifty recorded works commissioned by New Deal Arts Agencies have survived, a painting such as 'Going West' (*c*. 1934–38), clearly shows Pollock's ability to distance himself from the affirmative rhetoric of New Deal optimism that many artists, in all media, inserted into their work. In contrast to the closing scene of John Ford's film *The Grapes of Wrath*, in which Ma Joad evokes a never-say-die spirit of pioneering fortitude, Pollock's version of such creation myths is a landscape in which the basic elements of the myth have ground to a halt. The immigrant wagon, so often the image of pioneer optimism, lies abandoned and motionless, and a mule-train buckles under the strain of hauling a log. The atmosphere is one of stasis, dehumanisation and redundancy (Plate 4). What is interesting and contradictory is that the swirling curvilinear design of this painting from the 1930s reappears as a source of kinetic energy in the abstract paintings of the late 1940s. The relationship between 1930s realism and the shift into abstraction by many American painters in the 1940s and 1950s has become a critical *cause célèbre*, particularly in the work of the art critics, Clement Greenberg and Harold Rosenberg. Their essays on Pollock and the Abstract Expressionists played a considerable part in establishing the international reputation of New York avant-garde painting in the post-war period.

Clement Greenberg first drew attention to Jackson Pollock in a series of articles he wrote for a monthly journal, *The Nation* magazine, beginning in 1943. Pollock's intense preoccupation with new techniques coincided with Greenberg's search for an avant-garde model of creativity and practice that could disrupt the dominance, in modern industrial society, of mass culture. Greenberg's definition of the role of an avant-garde in a modern mass society was developed in a famous essay, 'Avant-Garde and Kitsch', first published in *Partisan Review* in 1939. The essay is a ringing declaration of support for the complex innovations and experiments of 'avant-garde aesthetics' (*AC*, p. 7). The main quality that Greenberg isolates within avant-garde practice is its ability to create an independent field of meaning and activity: 'Something valid solely on its own terms, in the way nature itself is valid, in the way a landscape – not its picture – is aesthetically valid; something given, increate, independent of meanings, similars or originals' (*AC*, p. 6). This drive to make the world of art an autonomous non-referential field had led avant-garde artists like Picasso away from an interest in content towards an interest in: 'the disciplines and processes of art and literature themselves' (*AC*, p. 6). By 'concentrating on the medium of his own craft', the avant-garde artist has created an aesthetic in which: 'content is to be dissolved so completely into form that the work of art or literature cannot be reduced in whole or in part to anything not itself' (*AC*, p. 6). Greenberg is unrepentant in his defence of this experimental non-representational avant-garde in which: 'Picasso, Braque, Mondrian, Miro, Kandinsky, Brancusi, even Klee, Matisse and Cezanne derive their chief inspiration from the medium they work in', and in which: 'Gide's most ambitious book is a novel about the writing of a novel' (*AC*, p. 7).

Greenberg's support for the small minority world of the avant-garde is all the more aggressive in that the avant-garde represents the only genuine alternative to the 'virulence' and 'irresistible attractiveness' (*AC*, p. 12) of the major cultural product of modern industrial society, a commodity that Greenberg calls 'kitsch'.

He gives the following examples of the varied forms kitsch can take:

> Popular, commercial art and literature with their chromeotypes, magazine covers, illustrations, ads, slick and pulp fiction, comics, Tin Pan Alley music, tap dancing, Hollywood movies, etc, etc. (*AC*, p. 9)

Kitsch, unlike avant-garde art, has no interest in the processes of art nor in ambiguity or complexity, it is only interested in emotional effects and: 'pre-digests art for the spectator and spares him effort, provides him with a short cut to the pleasure of art that detours what is necessarily difficult in genuine art' (*AC*, p. 15). Kitsch does have a relationship to avant-garde art but it is an entirely parasitic one:

> The pre-condition for kitsch, a condition without which kitsch would be impossible, is the availability close at hand of a fully matured cultural tradition, whose discoveries, acquisitions, and perfected self-consciousness kitsch can take advantage of for its own ends. It borrows from it devices, tricks, stratagems, rules of thumb, themes, converts them into a system, and discards the rest. (*AC*, p. 10) (See Plates 5 and 6)

The products of kitsch not only dominate in the field of mass culture, their corrosive operations can be detected in apparently unlikely places: 'A magazine like *The New Yorker*, which is fundamentally high-class kitsch for the luxury trade, converts and waters down a great deal of avant-garde material for its own use' (*AC*, p. 11). Kitsch because it 'has become an integral part of our productive system . . . capitalized at a tremendous investment' (*AC*, p. 11) needs an ever expanding market and obliterates any resistant alternatives it meets: 'Today the native of China, no less than the South American Indian, the Hindu, no less than the Polynesian, have come to prefer to the products of their native art, magazine covers, rotogravure sections and calendar girls' (*AC*, p. 12). For Greenberg the only counter to this tidal wave of kitsch, of 'vicarious experience and faked sensations' (*AC*, p. 10) is the avant-garde which, in his view, has to become the complex opposite of kitsch if genuine art is to survive at all in mass industrial society.

There is an important political dimension to the evolution of Greenberg's ideas, in that he arrived at his unrepentant defence of a minority avant-garde as a consequence of his involvement in the mass politics of the 1930s. Like Dwight Macdonald, Greenberg was dismayed not only by the repressive regime of Stalin but also by the cultural policy of the 'Popular Front' period during which an experimental modernism was denigrated as being pessimistic, lacking in mass appeal and therefore counter-revolutionary. The pages of *Partisan Review* in its anti-Stalinist Trotskyite period (1937–9) provided Greenberg with a platform to defend the revolutionary role of an experimental avant-garde that Stalin had repressed. This is the political context for Greenberg's account, in an essay on 'The Late Thirties in New York', of how the ground was prepared for the emergence of the New York School of painters: 'Some day it will have to be told how "anti-Stalinism", which started out more or less as "Trotskyism", turned into art for art's sake, and thereby cleared the way, heroically, for what was to come' (*AC*, p. 230). What came was Jackson Pollock and the Abstract Expressionists, whose status as the most important heirs of Cézanne and Picasso, Greenberg summarised in his 1955 essay ' "American-Type" Painting'.

In this essay, the avant-garde advances that Greenberg documents in the work of Arshile Groky, Barnett Newman, Willem de Kooning, Hans Hofmann, Mark Rothko and Jackson Pollock are almost exclusively technical. Their work illustrates what Greenberg sees as 'a law of modernism . . . that the conventions not essential to the viability of a medium be discarded as soon as they are recognized' (*AC*, p. 208). One striking result of this search for new techniques among these painters was 'the most direct attack yet on the easel convention' (*AC*, p. 225). The large formats that Newman, Pollock and Rothko worked on created a scale to their paintings 'so large that its enclosing edges would lay outside or only on the periphery of the artist's field of vision as he worked' (*AC*, p. 219). In contrast, the smaller scale of easel painting created pictures that 'sit there in space like isolated, insulated objects' (*AC*, p. 227) whereas with painters like Newman and Rothko 'one reacts to an environment as much as to a picture on a wall' (*AC*, p. 226). Although Greenberg highlights the specifically technical innovations that developed out of this desire to push the scale of abstract painting to the limits, the artists themselves eschewed such purely technicist accounts. They were aware of an important spiritual content to their endeavours:

> The large format, at one blow destroyed the century-long tendency of the French to domesticize modern painting, to make it intimate. We replaced the nude girl and the French door with a modern Stonehenge, with a sense of the sublime and the tragic that had not existed since Goya and Turner.[21]

Greenberg's emphasis on technique and formal innovation so pervasive in the critical debates of the 1940s and 1950s has prompted Harold Rosenberg to characterise Greenberg's criticism as 'a popular melodrama of technical breakthrough, comparable to the invention of the transistor'.[22] In Rosenberg's criticism, the technical inventiveness of the New York painters has important ideological implications.

Rosenberg saw Jackson Pollock and the Abstract Expressionist School as 'action' painters who had arrived at their individual avant-garde distinctiveness after the following journey:

> Many of the painters were 'Marxists' (WPA unions, artists' congresses) they had been trying to paint society. Others had been trying to paint Art (Cubism, Post-Impressionism) – it amounts to the same thing. The big moment came when it was decided to paint . . . just to paint. The gesture on the canvas was a gesture of liberation, from value – political, esthetic, moral.[23]

In the same way that in Pirandello's plays the playwright appears on the stage as a character who is writing plays, thereby calling attention to the processes by which illusion is created, Rosenberg calls attention to the way that in action painting the painter's 'activity and state of mind while painting are exposed in his brush strokes, his splashes, or the recurrence of characteristic shapes'.[24] For Rosenberg, this is not a purely aesthetic gesture, signalling ideological retreat. In a very specific sense, when action painters like Pollock, Gorky or de Kooning leave visible signs of the process by which the unprimed canvas is transformed, they are making a political statement:

> The outlines of art as action began to emerge in the nineteenth century. Marx speaks of the liberation of work, and defines free work as work for the sake of the worker, as distinguished from work for the sake of the product. In this idea, which puts creation above the object, whether artifact or commodity, Marx anticipates the thought of Klee and of the Action Painters . . . a dynamic world dominated no longer by things but by the activities of men.[25]

The aesthetic and political contexts that Greenberg and Rosenberg created for the New York painters of the late 1940s and 1950s have been subjected to two main revisionary analyses. Max Kozloff has a less positive view of the move towards transcendental ideas of 'the sublime and tragic' than Robert Motherwell. Unlike Léger and Mondrian, who directly confronted the modern industrial world of machine technology, or Francis Bacon and Jean Dubuffet 'whose works flared with atrocious memories', many of these New York artists turned their backs on contemporary history and sought in 'primitive icons drawn from many cultures, Southwest Indian or Imperial Roman . . . "universal" symbols for their own alienation'.[26] The viewer of such transcendental painting is absorbed into mystical space which seems to have no ideological point of view. A more technical history of art revision can be found in the work of Leo Steinberg, who questions one of Greenberg's basic propositions about the New York painters. Greenberg finds in the advanced modernism of these painters a whole range of effects not found in traditional painting. Throughout Greenberg's writings, he disparages the techniques of the realist 'old masters', whose mechanical style had monolithically dominated painting since the Renaissance: 'From Giotto to Courbet, the painter's first task had been to hollow out an illusion of three-dimensional space on a flat surface. One looked through this surface as through a proscenium onto a stage.'[27] In Greenberg's view it is only with the advent of Cézanne and the modernist movement from Picasso to Pollock that these mechanical realist techniques of reproduction began to be challenged and disrupted. Steinberg finds Greenberg's contrast between a modernist tradition that uniquely exposes and examines the processes of artistic artifice, and a realist 'old master' tradition that mechanically reproduces static three-dimensional images, unproven. He cites Michelangelo and the Sistine Chapel Ceiling as an example of an 'old master' who:

> delights in calling attention to and examining the process by which illusion is created. The ceiling is a battleground for local illusion, counter-illusion, and emphasized architectural surface – art turning constantly back on itself.[28]

In Steinberg's view, the all-over polyphonic design of an Abstract Expressionist canvas is not technically unique, and therefore Greenberg's famous distinction between an inventive modernism and a mechanical realism is open to challenge. The revival of the practices of realism in much avant-garde art in America and Europe since the 1960s has further subverted the neatness and validity of Greenberg's equation of abstraction with an innovating avant-garde and realism with a kitsch-dominated mass culture.[29]

The rigid distinction between high and mass culture, avant-garde and kitsch, had been tenaciously asserted and maintained by a whole range of cultural commentators, whose judgements dominated the 1940s and 1950s. The sheer volume of the activities of Criticism, Inc. has been succinctly catalogued by Daniel Bell:

> The New Criticism of John Crowe Ransom, the textual criticism of R. P. Blackmur, the moral criticism of Lionel Trilling, the socio-historical criticism of Edmund Wilson, the dramaturgical stance of Kenneth Burke, the linguistic analysis of I. A. Richards, the mythopeic criticisms of Northrop Frye. (*CCC*, p. 129)

The main impact of this age of criticism had been to establish clear-cut models of evaluative standards against which new work was judged. One of the major critics who challenged what were felt to be the repressive models and hierarchies of this age of criticism was Susan Sontag. In a famous essay, entitled 'Against Interpretation' (1966), she called for a 'new sensibility' in the arts in which greater emphasis would be given to active physical participation and sensuous erotic experience. The essay is not a dionysiac call to burn the books of criticism, rather it seeks to restore the importance of sensory experience to a culture that has become excessively literary, mental and critical. Much of Sontag's critique derives from her assessment that literature has gained an unhealthy dominance in modern culture. This elevation of literature and language over other forms of artistic activity had been a major feature of the age of criticism. Following on from I. A. Richards' firm belief that language is 'the instrument of all our distinctively human development, of everything in which we go beyond the animal',[30] literary criticism had achieved a major arbitrating role in modern culture. Characteristically, Susan Sontag tries to divert attention away from literature with its 'heavy burden of "content" ' towards what she sees as 'the model arts of our time . . . those with much less content, and a much cooler mode of moral judgement – like music, films, dance, architecture, painting, sculpture'.[31] The fact that these 'model arts' involve a much greater appeal to sense impressions of sound, shape, space and form than literature does, makes them 'the locus of the new sensibility'.[32] Sontag's promotion and analysis of 'the new sensibility' draws into its orbit a whole range of developments in contemporary American culture, making her work an important guide to the proliferation of attitudes and activities that ensued in America once the rigid aesthetic and critical categories, established in the 1940s and 1950s, no longer held dominant sway.

16. Susan Sontag: Against Interpretation

In his genealogical tree of the New York Jewish Intellectuals *c*.1935–*c*.1965, Daniel Bell places Susan Sontag in the generation that comes 'of age in the late 1940s and early 1950s'.[1] Though clearly affiliated to this group and sharing many of their assumptions about culture and politics, Susan Sontag questioned a number of the group's shibboleths. She does not concur with their outright rejection of an aesthetically degraded and potentially totalitarian mass culture, nor does she believe that the arts have a sacred mission to provide models of ethical and spiritual behaviour. For critics and social theorists of Hannah Arendt's and Lionel Trilling's generation, the arts had responsibilities to deal with a set of moral and social themes that Daniel Bell has summarised as follows:

> How one meets death, the meaning of tragedy, the nature of obligation, the character of love – these recurrent questions which are, I believe cultural universals, to be found in all societies where men have become conscious of the finiteness of existence.[2]

In her famous essay, 'Against Interpretation', in the book to which it gives its name, Sontag argued that the arts had other less transcendental responsibilities than those enunciated by Daniel Bell. Sontag calls for an 'erotics of art', which will enable people 'to see more, to hear more, to feel more'.[3] Instead of moral content, she celebrates sensuous form and experience. In the essay, Sontag also argued that cognitive criticism and interpretation, which the New York intelligentsia produced in great volume, occupied far too much space and prestige in contemporary culture, to the detriment of the creative arts.

Sontag was particularly alarmed by the influence of Marx and Freud on the arts. Marxist and Freudian models of analysis, so fundamental to the ideas of the New York Jewish intelligentsia, proposed that the real meaning to historical and psychological phenomena lay hidden beneath the surface. Only criticism could unearth the buried meaning. When applied to the arts, this methodology had grossly distorted the primary role of art, which in Sontag's view is not to carry cryptic moral messages, but to enable people 'to recover their senses'.[4] The spirit of Sontag's ideas is expressed in the quotation from Oscar Wilde, with which she prefaces 'Against Interpretation': 'It is only shallow people who do not judge by appearances. The mystery of the world is the visible, not the invisible'.[5]

As a counter to the negative influences of Criticism, Inc., Sontag enthusiastically promoted those art forms such as cinema, painting, theatre and music, which she felt made a direct sensuous appeal to eye and ear. In particular, she saw the avant-garde experimentalism that flourished in New York from the late 1950s onwards as a progressive antidote to an age of criticism that: 'Like the fumes of the automobile and of heavy industry which befoul the urban atmosphere . . ., poisons our sensibilities'.[6] In such a situation, the Pop Art of Andy Warhol and Jasper Johns and the mixed media 'happenings' of theatrical spectacle and painting represented a liberating new sensibility that was 'light, pretty, playful'.[7] Sontag's promotion of an experimental avant-garde was in line with the thinking of that section of the New York intelligentsia, led by the art critics Clement Greenberg and Harold Rosenberg, who had committed such influential journals as *Partisan Review* to the support of avant-garde practice, particularly in the field of painting. Greenberg and Rosenberg had enthusiastically promoted Jackson Pollock and the Abstract Expressionists. However, unlike Sontag they were less sure about the avant-garde status of Pop Art and 'happenings'. Greenberg, whose aesthetic was steeped in 'the great values the cultivated find in Picasso' (*AC*, p. 14), could not see Pop Art as part of that heroic inventive avant-garde to which Jackson Pollock belonged. In Greenberg's view, Warhol's use of imagery and reprographic techniques derived from the world of commercial advertising placed his work firmly in the shoddy world of kitsch. Warhol's unashamed use of the technical resources of industrialisation with their ability to produce multiple copies of a single image, was an affront to Greenberg's high-culture idea of the single artist producing individual masterpieces in a studio. Warhol deliberately attacked the conventions of high art by calling his studio a 'factory', which was not only the production base for Warhol's silkscreens, but also for a rock group, The Velvet Underground, and an underground movie company. Warhol's anarchism often exposed the degree to which all art, including that produced by an experimental avant-garde, was a commodity. This is one of the messages of the multiple versions of Marilyn Monroe, Brillo pads or Coke bottles, that Warhol's 'factory' produced. By pushing the ideology of capitalist consumption and interchangeability to its furthest extreme, Warhol sent tremors throughout the art establishment. On one occasion, he casually remarked that it was not necessary for him personally to create and supervise each of his images, since in his factory he could technically delegate the creative process to one of his many assistants. As a consequence of this remark, many owners of his works panicked at the thought that the Warhol commodity they owned might just be the mechanical reproduction of an assembly line rather than the unique expression of a single artist's creativity. When one compares Warhol's concept of the role of art in society with those of the Abstract Expressionists, the gap between them widens into a chasm. In a famous letter to the *New York Times* in 1943, several of the Abstract Expressionists signed the following declaration: 'We assert that the subject is crucial and only that subject matter is valid which is tragic and timeless. That is why we profess spiritual kinship with primitive and archaic art.'[8] Warhol, the parodist of a throwaway consumer culture of Coke bottles and popular celebrities, debunked the spiritual pretensions of high art. In conversation with G. Swenson in 1963, Warhol gave the following resumé of his views:

AW: I think everybody should be a machine. I think everybody should like everybody.

GS: Is that what Pop Art is about?

AW: Yes. It's liking things.

GS: And liking things is like being a machine.

AW: Yes, because you do the same thing every time. You do it over and over again.[9]

The striking differences between the Abstract Expressionists and the sublime status they assigned to their work, and the ironic irreverence of Warhol, Robert Rauschenberg and Jasper Johns, led many critics to argue that American artists of the 1960s had devalued the high commitments expected of a genuine avant-garde. To critics such as Greenberg and Rosenberg, a major characteristic of the avant-garde tradition resided in its adversary stance towards the values of mass technological society. They therefore interpreted the use, by American painters of the 1960s, of mass-culture imagery derived from advertising, cartoons or Hollywood, their delight in the potentialities of modern technologies of image production, and the absence of an explicit ethical and spiritual programme to their work, as representing a dangerous assimilation of the artist into a treacherous Midcult mainstream. Unlike Clement Greenberg and Harold Rosenberg, who actively demoted the Pop Artists and other avant-garde groups that emerged in the 1960s, Susan Sontag welcomed the work of this 1960s avant-garde as a liberating sensuous antidote to the prevailing rigidity of aesthetic and moral categories.

One particular aspect of this rigidity that Sontag singles out for attack is the totally unjustified prestige that realism and its conventions enjoy in western culture. By realism, Sontag means that form of aesthetic organisation particularly associated with the nineteenth-century novel, which sees the world as 'the unfolding of the destinies of sharply individualized "characters" in familiar socially dense situations within the conventional notation of chronological experience'.[10] Other important conventions of realism demand that a work of art should exhibit 'cause-and-effect sequences of events, climactic scenes, logical denouements'.[11] This model of artistic representation has not only come to dominate the novel, but has also prevailed in cinema and theatre. Realism also proposes a constricting model of how a work of art should impact on an audience: 'to induce in the audience a certain sequence of experience: first arousing, then manipulating, and eventually fulfilling emotional expectations'.[12] Sontag provides a clear indication of how avant-garde art can and should enable an audience to escape the arbitrary controls imposed by realism, in her essay on 'Happenings: An Art of Radical Juxtaposition'. The main aim of a Happening is not to create characters with which the audience can identify, or sequences of narrative action that the audience can follow. A 'Happening' seeks to expand an audience's sensory faculties. This repertoire of sensuous effects cannot be communicated if the audience sits in darkness separated from the action as they are if the play is constructed according to the conventions of theatrical realism. Although realism does permit the audience, through its imagination, to experience and identify with the emotions and events taking place within the staged illusion they are watching, the audience will always be at one remove. The audience-participants of a 'Happening' are treated in a totally different way:

> The performers may sprinkle water on the audience, or fling pennies or sneeze-producing detergent powder at it. . . . The audience may be made to stand uncomfortably in a crowded room, or fight for space to stand on boards laid in a few inches of water.[13]

'Happenings' are close to paintings in form, in that the audience is involved with materials 'hard and soft, dirty and clean',[14] rather than with characters and plot. Sontag does not claim that Happenings, pioneered in America by John Cage and others at Black Mountain College and by Allan Kaprow in New York, are a unique post-war development. They are an extension of European Surrealism and Antoin Artaud's Theatre of Cruelty, and an important element within the new anti-realist sensibility.

Sontag's promotion of this 'new sensibility' of sensory experience rather than moral commentary made her a particular advocate of those art forms, such as cinema, dance, painting, sculpture and music, in which visual, plastic or performance techniques were in the ascendancy over literary ones. Literature and the verbal text which for the New Critics of the 1940s and 1950s had constituted the supreme guarantors of a complex civilisation, were not accorded the same status by Sontag. 'Happenings', for example, do not depend for their survival or performance on the existence of a fixed written text or script. Sontag, like Mcluhan, felt that the arts in western society were unjustifiably dominated by literature and the printed book. Instead of expanding and enriching all five senses, western culture, through its concentration on the skills of literacy and verbal comprehension, promoted sensory poverty. This dominance of print and literature had been achieved at the expense of a whole range of non-verbal faculties, which the 'new sensibility' actively promotes.

The idea that the arts could provide a utopian model of humanist morality or sensory plenitude is a basic theme in twentieth-century criticisms. Whether it is John Crowe Ransom's idea of 'fulness', or F. R. Leavis' 'great tradition' of 'moral intensity', the arts were seen as radical, alternative forms of consciousness to those provided by a repressive industrial society. One of the largest claims made on behalf of the 'new sensibility' was probably Marcuse's idea that it was an:

> Affirmation of the right to build a society in which the abolition of poverty and toil terminates in a universe where the sensuous, the playful, the calm, and the beautiful become forms of existence and thereby the Form of society itself. (*EL*, p. 25)

Like Marcuse, Sontag saw a complex avant-garde modernism as a prime agency of the new sensibility. This sets her apart from those populist tendencies in the counter-culture of the 1960s which, echoing the debates of the 1930s, saw the complexities of avant-garde modernism as elitist and counter-revolutionary. Sontag does not advocate an anti-technological ideology, in which the arts are valued as a humanistic defence against the dehumanising values of modern science and technology. In her view, the avant-garde arts have many of the characteristics of scientific disciplines:

> The music of Milton Babbitt and Morton Feldman, the painting of Mark Rothko and Frank Stella, the dance of Merce Cunningham and James Waring demands an education of sensibility whose difficulties and length of apprenticeship are at least comparable to the difficulties of mastering physics or engineering.[15]

The list of artists in this quotation, all in varying ways the product of the metropolitan avant-garde that had proliferated in the affluent economy of New York since the 1940s, indicates an important context to the evolution of Sontag's ideas. New York, with its ability to sustain a plethora of cultural centres, critical journals and debates, did become, in the post-Second World War era, a dominant centre of artistic activity, particularly of the experimental avant-garde. Sontag's commitment to the values of this minority avant-garde culture which is 'reflective, critical and pluralistic',[16] coincides with and is a product of New York's post-war culture boom. The sheer scale of the expansion is worth noting. One of the orthodox interpretations of the evolution of the American arts in the twentieth century often highlights the weakness of the arts, particularly in the field of the avant-garde, even in the New York of the 1930s. The story since the 1930s is spectacularly different. If the scale of the differences between the 1930s and the period from 1950 onwards is arbitrarily limited to an index of the construction and extension of art museums and centres, the level of expansion in the United States is staggering:

> It can be said that since 1950, a minimum grand total of $561,700,000 has been committed to the construction of at least 10.2 million square feet of total space at 123 American art museums and visual arts centers; more than a third of that (3.5 million square feet) comprises gallery space. Taking the figure of 750,000 square feet for the total size of the Louvre, one can calculate that the total square footage is the equivalent of 13.6 Louvres, or, to make a more parochial comparison, the equivalent of 1,643.7 football fields.[17]

New York, along with Washington, DC, has probably been the major recipient of this expansion. New York has witnessed the founding of the Museum of Modern Art in 1929 (considerably expanded as recently as 1983), followed in 1959 by The Guggenheim Museum, designed by Frank Lloyd Wright, the opening of the new Whitney Museum in 1970, and the almost continual expansion of the Metropolitan Museum. Museums are also a natural magnet for artists and gallery owners, who cluster in artistic neighbourhoods like Greenwich Village and Soho, thus creating concentrated centres of artistic activity and discrimination.[18]

A significant part of this general expansion has been devoted to the display and promotion of modernist avant-garde art of the twentieth century. The Guggenheim Museum, designed by Frank Lloyd Wright, is a distinctive symbol of this commitment to modernism (Plate 7). Wright's definition of this connection between the building and twentieth-century art is worth noting:

> The building was intended by Solomon R. Guggenheim to make a suitable place for exhibition of an advanced form of painting wherein line, color and form are a language in themselves ... independent of representation of objects animate or inanimate, thus placing painting in a realm enjoyed hitherto by music alone.[19]

Susan Sontag and her fellow New York intellectuals live and interact in this dense capital of culture. However, she has no illusions as to the separateness and un-Americanness of New York's status as a cornucopia of the arts, a unique island in a philistine mainstream that is largely indifferent and hostile to avant-garde culture. This philistine mainstream is dominated by 'a decentralised electorate mainly pre-occupied with local issues'[20] that holds 'man's biological as well as his historical future in its King Kong paws'.[21] The ability of this populist capitalist mainstream to control and neutralise the arts is the subject of her most recent extended piece of cultural analysis, the series of essays published together as *On Photography*.

The essays, first published in the *New York Review of Books*, mark a major shift in Sontag's cultural criticism. Up to these essays a central theme to her work had been the belief in the ability of the individual artist to generate rival and more complex images and experiments than those provided by a commercial mass society. Photography cannot be enlisted in this way for a number of reasons. Firstly, because: 'Recently, photography has become almost as widely practiced an amusement as sex and dancing – which means that, like every mass art form, photography is not practiced by most people as an art'.[22] Other factors that affect the aesthetic status of photography are caused by technology. From its beginnings in 1839 the camera mounted a number of challenges to the idea of individual creative vision, culminating in the sales pitch for the first Kodak in 1888: 'You press the button, we do the rest' (*OP*, p. 53). The technology of the camera offers to abolish the danger of human error and the need for individual creativity. This 'instamatic' promise and bias was quickly converted into a set of mass social uses that have far outweighed the role of individual photographers. For example, among the first employers of the unique documentary powers of photography were police forces, whose mug shots of criminals presaged the passport and identity photos that modern states use to keep track of their citizens. Two other, more complex examples that Sontag gives of photography's major role as an agency of social control and conformity are the cult of the family photograph, and tourism's role in the history of photography. In both instances, Sontag argues that photography anaesthetises and disfigures reality:

> Photography becomes a rite of family life just when, in the industrializing countries of Europe and America, the very institution of the family starts undergoing radical surgery. As that claustrophobic unit, the nuclear family, was being carved out of a much larger family aggregate, photography came along to

memorialize, to restate symbolically, the imperilled continuity and vanishing extendedness of family life. (*OP*, pp. 8–9)

The same process is evident when photography is placed in the context of the growth of mass tourism, which limits 'experience to a search for the photogenic, by converting experience into an image, a souvenir. Travel becomes a strategy for accumulating photographs (*OP*, p. 9). Sontag summarises the social and political impact of photography as follows:

Cameras define reality in two ways essential to the workings of an advanced industrial society: as a spectacle (for masses) and as an object of surveillance (for rulers). The production of images also furnishes a ruling ideology. Social change is replaced by a change in images. The freedom to consume a plurality of images and goods is equated with freedom itself. (*OP*, pp. 178–9)

Sontag's thesis that the camera converts all experience, however intractable, into socially and aesthetically acceptable forms and images, is also applied to the short history of individual American photographers that she provides in the essay 'America Seen Through Photographs, Darkly'. The key figure in Sontag's history, who provides the ideological context for American photographers, is not a photographer but a nineteenth-century poet, Walt Whitman. Whitman's famous declaration that: 'the United States themselves are essentially the greatest poem' expresses the spirit of a programme that sought to abolish all hierarchies and artificial distinctions 'between beauty and ugliness, importance and triviality' (*OP*, p. 27). Whitman wanted to embrace and convert all experience into a humanist democratic unity, to close the gaps between people, and between material objects. Sontag argues that 'this Whitmanesque mandate to record in its entirety the extravagant candors of actual American experience' (*OP*, p. 29) has been the major guiding motif for American photographers. From Lewis Hine's early twentieth-century photographs of Italian immigrants and workers that sought to establish their rights to the same dignity and status that more established Americans enjoyed, to Walker Evans's photographs of poor white tenant farmers and their cabins of the 1930s, American documentary photography had been engaged in a compassionate humanising mission (Plate 8). Evans in particular embodies this ideology, which can convert and therefore anaesthetise poverty and distress into aesthetically pleasing forms. Sontag notes that the following quotation from Whitman was attached to a book of Walker Evans's photographs, published by the Museum of Modern Art:

> I do not doubt but the majesty and beauty of the world are latent in any iota of the world . . . I do not doubt there is far more in trivialities, insects, vulgar persons, slaves, dwarfs, weeds, rejected refuse, than I have supposed. . . . (*OP*, p. 29)

The 'Whitmanesque mandate' had a particular appeal to photographers like Evans, who wanted to democratise and extend the range of subject matter that the visual fine arts had hitherto encompassed. This tendency was powerfully reinforced by the technological ability of the camera, through such devices as the close-up, to isolate and idealise 'a corner of material reality that the eye doesn't see at all or can't normally isolate' (*OP*, p. 90). The democratising, ravenous eye of the camera revolutionised traditional ideas of aesthetic beauty and subject matter that in western art had often depended on aristocratic concepts of flawless purity of shape and line. Historically, these idealisations of form were sited either in an unspoiled nature or in a highly transformed manmade item of culture such as a neo-classical temple. Whitman's programme of 'populist transcendence, of the democratic transvaluation of beauty and ugliness' (*OP*, p. 27) aspired to change these traditional equations.

This democratising drive is also apparent in another tradition of American photography, the fine-art style of Alfred Stieglitz, that is often seen in opposition to the documentary tradition of Lewis Hine and Walker Evans. When viewed through Sontag's perspective, the fine-art and documentary traditions have similar effects. Alfred Stieglitz's famous 1893 photography, 'New York, 5th Avenue, Winter', transforms and idealises the manmade city into a soft impressionistic pastoral in a way that is reminiscent of Hine's idealised immigrants. The same process of transformation and idealisation occurs in Edward Steichan's 1915 fine-art photographs of a milk bottle on a tenement fire escape, and in Edward Weston's 1925 series of pictures of the 'elegant form of a toilet bowl or his studies of peppers of 1929 and 1930' (*OP*, p. 98).

In Sontag's short history of American photography the Whit-

manesque programme collapses into absurdity and parody after the
Second World War. She cites two exhibitions, both staged at New
York's Museum of Modern Art, as witness to this collapse. In 1955,
Edward Steichen organised a show of 503 photographs from 68
countries, entitled 'Family of Man'. The message of the show, which
reached a worldwide audience when toured by the United States
Information Agency, was a crude and sentimental humanism.
Through photography, explicit and intractable differences of race,
class, culture and economic status were converted into images of
universal kinship in order: 'to prove that humanity is "one" and that
human beings, for all their flaws, and villainies, are attractive
creatures' (*OP*, p. 32). The second exhibition that Sontag cites is the
retrospective devoted to Diana Arbus, staged at the Museum of
Modern Art in 1972. Instead of providing 'the reassuring warmth of
Steichen's material', Arbus 'lined up assorted monsters and border-
line cases – most of them ugly; wearing grotesque or unflattering
clothing' (*OP*, p. 32). Arbus, by removing the compassionate
perspective, reveals human society as a series of isolated grotesques.
In a photograph like 'A Jewish Giant at Home with his Parents in the
Bronx, NY, 1970', Arbus does not seek to enlist sympathy for the plight
of the son or for the parents. She does not plead for their dignity.
Instead of compassionate concern, the photograph highlights the
visual incongruity not only of the son's size in relation to the room, but
of the way his size transforms the parents into midgets (Plate 9). The
Arbus show parodies the Whitmanesque idea of common kinship: 'In
photographing dwarfs, you don't get majesty and beauty. You get
dwarfs' (*OP*, p. 29).

Sontag does not derive much comfort from Arbus's 'anti-humanist
message' (*OP*, p. 32). Her attitudes are as disquieting as those
mediated by Steichen's folksy humanism in that she expresses 'a
leading tendency of high art in capitalist countries: to suppress, or at
least reduce, moral and sensory queasiness' (*OP*, p. 40). The Arbus
show is further evidence for Sontag's general theory of the role of
images: 'A capitalist society requires a culture based on images. It
needs to furnish vast amounts of entertainment in order to stimulate
buying and anesthetize the injuries of class, race, and sex' (*OP*, p.
178).

Sontag's essays represent a particular set of departures within the
tradition of cultural criticism under review. Unlike Daniel Bell she
does not see modernism and the avant-garde as 'exhausted'. Indeed

she has argued that it should be: 'mandatory for any responsible critic today', to show 'an intelligent involvement with the problems and objectives of "modernism" in the arts'.[23] She also rejects the premises of liberal humanism basic to the cultural criticism of such figures as Lionel Trilling, who argue that the arts should provide a moral commentary on civilisation. Rather Sontag identifies herself with artists and critics who have often been described as post-humanist and post-modern. In this post-modernist world of the paintings of Jackson Pollock, the fictions of Thomas Pynchon and the dance of Merce Cunningham, there are no reliable points of view, no explicit moral commentaries, no sharply differentiated individuals or causally related narratives. In post-modernist culture that has refined and expanded the programme of Picasso and his avant-garde contemporaries at the beginning of the twentieth century, the critic has to be alert to a high degree of formal experiment and inventiveness, and be prepared for the calculated transgression of traditional boundaries such as those between high and mass art. As Christopher Butler has argued in his important book, *After the Wake: an essay on the Contemporary Avant-Garde*, there is a 'radical uncertainty' in the world of post-modernism: 'Thus in Beckett's *Watt*, the Galls are father and son, or perhaps stepfather and stepson, or perhaps not related at all; and the central symbol of Pynchon's V may be Victoria, Vera, Valletta, Vesuvius, Venezuela, or the V made by the receding line of lights in a street, or. . . .'[24] For Sontag a model post-modernist artist is the French film-maker Jean-Luc Godard whose films are: 'casually encyclopedic, anthologising, formally and thematically eclectic, and marked by a rapid turnover of styles and forms'. Godard's 'mixtures of tonalities, themes and narrative methods suggest something like the union of Brecht and Robbe-Grillet, Gene Kelly and Francis Ponge, Gertrude Stein and David Riesman, Orwell and Robert Rauschenberg, Boulez and Raymond Chandler, Hegel and rock 'n' roll'.[25] Sontag's own essays exhibit a similar alertness to developments across the whole field of the contemporary arts, making her work an ideal set of entrances to that field.

Notes

1. THE LEGACY OF THE THIRTIES

1. Matthew Joseph Bruccoli, *The Notebooks of F. Scott Fitzgerald* (New York: Harcourt, Brace Jovanovich, 1978), p. 58.
2. T. S. Eliot, *For Lancelot Andrewes* (London: Faber, 1928), p. ix.
3. Lillian Hellman, *Pentimento* (London: Quartet, 1976), p. 103.
4. Daniel Aaron, *Writers on the Left* (New York: Octagon, 1979), p. 440.
5. James Agee and Walker Evans, *Let Us Now Praise Famous Men* (London: Peter Owen, 1975), Preface p. xix. First published 1941.
6. Daniel Aaron, *Writers on the Left*, p. 447.
7. Arthur Schlesinger, *The Vital Centre, Our Purposes and Perils on the Tightrope of American Liberalism* (Cambridge: Riverside Press, 1949), p. 208.
8. F. O. Matthiessen, *American Renaissance* (New York: OUP, 1941), Preface p. vii.
9. Ibid., Preface, p. ix.
10. F. R. Leavis, *The Great Tradition* (Harmondsworth: Penguin Books, 1972), p. 18. First published 1948.
11. Matthiessen, *American Renaissance*, Preface, p. xii.
12. For a discussion of Faulkner's changing status, see Lawrence Schwartz, 'Malcolm Cowley's Path to William Faulkner', *Journal of American Studies*, 16, 2 (August 1982), 229–42.
13. Gerald Graff, 'An Ideological Map of American Literary Criticism', *Revue Française d'Etudes Americaines*, VIII, 16 (February 1983) 112.
14. Philip Rahv, 'The Myth and the Powerhouse', in *Literature and the Sixth Sense* (Boston: Houghton Mifflin, 1970), pp. 204–5. (Essay first published 1949.)
15. Bruce Kuklick, 'Myth and Symbol in American Studies', *American Quarterly*, XXIV, 4 (October 1972) 449.
16. Henry Nash Smith, *Virgin Land: The American West as Symbol and Myth* (Cambridge, Massachusetts: Harvard University Press, revised edition, 1970), p. 259.
17. R. W. B. Lewis, *The American Adam: Innocence, Tragedy, and Tradition in the Nineteenth Century* (Chicago: The University of Chicago Press, 1955), p. 5.
18. Leo Marx, *The Machine in the Garden: Technology and the Pastoral Ideal in America* (New York: Oxford University Press, 1964), p. 5.
19. Leslie A. Fiedler, *Love and Death in the American Novel* (London: Jonathan Cape, 1967), p. 29.

2. DANIEL BELL AND THE CULTURAL CONTRADICTIONS OF CAPITALISM

1. Daniel Bell, *The End of Ideology* (New York: Collier-Macmillan, 1965), p. 300.
2. Ibid.

3. Lionel Trilling, *A Gathering of Fugitives* (Oxford: Oxford University Press, 1980), p. 68.

4. Raymond Williams, *The Long Revolution* (Harmondsworth: Penguin Books, 1965), p. 94.

5. Lionel Trilling, *The Opposing Self* (London: Secker & Warburg, 1955), Preface, p. ix.

6. Lionel Trilling, *Beyond Culture* (Oxford: Oxford University Press, 1980), Preface, pp. 4, 5. First published 1965.

7. Daniel Bell, *The End of Ideology*, p. 299.

8. Ibid., pp. 402, 403.

9. Daniel Bell, *Sociological Journeys: Essays 1960–1980* (London: Heinemann, 1980), Preface, p. xiv. (*SJ* in future text references.)

10. Daniel Bell, *The Cultural Contradictions of Capitalism* (London: Heinemann, 1979), p. 16. (*CCC* in future text references.)

11. Bell, *The End of Ideology*, p. 35.

12. Susan Sontag, *Against Interpretation* (New York: Delta, 1981), p. 14. First published 1966.

13. Bell, *The End of Ideology*, p. 32.

14. A succinct analysis of neo-conservatism can be found in 'The Divisions of the Right', *The Economist* (3 January 1981), pp. 39–42.

15. John F. Kennedy, Speech at Yale (June 1962), quoted in Peter Steinfels, *The Neo-Conservatives* (New York: Simon & Schuster, 1980), p. 42.

3. THE FOUNDATIONS OF ANGLO-AMERICAN LITERARY THEORY

1. Malcolm Bradbury, 'The tense pre-occupation of "ism" and "wasm" ', *The Times Higher Education Supplement*, No. 432 (13 February 1981), p. 9.

2. T. S. Eliot, *Selected Essays* (London: Faber & Faber, 1976), p. 21. First published 1932. (*SE* in future text references.)

3. Karl Marx, 'The Eighteenth Brumaire of Louis Bonaparte' in *Surveys from Exile, Political Writings Vol. 2*, edited by David Fernbach (Harmondsworth: Penguin Books, 1981), p. 146.

4. T. S. Eliot, 'Ulysses, Order, and Myth', 1923, reprinted as 'Myth and Literary Classicism' in Richard Ellmann and Charles Feidelson, Jr. (eds), *The Modern Tradition: Background of Modern Literature* (New York: Oxford University Press, 1965), p. 681.

5. John Crowe Ransom, 'The South – Old or New?', *Sewanee Review*, XXXVI (April 1928), 147.

6. T. S. Eliot, *After Strange Gods: A Primer of Modern Heresy* (London: Faber & Faber, 1934), p. 38. (*ASG* in future text references.)

7. Daniel Bell, 'The "Intelligentsia" in American Society', in *Sociological Journeys*, pp. 119–37.

8. T. S. Eliot, 'A Commentary', *Criterion*, 10 (April 1931), 484–5.

4. FROM SOUTHERN AGRARIANISM TO CRITICISM, INC.

1. Marshall Mcluhan, *Culture is Our Business* (New York: McGraw-Hill, 1970), p. 45.

2. Matthew Arnold, *Culture and Anarchy* (London: Thomas Nelson, 1869), Preface, p. ii.

3. Matthew Arnold, 'The Study of Poetry', in Miriam Allott (ed.), *Matthew Arnold: Selected Poems and Prose* (London: J. M. Dent, 1978), pp. 242–3.

4. Matthew Arnold, *Culture and Anarchy*, pp. 74–127.

5. F. R. Leavis, *The Great Tradition*, p. 18.

6. Perry Anderson, 'Components of the National Culture', p. 225 in Alexander Cockburn and Robin Blackburn (eds), *Student Power* (Harmondsworth: Penguin Books, 1969).

7. I. A. Richards, *Practical Criticism: A Study of Literary Judgement* (London: Routledge & Kegan Paul, 1929), pp. 240–54. (*PC* in future text references.)

8. I. A. Richards, *Philosophy of Rhetoric* (New York: Galaxy Books, 1965), p. 131. First published 1936.

9. I. A. Richards, *Poetries and Sciences – a reissue of Science and Poetry with Commentary* (London: Routledge & Kegan Paul, 1970), p. 601. First published 1925.

10. Ibid., p. 78.

11. Richards, *Poetries and Sciences*, p. 38.

12. Ibid., p. 36.

13. John Fekete, *The Critical Twilight: Explorations in the Ideology of Anglo-American Literary Theory from Eliot to Mcluhan* (London: Routledge & Kegan Paul, 1978), p. 29.

14. John Crowe Ransom, *God Without Thunder: An Unorthodox Defence of Orthodoxy* (London: Gerald Howe, 1931), p. 103. (*GWT* in future text references.)

15. John Crowe Ransom, 'The South – Old or New?', *Sewanee Review*, XXXVI (April 1928), p. 147.

16. Letter to Allen Tate, cited in Fekete, *The Critical Twilight*, p. 60.

17. Fekete, *The Critical Twilight*, pp. 68–9.

18. Ibid., p. 69.

19. I. A. Richards, *Coleridge on Imagination* (London: Routledge & Kegan Paul, 1962), p. 227. First published 1934.

20. John Crowe Ransom, *The World's Body* (New York: Charles Scribner's Sons, 1938), p. 58. (*WB* in future text references.)

21. Fekete, *The Critical Twilight*, p. 89.

22. John Crowe Ransom, *The New Criticism* (Norfolk, Connecticut: New Directions, 1941), p. 95.

23. John Crowe Ransom, 'The Bases of Criticism', *Sewanee Review*, XLII (October 1944), p. 563.

24. Cleanth Brooks, *The Well Wrought Urn: Studies in the Structure of Poetry* (London: Denis Dobson, 1968), p. 1. First published 1947.

25. Ransom, *The New Criticism*, p. 95.

26. Brooks, *The Well Wrought Urn*, p. 169.

27. Ibid., p. 166.

28. Fekete, *The Critical Twilight*, p. 87.

29. Malcolm Bradbury and David Palmer (eds), *Contemporary Criticism* (London: Edward Arnold, 1970), p. 23.

5. THE DEBATE ON MASS CULTURE

1. I. A. Richards, *Principles of Literary Criticism* (London: Routledge & Kegan Paul, 1976), pp. 25–6. First published 1924.

2. Bernard Rosenberg and David Manning White (eds), *Mass Culture Revisited* (New York: Van Nostrand, 1971), Introduction, p. vii.

3. T. S. Eliot, *Notes Towards the Definition of Culture* (London: Faber & Faber, 1979), p. 45. First published 1948.

4. Dwight Macdonald, *Against the American Grain* (London: Victor Gollancz, 1963), pp. 34–5. (*AAG* in future text references.)

5. Theodor Adorno and Max Horkheimer, *Dialectic of Enlightenment* (London: Verso Editions, 1979), pp. 58–9. First published 1944.

6. Ibid., Introduction, p. xiv.

7. C. Wright Mills, *The Sociological Imagination* (Harmondsworth: Penguin, 1980), p. 21. First published 1959.

8. Erskine Caldwell and Margaret Bourke-White, *Say, is this the U.S.A.* (New York: Da Capo Press, 1977), pp. 10–12. First published 1941.

9. Bell, *The End of Ideology*, p. 306.

10. Dwight Macdonald, *The Responsibilities of Peoples and other essays in Political Criticism* (London: Victor Gollancz, 1957), p. 139.

11. Dwight Macdonald, *Henry Wallace: The Man and the Myth* (New York: The Vanguard Press, 1948), p. 36.

12. Ibid.

13. Ibid., p. 160.

14. Macdonald, *The Responsibilities of Peoples*, p. 122.

15. Bell, *The End of Ideology*, pp. 21–5.

16. Ibid., p. 25.

17. Eliot, *Notes Towards the Definition of Culture*, p. 9.

18. Denis Wrong, 'Far more chic than radical', *The Times Higher Education Supplement* (21 July 1978), No. 349, p. 10.

19. Dwight Macdonald, *On Movies* (New York: Da Capo Press, 1981) p. 240. First published 1969. (*OM* in future text references.)

6. ROBERT WARSHOW AND THE LEGACY OF THE 1930s

1. Robert Warshow, *The Immediate Experience: Movies, Comics, Theatre and other aspects of Popular Culture* (New York: Atheneum, 1971), p. 34. First published 1962. (*IE* in future text references.)

2. Michel Ciment, *Kazan on Kazan* (London: Secker & Warburg, 1973), p. 84.

3. See *Film Noir*, edited by Alain Silver and Elizabeth Ward (London: Secker & Warburg, 1980), for an assessment of the significance and extent of the form of *film noir*.

7. T. S. ELIOT AND MASS SOCIETY

1. George H. Nash, *The Conservative Intellectual Movement in America* (New York: Basic Books, 1979), p. 151. First published 1976.

2. T. S. Eliot, *The Idea of a Christian Society* (London: Faber & Faber, 1939), p. 78.

3. Ibid.

4. Roland Barthes, *Mythologies* (London: Jonathan Cape, 1972), p. 140.

5. Eliot, *The Idea of a Christian Society*, pp. 39–40.

6. Eliot, *Notes Towards the Definition of Culture*, p. 9. (*NTDC* in future text references.)

7. Raymond Williams, *Culture and Society 1780–1950* (Harmondsworth: Penguin Books, 1961), p. 230.

8. Eliot, *The Idea of a Christian Society*, pp. 39–40.

8. THE FRANKFURT SCHOOL: MARXISM, FASCISM AND MASS CULTURE

1. H. Stuart Hughes, *The Sea Change: The Migration of Social Thought, 1930–1965* (New York: McGraw-Hill, 1975), p. 1.

2. Martin Jay, *The Dialectical Imagination: A History of the Frankfurt School and the Institute of Social Research 1923–1950* (London: Heinemann Educational Books, 1976), p. 29.

3. Ibid., p. 220.

4. Adorno and Horkheimer, *Dialectic of Enlightenment*, p. 4. (*DE* in future text references.)

5. Jay, *The Dialectical Imagination*, pp. 240–3.

6. T. W. Adorno, Else Frenkel-Brunswick, Daniel J. Levinson and R. Nevitt Sanford, *The Authoritarian Personality* (New York: Harper & Row, 1950), pp. 1, 664–5, 695, 759–60.

7. Hughes, *The Sea Change*, p. 119.

8. Leo Lowenthal, *Literature, Popular Culture and Society* (Palo Alto: Pacific Books, 1968), Preface, p. xii. (*LPCS* in future text references.)

9. Norman H. Baynes (ed.), *The Speeches of Adolf Hitler, 1922–39* (London: Oxford University Press, 1942), Vol. 1, pp. 871–2.

10. For other less pessimistic assessments of Afro-American culture, see Leroi Jones, *Blues People: Negro Music in White America* (New York: William Morrow, 1963) and Lawrence W. Levine, *Black Culture and Black Consciousness: Afro-American Folk Thought from Slavery to Freedom* (New York: Oxford University Press, 1977).

11. Theodor Adorno, *Prisms*, translated by Samuel and Shierry Weber (London: Neville Spearman, 1967), p. 121.

12. Donald Fleming and Bernard Bailyn (eds), *The Intellectual Migration: Europe and America, 1930–1960* (Cambridge: Harvard University Press, 1969), p. 338.

13. Ibid., p. 369.

9. HERBERT MARCUSE: FROM AFFIRMATION TO LIBERATION

1. Herbert Marcuse, *Eros and Civilization* (Boston: Beacon Press, 1974), p. 17. First published 1955. (*EC* in future text references.)

2. Sigmund Freud, *Civilization and its Discontents* (London: The Hogarth Press, 1979), p. 26. First published 1930. (*CD* in future text references.)

3. Hendrick K. M. Ruitenbeek, *Freud and America* (New York: Macmillan, 1966), p. 20.

4. Herbert Marcuse, *Negations* (Harmondsworth: Penguin University Books, 1972), pp. 98–9.

5. Ibid., p. 95.

6. Herbert Marcuse, *One-Dimensional Man: Studies in the Ideology of Advanced Industrial Society* (Boston: Beacon Press, 1964), p. 10.

7. Ibid., p. 8.

8. Marcuse, *One-Dimensional Man*, Introduction, p. xv.

9. Robert Paul Wolff, Barrington Moore Jr, Herbert Marcuse, *A Critique of Pure Tolerance* (London: Jonathan Cape, 1969), p. 21.

10. Ibid., p. 98.

11. Ibid., p. 99.

12. Ibid., p. 102.

13. Marcuse, *Negations*, pp. 98–9.

14. Ibid., p. 98.

15. Ibid., p. 99.

16. Marcuse, *Negations*, p. 110.

17. Marcuse, *Negations*, p. 117.

18. Ibid., p. 116.

19. Karl Marx and Frederick Engels, *The German Ideology, Part One*, edited by C. J. Arthur (London: Lawrence & Wishart, 1974), p. 64.

20. Herbert Marcuse, *An Essay on Liberation* (Boston: Beacon Press, 1969), p. 38. (*EL* in future text references.)

21. Herbert Marcuse, *Five Lectures: Psychoanalysis, Politics, and Utopia* (Boston: Beacon Press, 1970), p. 39.

22. Hughes, *The Sea Change*, p. 195.

23. Wolff, Moore Jr, Marcuse, *A Critique of Pure Tolerance*, p. 25.

24. Recent scholarship has challenged the reliability of Mead's fieldwork in Samoa. See Derek Freeman, *Margaret Mead and Samoa: The Making and Unmaking of an Anthropological Myth* (Cambridge, Mass.: Harvard University Press, 1983).

25. Philip Gleason, 'Americans All: Ethnicity, Ideology and American Identity in the Era of World War II', in Rob Kroes (ed.), *The American Identity: Fusion and Fragmentation* (Amsterdam: Amerika Institute, University of Amsterdam, 1980), p. 237.

26. Ibid., p. 239.

27. Ibid., p. 245.

28. Lionel Trilling, *E. M. Forster* (New York: Harcourt Brace Jovanovich, 1980), p. 7. First published 1943.

10. THE LONELY CROWD: DAVID RIESMAN AND AMERICAN SOCIETY

1. David Riesman, *The Lonely Crowd: A Study of the Changing American Character* (New Haven and London: Yale University Press, revised edition, 1970), 1961 Preface, p. xliii. First published 1950. (*LC* in future text references.)

2. Arthur J. Brodbeck, 'Values in The Lonely Crowd: Ascent or Descent of Man', in Seymour Martin Lipset and Leo Lowenthal (eds), *Culture and Social Character: The Work of David Riesman Reviewed* (New York: Free Press, 1961), p. 58.

3. Margaret Mead, review of *The Lonely Crowd*, in *American Journal of Sociology*, 56 (March 1951), 496–7.

4. Lionel Trilling, *The Last Decade: Essays and Reviews, 1965–75* (New York: Harcourt Brace Jovanovich, 1979), p. 239. (*LD* in future text references.)

5. The problems of this kind of ideological analysis of a writer are discussed in George Orwell's essay, 'Charles Dickens', in *The Collected Essays, Journalism and Letters of George Orwell, Vol. 1* (Harmondsworth: Penguin Books, 1971), pp. 454–504.

6. Aaron, *Writers on the Left*, p. 239.

7. Bell, *The End of Ideology*, p. 300.

8. Lionel Trilling, *Matthew Arnold* (London: Unwin University Books, 1963), pp. 180–1. First published 1939.

9. Lionel Trilling, *Sincerity and Authenticity* (London: Oxford University Press, 1972), p. 122.

10. Ibid., pp. 124–5.

11. Lionel Trilling, *The Liberal Imagination: Essays on Literature and Society* (Oxford: Oxford University Press, 1981), p. 249. First published 1950. (*LI* in future text references.)

12. Adorno, *Prisms*, p. 34.

13. Lionel Trilling, *Beyond Culture: Essays on Literature and Learning* (Oxford: Oxford University Press, 1980), Preface, pp. iv–v.

14. See Raymond Williams, *The Long Revolution*, pp. 19–56.

15. See Ian P. Watt, *The Rise of the Novel: Studies in Defoe, Richardson and Fielding* (London: Chatto & Windus, 1957).

16. I. A. Richards, *Poetries and Sciences*, p. 38.

17. Ibid., p. 61.

18. Trilling, *Sincerity and Authenticity*, p. 24.

19. Ibid., p. 25.

20. Lionel Trilling, *The Opposing Self: Nine Essays in Criticism* (Oxford: Oxford

University Press, 1980), Preface p. 2. First published in 1955. (*OS* in future text references.)

21. Trilling, *Sincerity and Authenticity*, p. 79.

22. Ibid.

23. Trilling, *Matthew Arnold*, p. 180.

24. Trilling, *Sincerity and Authenticity*, p. 55.

25. Stan Smith, *A Sadly Contracted Hero: The Comic Self in Post-war American Fiction* (British Association for American Studies Pamphlets, 1981), p. 8.

11. MARSHALL MCLUHAN: THE MODERNISM OF THE MASS MEDIA

1. Tom Wolfe, *The Pump House Gang* (New York: Bantam Books, 1969), p. 110.

2. Fekete, *The Critical Twilight*, p. 174.

3. Marshall Mcluhan, *Playboy* magazine interview (March 1969), p. 60.

4. Marshall Mcluhan, *Understanding Media: The Extensions of Man* (London: Routledge & Kegan Paul, 1969), p. 23. First published 1964. (*UM* in future text references.)

5. Marshall Mcluhan, 'The Southern Quality', *Sewanee Review*, LV, No. 1 (July 1947), 374.

6. Jonathan Miller, *Mcluhan* (London: Fontana Books, 1971), p. 63.

7. Marshall Mcluhan and Harley Parker, *Through the Vanishing Point: Space in Poetry and Painting* (New York: Harper & Row, 1969), p. 209.

8. Marshall Mcluhan, *The Mechanical Bride: Folklore of Industrial Man* (London: Routledge & Kegan Paul, 1967), p. 3. First published in 1951.

9. Ibid., p. 156.

10. Ibid., p. 157.

11. Fekete, *The Critical Twilight*, p. 186.

12. Herbert I. Schiller, *Mass Communications and American Empire* (New York: Augustus M. Kelley, 1970), p. 2.

12. TOM WOLFE AND THE NEW JOURNALISM

1. Hunter S. Thompson, *Hell's Angels* (Harmondsworth: Penguin Books, 1967), p. 283.

2. Ibid., p. 284.

3. Robert Atwan, Barry Orton and William Vesterman (eds), *American Mass Media Industries and Issues* (New York: Random House, 1978), p. 212.

4. Ibid., p. 213.

5. Ibid., p. 210.

6. Ibid., p. 245.

7. Tom Wolfe, *The Painted Word* (New York: Bantam Books, 1976), p. 3.

8. Ibid., p. 4.

9. Tom Wolfe, *From Bauhaus to Our House* (New York: Farrar, Straus & Giroux, 1981), p. 4.

10. Ibid., p. 23.

11. Tom Wolfe, *The New Journalism* (London: Picador-Pan Books, 1975), p. 56. (*NJ* in future text references.)

12. Larry L. King, 'You Must Be Kidding', *New Republic* (21 May 1969), pp. 24–5.

13. Herbert J. Gans, *Deciding What's News: A Study of C.B.S. Evening News, N.B.C. Nightly News, Newsweek and Time* (New York: Vintage Books, 1980), pp. 68–9.

14. Atwan, Orton and Vesterman (eds), *American Mass Media*, pp. 229–36.

15. Herbert J. Gans, *Popular Culture and High Culture: An Analysis and Evaluation of Taste* (New York: Basic Books, 1974), pp. 67–8.

16. Stanley Aronowitz, *False Promises: The Shaping of American Working Class Consciousness* (New York: McGraw-Hill, 1973), p. 100.

17. Christopher Lasch, *The Agony of the American Left: One Hundred Years of Radicalism* (Harmondsworth: Pelican Books, 1973), p. 118.

18. Aronowitz, *False Promises*, p. 107.

19. Herbert G. Gutman, *Work, Culture, and Society in Industrializing America* (Oxford: Oxford University Press, 1977), pp. 44–5.

20. Aronowitz, *False Promises*, pp. 303–4.

21. Quoted in Dwight Macdonald, *Against the American Grain*, p. 29.

22. Aronowitz, *False Promises*, p. 100.

23. Ibid., p. 101.

24. Ibid., p. 110.

13. NORMAN MAILER AND MASS AMERICA

1. Norman Mailer, *The Naked and the Dead* (St Albans: Panther Books, 1964), p. 277. First published in 1948.

2. Ibid., p. 606.

3. Leo Braudy (ed.), *Norman Mailer: A Collection of Critical Essays* (New Jersey: Prentice-Hall, 1972), p. 50.

4. Ibid., p. 55.

5. Norman Mailer, *Advertisements for Myself* (London: Corgi Books, 1963), p. 259. First published in 1959.

6. Hughes, *The Sea Change*, p. 120.

7. Norman Mailer, *The Presidential Papers* (St Alban's: Panther Books, 1976), p. 291. First published 1963. (*PP* in future text references.)

8. Mailer, *Advertisements for Myself*, p. 244.

9. Ibid., p. 257.

10. Ibid., p. 204.

11. Norman Mailer, *The Armies of the Night: History as a Novel, the Novel as History* (Harmondsworth: Penguin Books, 1968), p. 31. (*AN* in future text references.)

12. Mailer, *Advertisements for Myself*, p. 157.

13. Ibid., p. 156.

14. Bell, *The End of Ideology*, p. 283.

15. Ibid., p. 31.

16. Norman Mailer, *Miami and the Siege of Chicago: An informal history of the American political conventions of 1968* (Harmondsworth: Penguin Books, 1969), p. 36.

17. Daniel Boorstin, *The Image or What Happened to the American Dream* (London: Weidenfeld & Nicholson, 1962), p. 11.

18. Ibid., p. 22.

19. Arthur M. Schlesinger Jr, *A Thousand Days: John F. Kennedy in the White House* (London: André Deutsch, 1965), p. 107.

20. David Halberstam, *The Powers That Be* (New York: Alfred A. Knopf, 1979), p. 8.

21. Ibid., p. 9.

22. William Stott, *Documentary Expression and Thirties America* (New York: Oxford University Press, 1973), p. 79.

23. Ibid., p. 82.

24. Hunter S. Thompson, *Fear and Loathing on the Campaign Trail '72* (New York: Fawcett Books, 1974), p. 18.

25. Ibid., p. 502.

26. The League of Women Voters, *Choosing the President 1980* (Nashville: Thomas Nelson Publishers, 1980), p. 33.

27. David Lodge, 'The Language of Modernist Fiction: Metaphor and Metonymy', in *Modernism*, edited by Malcom Bradbury and James McFarlane (Harmondsworth: Penguin Books, 1981), p. 481.

28. Mailer, *Miami and the Siege of Chicago*, p. 210.

29. Norman Mailer, *Marilyn: A Biography* (London: Hodder & Stoughton, 1973), p. 18.

30. Mailer, *Miami and the Siege of Chicago*, p. 89.

31. Norman Mailer, *Cannibals and Christians* (London: Sphere Books, 1969), p. 56. First published 1966.

32. Norman Mailer, *The Executioner's Song* (New York: Warner Books, 1980), p. 580.

33. Ibid., p. 379.

34. Ibid., p. 805.

14. COMING TO TERMS WITH HOLLYWOOD: FROM MASS TO AUTEUR THEORY

1. Peter Wollen, *Signs and Meanings in the Cinema* (London: Secker & Warburg, third edition, revised and enlarged, 1972), p. 10.

2. Andrew Sarris, *Politics and Cinema* (New York: Columbia University Press, 1978), p. 206.

3. Andrew Sarris, *The Primal Screen: Essays on Film and Related Subjects* (New York: Simon & Schuster, 1973), p. 48.

4. Andrew Sarris, *The American Cinema: Directors and Directions 1929–1968* (New York: E. P. Dutton, 1968), p. 21.

5. Ibid., p. 38.

6. Warshow, *The Immediate Experience*, p. 129.

7. For examples of this enhancement of Hollywood's status that includes a range of critical strategies, genre and auteur, see Robin Wood, *Howard Hawks* (London: British Film Institute, revised edition, 1981), and Jim Kitses, *Horizons West* (London: Thames & Hudson, 1969).

8. Ed Buscombe, 'The Idea of Genre in American Cinema', *Screen Magazine*, 11, No. 2 (1970), 37.

9. Andrew Sarris, *Confessions of a Cultist: On the Cinema, 1955/1969* (New York: Simon & Schuster, 1970), p. 13.

10. Sarris, *The Primal Screen*, p. 50.

11. Sarris, *Politics and Cinema*, p. 6.

12. Sarris, *The American Cinema*, p. 58.

13. Ibid., pp. 58–9.

14. Ibid., p. 38.

15. For examples of European enthusiasm for selected Hollywood directors, see 'Génie de Howard Hawks', Jacques Rivette, *Cahiers du Cinéma*, no. 23 (May 1953) translated in Joseph McBride (ed.), *Focus on Howard Hawks* (New Jersey: Prentice-Hall, 1972), pp. 70–7, and Francois Truffaut with the collaboration of Helen G. Scott, *Hitchcock* (London: Secker & Warburg, 1968).

16. Sarris, *The American Cinema*, p. 55.

17. Ibid., p. 155.

18. Sarris, *The Primal Screen*, p. 58.

19. Sarris, *Confessions of a Cultist*, p. 13.

20. Sarris, *The American Cinema*, p. 56.

21. Geoffrey Nowell-Smith, 'Visconti', in John Caughie (ed.), *Theories of Authorship* (London: Routledge & Kegan Paul, 1981), p. 137.

22. Philip French, *Westerns: Aspects of a Movie Genre* (London: Secker & Warburg, 1977), p. 57.

23. Sarris, *The Primal Screen*, p. 152.

24. *The Man Who Shot Liberty Valance*, directed by John Ford (Paramount Pictures: 1962), British Film Institute Script Library.

25. Ibid.

26. Peter Wollen, 'John Ford', in John Caughie (ed.), *Theories of Authorship: A Reader* (London: Routledge & Kegan Paul, 1981), p. 102. First published in *New Left Review*, No. 29, January/February 1965.

27. Christine Gledhill, 'Klute 1: a contemporary film noir and feminist criticism', in E. Ann Kaplan (ed.), *Women in Film Noir* (London: British Film Institute, 1981), p. 11.

28. For parts of this analysis of Hollywood cinema and *The Man Who Shot Liberty Valance*, I am indebted to Robert Ray, who kindly allowed me to read his forthcoming book *A Certain Tendency of the American Cinema: The Movies 1930–1980* and to Michael Wood's paper on the Western and the discussion afterwards at the BAAS Conference, 1982.

29. Daniel Boorstin, *The Americans: The National Experience* (London: Weidenfeld & Nicholson, 1966), p. 337.

30. Lewis, *The American Adam*, p. 5.

31. Henry Nash Smith, *Virgin Land*, p. 89.

32. Lindsay Anderson, *About John Ford* (London: Plexus Publishing, 1981), p. 20.

33. Sarris, *The Primal Screen*, p. 149.

34. Wollen, 'John Ford', p. 102.

35. Christopher Lasch, *The Culture of Narcissism: American Life in an Age of Diminishing Expectations* (New York: W. W. Norton, 1978), p. 10–11.

15. THE POLITICS AND AESTHETICS OF MODERNISM

1. Herbert J. Gans, *Popular Culture and High Culture: An Analysis and Evaluation of Taste* (New York: Basic Books, 1974), p. 77.

2. Leo Lowenthal, 'Historical Perspectives of Popular Culture', in Bernard Rosenberg and Daniel M. White (eds), *Mass Culture: The Popular Arts in America* (Glencoe, Ill.: The Free Press, 1957), p. 55.

3. Christopher Butler, *After the Wake: An Essay on the Contemporary Avant-garde* (Oxford: Clarendon Press, 1980), p. 125.

4. Milton W. Brown, *The Story of the Armory Show* (Greenwich, Conn.: New York Graphic Society, 1963).

5. Royal Cortissoz, *American Painters* (New York: Charles Scribner's Sons, 1923), p. 17.

6. Raymond Williams, *Culture* (Glasgow: Fontana Paperbacks, 1981), p. 84.

7. Harold Rosenberg, *The Tradition of the New* (New York: McGraw-Hill, 1960), p. 47.

8. Ibid.

9. Ibid., p. 42.

10. Ibid.

11. Harold Rosenberg, *The Anxious Object: Art Today and its Audience* (London: Thames & Hudson, 1965), p. 77.

12. For an assessment of this early period of American modernism see Abraham A. Davidson, *Early American Modernist Painting 1910–1935* (New York: Harper & Row, 1981).

13. Barry Ulanov, *The Two Worlds of American Art: The Private and the Popular* (London: Collier-Macmillan, 1967), p. 85.

14. Taken from the film *Jackson Pollock* by Paul Falkenberg and Hans Namuth, 1951, Arts Council Film Library.

15. See Tom Wolfe, *The Painted Word* (New York: Bantam Books, 1976).

16. Max Kozloff, 'American Painting During the Cold War', *Artforum* (May 1973), 44.

17. Quoted in B. H. Friedman, *Jackson Pollock: Energy Made Visible: A Biography* (New York: McGraw-Hill, 1972), p. 131.

18. Excerpt from the artist's written answer to a questionnaire published in *Arts and Architecture*, LXI (February 1944). Reprinted in Herschel B. Chipp, *Theories of Modern Art: A Source Book by Artists and Critics* (Berkeley: University of California Press, 1968), p. 546.

19. Clement Greenberg, *Art and Culture* (Boston: Beacon Press, 1961), p. 137. (*AC* in future text references.)

20. Herschel B. Chipp, *Theories of Modern Art*, p. 546.

21. Max Kozloff, 'An Interview with Robert Motherwell', *Artforum* (September 1965), 37.

22. Harold Rosenberg, *The Anxious Object*, p. 43.

23. Rosenberg, *The Tradition of the New*, p. 30.

24. Rosenberg, *The Anxious Object*, p. 101.

25. Harold Rosenberg, *Artworks and Packages* (London: Thames & Hudson, 1969), p. 220.

26. Kozloff, 'American Painting During the Cold War', p. 45.

27. Clement Greenberg, 'Abstract, Representational and so forth', in *Art and Culture*, p. 136.

28. Leo Steinberg, *Other Criteria: Confrontations with Twentieth-Century Art* (London: Oxford University Press, 1979), p. 71.

29. See the essays on 'Realism' in *Art in America* (September 1981), 69, No. 7.

30. I. A. Richards, *Philosophy of Rhetoric*, p. 131.

31. Susan Sontag, 'One Culture and the New Sensibility'. 1965, in Susan Sontag, *Against Interpretation* (New York: Delta Books, 1981), pp. 298–9.

32. Ibid., p. 299.

16. SUSAN SONTAG: AGAINST INTERPRETATION

1. Daniel Bell, *Sociological Journeys*, p. 128.

2. Ibid., p. 333.

3. Sontag, *Against Interpretation*, p. 14.

4. Ibid.

5. Ibid., p. 3.

6. Ibid., p. 7.

7. Marcuse, *An Essay on Liberation*, p. 26.

8. Herschel B. Chipp, *Theories of Modern Art; A Source Book by Artists and Critics* (Berkeley: University of California Press, 1968), p. 545.

9. Ellen H. Johnson (ed.), *American Artists on Art: From 1940 to 1980* (New York: Harper & Row, 1982), p. 86.

10. Susan Sontag, *Styles of Radical Will* (London: Secker & Warburg, 1969), p. 41.

11. Ibid., p. 157.

12. Ibid., p. 26.

13. Sontag, *Against Interpretation*, p. 265.

14. Ibid., p. 267.

15. Sontag, *Against Interpretation*, p. 295.

16. Susan Sontag, *Under the Sign of Saturn* (New York: Farrar, Straus & Giroux, 1980), p. 89.

17. Karl E. Meyer, *The Art Museum: Power, Money, Ethics* (New York: William Morrow, 1979), p. 271.

18. See article on New York in *The Economist* (2 April 1983), Vol. 287, No. 7283, pp. 58–9.

19. *The Solomon R. Guggenheim Museum, Architect Frank Lloyd Wright* (New York: Horizon Press, 1960), p. 17.

20. Sontag, *Styles of Radical Will*, p. 198.

21. Ibid., p. 194.

22. Susan Sontag, *On Photography* (Harmondsworth: Penguin Books, 1980), p. 8. (*OP* in future text references.)

23. Sontag, *Against Interpretation*, p. 92.

24. Christopher Butler, *After the Wake: an essay on the Contemporary Avant-Garde* (Oxford University Press, 1980), p. 148.

25. Susan Sontag, *Styles of Radical Will* (London: Secker & Warburg, 1969), pp. 156–7.

Selected Bibliography

(Including books not referred to in the text)

1. THE LEGACY OF THE THIRTIES

Daniel Aaron, *Writers on the Left* (New York: Octagon, 1979).

Daniel Aaron and Robert Bendiner (eds), *The Strenuous Decade: A Social and Intellectual Record of the Nineteen-Thirties* (New York: Anchor Books, 1970).

Malcolm Bradbury and Howard Temperley (eds), *An Introduction to American Studies* (London: Longman, 1981).

David Caute, *The Great Fear: The Anti-Communist Purge Under Truman and Eisenhower* (New York: Simon & Schuster, 1978).

Leslie A. Fiedler, *Love and Death in the American Novel* (London: Jonathan Cape, 1967).

James Gilbert, *Writers and Partisans: A History of Literary Radicalism in America* (New York: John Wiley, 1968).

Lillian Hellman, *Pentimento* (London: Quartet, 1976).

Christopher Lasch, *The New Radicalism in America 1889–1963: The Intellectual as a Social Type* (New York: Vintage Books, 1965).

R. W. B. Lewis, *The American Adam: Innocence, Tragedy, and Tradition in the Nineteenth Century* (Chicago: University of Chicago Press, 1955).

Jerre Mangione, *The Dream and the Deal: The Federal Writers' Project 1935–1943* (Boston: Little, Brown, 1972).

Leo Marx, *The Machine in the Garden: Technology and the Pastoral Ideal in America* (New York: Oxford University Press, 1964)

F. O. Matthiessen, *American Renaissance* (New York: OUP, 1941).

Eric Mottram and Malcolm Bradbury (eds), *United States and Latin American Literature, Penguin Companion to Literature No. 3* (Harmondsworth: Penguin Books, 1971).

Victor S. Navasky, *Naming Names* (London: John Calder, 1982).

Richard H. Pells, *Radical Visions and American Dreams: Culture and Social Thought in the Depression Years* (New York: Harper & Row, 1973).

Henry Nash Smith, *Virgin Land: The American West as Symbol and Myth* (Cambridge: Harvard University Press, 1970).

2. DANIEL BELL AND THE CULTURAL CONTRADICTIONS OF CAPITALISM

Daniel Bell, *The End of Ideology* (New York: Collier-Macmillan, 1965).

——, *The Coming of Post-Industrial Society: A Venture in Social Forecasting* (London: Heinemann Educational, 1974).

——, *The Cultural Contradictions of Capitalism* (London: Heinemann, 1979).

——, *Sociological Journeys: Essays 1960–1980* (London: Heinemann, 1980).

227

John P. Diggins, *Up from Communism: Conservative Odysseys in American Intellectual History* (New York: Harper & Row, 1975).

Chester E. Eisinger (ed.), *The 1940s: Profile of a Nation in Crisis* (New York: Anchor Books, 1969).

Godfrey Hodgson, *America in Our Time: From World War II to Nixon: What Happened and Why* (New York: Vintage Books, 1978).

Daniel Hoffman (ed.), *Harvard Guide to Contemporary American Writing* (Cambridge, Massachusetts: Harvard University Press, 1979).

Norman Podhoretz, *Breaking Ranks: A Political Memoir* (London: Weidenfeld & Nicholson, 1980).

Peter Steinfels, *The Neo-Conservatives* (New York: Simon & Schuster, 1980).

3. THE FOUNDATIONS OF ANGLO-AMERICAN LITERARY THEORY

4. FROM SOUTHERN AGRARIANISM TO CRITICISM, INC.

Elmer Borklund, *Contemporary Literary Critics* (London: St James Press, 1977).

Cleanth Brooks, *The Well Wrought Urn: Studies in the Structure of Poetry* (London: Denis Dobson, 1968).

William H. Chace, *The Political Identities of Ezra Pound and T. S. Eliot* (Stanford: Stanford University Press, 1973).

Terry Eagleton, *Literary Theory: An Introduction* (Oxford University Press, 1983).

T. S. Eliot, *After Strange Gods: A Primer of Modern Heresy* (London: Faber & Faber, 1934)

———, *Selected Essays* (London: Faber & Faber, 1976).

Lillian Feder, *Ancient Myth in Modern Poetry* (Princeton: Princeton University Press, 1971).

John Fekete, *The Critical Twilight: Explorations in the Ideology of Anglo-American Literary Theory from Eliot to Mcluhan* (London: Routledge & Kegan Paul, 1978).

Arnold L. Goldsmith, *American Literary Criticism 1905–1965* (Boston: Twayne Publishers, 1979).

Richard Gray, *The Literature of Memory, Modern Writers of the American South* (London: Edward Arnold, 1979).

John Crowe Ransom, *God Without Thunder: An Unorthodox Defence of Orthodoxy* (London: Gerald Howe, 1931).

———, *The World's Body* (New York: Charles Scribner's Sons, 1938).

———, *The New Criticism* (Norfolk, Connecticut: New Directions, 1941).

I. A. Richards, *Practical Criticism: A Study of Literary Judgement* (London: Routledge & Kegan Paul, 1929).

———, *Poetries and Sciences – A Re-Issue of Science and Poetry with Commentary* (London: Routledge & Kegan Paul, 1970).

———, *Principles of Literary Criticism* (London: Routledge & Kegan Paul, 1976).

5. THE DEBATE ON MASS CULTURE

6. ROBERT WARSHOW AND THE LEGACY OF THE 1930s

Hannah Arendt, *The Origins of Totalitarianism* (Cleveland: World Publishing, 1962).

Salvador Giner, *Mass Society* (London: Martin Robertson, 1976).

Edith Kurzweil and William Phillips (eds), *Writers and Politics: an anthology from* Partisan Review (London: Routledge & Kegan Paul, 1983).
Dwight Macdonald, *The Responsibilities of Peoples and Other Essays in Political Criticism* (London: Victor Gollancz, 1957).
——, *Against the American Grain* (London: Victor Gollancz, 1963).
——, *On Movies* (New York: Da Capo Press, 1981).
C. Wright Mills, *The Sociological Imagination* (Harmondsworth: Penguin Books, 1980).
Bernard Rosenberg and David H. White (eds), *Mass Culture: The Popular Arts in America* (Glencoe, Illinois: The Free Press, 1957).
Alain Silver and Elizabeth Ward (eds), *Film Noir* (London: Secker & Warburg, 1980).
Robert Warshow, *The Immediate Experience: Movies, Comics, Theatre and Other Aspects of Popular Culture* (New York: Atheneum, 1971).

7. T. S. ELIOT AND MASS SOCIETY

8. THE FRANKFURT SCHOOL: MARXISM, FASCISM AND MASS CULTURE

Theodor Adorno, *Prisms* (London: Neville Spearman, 1967).
Theodor Adorno and Max Horkheimer, *Dialectic of Enlightenment* (London: Verso Editions, 1979).
Roland Barthes, *Mythologies* (London: Jonathan Cape, 1972).
Richard Dyer, *Stars* (London: British Film Institute, 1979).
——, *Marilyn Monroe: Star Dossier One* (London: British Film Institute, 1980).
T. S. Eliot, *The Idea of a Christian Society* (London: Faber & Faber, 1939).
——, *Notes Towards the Definition of Culture* (London: Faber & Faber, 1979).
H. Stuart Hughes, *The Sea Change: The Migration of Social Thought, 1930–1965* (New York: McGraw-Hill, 1972).
Martin Jay, *The Dialectical Imagination: A History of the Frankfurt School and the Institute of Social Research 1923–1950* (London: Heinemann Educational, 1976).
Leo Lowenthal, *Literature, Popular Culture and Society* (Palo Alto: Pacific Books, 1968).
Lary May, *Screening Out the Past: The Birth of Mass Culture and the Motion Picture Industry* (New York: Oxford University Press, 1980).

9. HERBERT MARCUSE: FROM AFFIRMATION TO LIBERATION

Morris Dickstein, *Gates of Eden: American Culture in the Sixties* (New York: Basic Books, 1977).
Sigmund Freud, *Civilization and its Discontents* (London: The Hogarth Press, 1979).
Herbert Marcuse, *One-Dimensional Man: Studies in the Ideology of Advanced Industrial Society* (Boston: Beacon Press, 1964).
——, *An Essay on Liberation* (Boston: Beacon Press, 1969).
——, *Five Lectures: Psychoanalysis, Politics, and Utopia* (Boston: Beacon Press, 1970).
——, *Negations* (Harmondsworth: Penguin University Books, 1972).
——, *Eros and Civilization* (Boston: Beacon Press, 1974).
——, *The Aesthetic Dimension: Towards a Critique of Marxist Aesthetics* (London: Macmillan, 1979).
William L. O'Neill, *Coming Apart: An Informal History of America in the 1960s* (New York: Quadrangle Books, 1978).
Theodor Roszak, *The Making of a Counter-Culture: Reflections on the Technocratic Society and its Youthful Opposition* (New York: Anchor Books, 1969).
Hendrick K. H. Ruitenbeek, *Freud and America* (New York: Macmillan, 1966).

10. THE LONELY CROWD: DAVID RIESMAN AND AMERICAN SOCIETY

Paul Goodman, *Growing Up Absurd: Problems of Youth in the Organized System* (London: Victor Gollancz, 1961).
Seymour Martin Lipset and Leo Lowenthal (eds), *Culture and Social Character: The Work of David Riesman Reviewed* (New York: Free Press, 1961).
C. Wright Mills, *The Power Elite: On the Ruling Groups in the United States* (New York: Oxford University Press, 1956).
David Riesman, *Individualism Reconsidered, and other essays* (Glencoe, Illinois: Free Press, 1954).
——, *Abundance for What?, and other essays* (London: Chatto & Windus, 1964).
——, *The Lonely Crowd: A Study of the Changing American Character* (New Haven and London: Yale University Press, revised edition, 1970).
Edward Joseph Shoben Jr, *Lionel Trilling* (New York: Frederick Ungar, 1981).
Lionel Trilling, *Matthew Arnold* (London: Unwin University Books, 1963).
——, *Sincerity and Authenticity* (London: Oxford University Press, 1972).
——, *The Last Decade: Essays and Reviews, 1965–75* (New York: Harcourt Brace Jovanovich, 1979).
——, *E. M. Forster* (New York: Harcourt Brace Jovanovich, 1980).
——, *The Opposing Self: Nine Essays in Criticism* (Oxford: Oxford University Press, 1980).
——, *A Gathering of Fugitives* (Oxford: Oxford University Press, 1980).
——, *Beyond Culture: Essays on Literature and Learning* (Oxford: Oxford University Press, 1980).
——, *The Liberal Imagination: Essays on Literature and Society* (Oxford: Oxford University Press, 1981).
Raymond Williams, *Culture and Society 1780–1950* (Harmondsworth: Penguin Books, 1961).
——, *The Long Revolution* (Harmondsworth: Penguin Books, 1965).

11. MARSHALL MCLUHAN: THE MODERNISM OF THE MASS MEDIA

12. TOM WOLFE AND THE NEW JOURNALISM

Stanley Aronowitz, *False Promises: The Shaping of American Working Class Consciousness* (New York: McGraw-Hill, 1973).
Robert Atwan, Barry Orton and William Vesterman (eds), *American Mass Media: Industries and Issues* (New York: Random House, 1978).
Herbert J. Gans, *Popular Culture and High Culture: An Analysis and Evaluation of Taste* (New York: Basic Books, 1974).
——, *Deciding What's News: A Study of C.B.S. Evening News, N.B.C. Nightly News, Newsweek and Time* (New York: Vintage Books, 1980).
William Kuhns, *The Post-Industrial Prophets: Interpretations of Technology* (New York: Weybright & Talley, 1971).
Christopher Lasch, *The Agony of the American Left: One Hundred Years of Radicalism* (Harmondsworth: Pelican Books, 1973).
Marshall Mcluhan, *The Gutenberg Galaxy: The Making of Typographic Man* (London: Routledge & Kegan Paul, 1962).
——, *Understanding Media: The Extensions of Man* (London: Routledge & Kegan Paul, 1964).
——, *The Mechanical Bride: Folklore of Industrial Man* (London: Routledge & Kegan Paul, 1967).

——, *The Medium is the Massage* (Harmondsworth: Allen Lane, Penguin Press, 1967).
——, with Harley Parker, *Through the Vanishing Point: Space in Poetry and Painting* (New York: Harper & Row, 1969).
——, *Culture is Our Business* (New York: McGraw-Hill, 1970).
Jonathan Miller, *Mcluhan* (London: Fontana Books, 1971).
Herbert I. Schiller, *Mass Communications and American Empire* (New York: Augustus M. Keeley, 1970).
Gerald Emanuel Stearn (ed.), *Mcluhan Hot and Cool: A Primer for the Understanding of and a critical symposium with responses by Mcluhan* (Harmondsworth: Penguin Books, 1968).
Hunter S. Thompson, *Hell's Angels* (London: Penguin Books, 1967).
——, *Fear and Loathing in Las Vegas* (St Alban's: Paladin Books, 1972).
——, *Fear and Loathing on the Campaign Trail '72* (New York: Fawcett Books, 1974).
——, *The Great Shark Hunt* (London: Picador Books, 1980).
Tom Wolfe, *The Pump House Gang* (New York: Bantam, 1969).
——, *The Electric Kool-Aid Acid Test* (New York: Bantam, 1969).
——, *Radical Chic and Mau-Mauing the Flak Catchers* (New York: Bantam, 1971).
——, *The Painted Word* (New York: Bantam, 1976).
——, *Mauve Gloves and Madmen, Clutter and Vine* (New York: Bantam, 1977).
——, *The New Journalism* (London: Picador Books, 1977).
——, *The Kandy-Kolored Tangerine-Flake Streamline Baby* (London: Picador Books, 1981).
——, *The Right Stuff* (New York: Bantam, 1981).
——, *From Bauhaus to Our House* (New York: Farrar, Straus & Giroux, 1981).

13. NORMAN MAILER AND MASS AMERICA

Jennifer Bailey, *Norman Mailer: Quick-Change Artist* (New York: Barnes & Noble, 1979).
Leo Braudy (ed.), *Norman Mailer: A Collection of Critical Essays* (New Jersey: Prentice-Hall, 1972).
Norman Mailer, *Advertisements for Myself* (London: Corgi Books, 1963).
——, *The Naked and the Dead* (St Alban's: Panther Books, 1964).
——, *The Armies of the Night: History as a Novel, the Novel as History* (Harmondsworth: Penguin Books, 1968).
——, *Cannibals and Christians* (London: Sphere Books, 1969).
——, *Miami and the Siege of Chicago: An informal history of the American political conventions of 1968* (Harmondsworth: Penguin Books, 1969).
——, *Of a Fire on the Moon* (New York: Signet Books, 1971).
——, *Marilyn: A Biography* (London: Hodder & Stoughton, 1973).
——, *The Presidential Papers* (St Alban's: Panther Books, 1976).
——, *The Executioner's Song* (New York: Warner Books, 1980).
Arthur M. Schlesinger Jr, *A Thousand Days: John F. Kennedy in the White House* (London: André Deutsch, 1965).

14. COMING TO TERMS WITH HOLLYWOOD: FROM MASS TO AUTEUR THEORY

Lindsay Anderson, *About John Ford* (London: Plexus Publishing, 1981).
Peter Bogdanovich, *John Ford* (Berkeley: University of California Press, 1968).
John Caughie (ed.), *Theories of Authorship* (London: Routledge & Kegan Paul, 1981).
Edward Countryman, 'Westerns and United States History', *History Today* (March 1983) 18–23.
Philip Davies and Brian Neve (eds), *Cinema, Politics and Society in America* (Manchester: Manchester University Press, 1981).

Phil Hardy, *The Western: the Complete Film Reference* (London: Aurum Press, 1983).

Jim Kitses, *Horizons West* (London: Thames & Hudson, 1969).

Christopher Lasch, *The Culture of Narcissism: American Life in an Age of Diminishing Expectations* (New York: W. W. Norton, 1978).

Andrew Sarris, *The American Cinema: Directors and Directions 1929–1968* (New York: E. P. Dutton, 1968).

——, *Confessions of a Cultist: On the Cinema, 1955–1969* (New York: Simon & Schuster, 1970).

——, *The Primal Screen: Essays on Film and Related Subjects* (New York: Simon & Schuster, 1973).

——, *The John Ford Movie Mystery* (London: Secker & Warburg, 1976).

——, *Politics and Cinema* (New York: Columbia University Press, 1978).

Michael Stern, *Douglas Sirk* (Boston: Twayne Publishers, 1979).

Peter Wollen, *Signs and Meaning in the Cinema* (London: Secker & Warburg, third edition, revised and enlarged, 1972).

Robin Wood, *Howard Hawks* (London: British Film Institute, revised edition, 1981).

15. THE POLITICS AND AESTHETICS OF MODERNISM

Dore Ashton, *The New York School: A Cultural Reckoning* (New York: Penguin Books, 1980).

——, *American Art Since 1945* (London: Thames & Hudson, 1982).

John Berger, *The Moment of Cubism and Other Essays* (London: Weidenfeld & Nicholson, 1969).

Malcolm Bradbury and James McFarlane (eds), *Modernism* (Harmondsworth: Penguin Books, 1981).

Christopher Butler, *After the Wake: An Essay on the Contemporary Avant-Garde* (Oxford: Clarendon Press, 1980).

Herschel B. Chipp, *Theories of Modern Art: A Source Book by Artists and Critics* (Berkeley: University of California Press, 1968).

Abraham Davidson, *Early American Modernist Painting 1910–1935* (New York: Harper & Row, 1981).

B. H. Friedman, *Jackson Pollock: Energy Made Visible, A Biography* (New York: McGraw-Hill, 1972).

Peter Fuller, *Beyond the Crisis in Art* (London: Writers and Readers Publishing Cooperative, 1980).

Clement Greenberg, *Art and Culture* (Boston: Beacon Press, 1961).

Peggy Guggenheim, *Out of this Century: Confessions of an Art Addict* (New York: Anchor Books, 1980).

Robert Hughes, *The Shock of the New: Art and the Century of Change* (London: British Broadcasting Corporation, 1980).

Max Kozloff, 'American Painting During the Cold War', *Artforum* (May 1973).

Karal Ann Marling, *Wall-to-wall America: a cultural history of post-office murals in the Great Depression* (Minneapolis: University of Minnesota Press, 1982), pp. 45–8.

Francis V. O'Connor (ed.), *Art for the Millions: Essays from the 1930s by Artists and Administrators of the WPA Federal Art Project* (Boston: New York Graphic Society, 1975).

Francis Valentine O'Connor and Eugene Victor Thaw (eds), *Jackson Pollock: A Catalogue Raisonné of Paintings, Drawings and Other Works* (New Haven: Yale University Press, 1978).

Bryan Robertson, *Jackson Pollock* (London: Thames & Hudson, 1960).

Barbara Rose, *American Art Since 1900* (New York: Holt, Rinehart & Winston, 1975).

——, *Readings in American Art* (New York: Holt, Rinehart & Winston, 1975).
Harold Rosenberg, *The Tradition of the New* (New York: McGraw-Hill, 1960).
——, *The Anxious Object: Art Today and its Audience* (London: Thames & Hudson, 1965).
——, *Artworks and Packages* (London: Thames & Hudson, 1969).
Irving Sandler, *The Triumph of American Painting: A History of Abstract Expressionism* (New York: Harper & Row, 1970).
——, *The New York School: The Painters and Sculptors of the Fifties* (New York: Harper & Row, 1978).
Lee Seldes, *The Legacy of Mark Rothko* (New York: Penguin Books, 1979).
Leo Steinberg, *Other Criteria: Confrontations with Twentieth-Century Art* (London: Oxford University Press, 1979).
John Tagg, 'American Power and American Painting: The development of Vanguard Painting in the United States since 1945', *Praxis*, 1, No. 2 (Winter 1976).
Raymond Williams, *Culture* (Glasgow: Fontana Paperbacks, 1981).

Films

Painters Painting: Directed by Emil de Antonio, 1973. A series of interviews with the artists, critics and collectors associated with the New York School. Many of the sequences in this 115-minute documentary show the artists at work in their studios. The artists include Willem de Kooning, Helen Frankenthaler, Jasper Johns and Andy Warhol. Available from Cinegate Films, Gate Cinema, Notting Hill Gate, London.
Jackson Pollock: Made by Paul Falkenberg and Hans Namuth, 1951, available through Arts Council Film Library, London.

16. SUSAN SONTAG: AGAINST INTERPRETATION

Stewart Buettner, *American Art Theory 1945–1970* (Ann Arbor, Michigan: UMI Research Press, 1981).
Lucy R. Lippard (ed.), *Pop Art* (New York: Praeger, 1966).
Karl E. Meyer, *The Art Museum: Power, Money, Ethics* (New York: William Morrow, 1979).
Susan Sontag, *Styles of Radical Will* (London: Secker & Warburg, 1969).
——, *Under the Sign of Saturn* (New York: Farrar, Straus & Giroux, 1980).
——, *On Photography* (Harmondsworth: Penguin Books, 1980).
——, *Against Interpretation* (New York: Delta, 1981).
——, *A Susan Sontag Reader* (Harmondsworth: Penguin Books, 1983).
Edward Steichen (ed.), *The Family of Man* (New York: Museum of Modern Art, 1955).
John Szarkowski (ed.), *Walker Evans* (New York: Museum of Modern Art, 1971).
Andy Warhol and Pat Hackett, *Popism: The Warhol '60s* (New York: Harcourt Brace Jovanovich, 1980).

Selected Journals of Opinion

Journal	Founded	Circulation	Frequency	Main contents and/or Ideological slant
Artforum	1962	25,000	Monthly	Avant-garde
Commentary	1945	55,000	Weekly	Jewish neo-conservative
Commonweal	1924	18,000	Twice monthly	Catholic
Dissent	1954	5,000	Quarterly	Democratic socialist
Harper's	1850	293,187	Monthly	Current events and general culture
National Review	1955	103,677	Weekly	Conservative
New Republic	1914	96,244	Weekly	Liberal
New York Review of Books	1963	118,000	Weekly	Liberal/literary
New Yorker	1925	506,038	Weekly	Current events and general culture
Partisan Review	1934	8,000	Quarterly	Anti-Stalinist radical
Rolling Stone	1967	753,669	Twice monthly	Counter-cultural/investigative
The Nation	1865	48,000	Weekly	Liberal-radical
The Progressive	1909	35,000	Weekly	Old Left
The Public Interest	1965	12,000	Quarterly	Neo-conservative
Village Voice	1955	156,035	Weekly	Liberal hedonist

Index